# National Human Rights Institutions in Southeast Asia

James Gomez • Robin Ramcharan
Editors

# National Human Rights Institutions in Southeast Asia

## Selected Case Studies

palgrave
macmillan

*Editors*
James Gomez
128/183 Phayathai Plaza Building
Asia Centre
Bangkok, Thailand

Robin Ramcharan
128/183 Phayathai Plaza Building
Asia Centre
Bangkok, Thailand

ISBN 978-981-15-1073-1    ISBN 978-981-15-1074-8 (eBook)
https://doi.org/10.1007/978-981-15-1074-8

The print edition is not for sale in Malaysia and Singapore. Customers from Malaysia and Singapore please order the print book from: GB Gerakbudaya Enterprise Sdn Bhd.
ISBN of the Co-Publisher's edition: 978-967-2165-880



This Palgrave Macmillan imprint is published by the registered company Springer Nature Singapore Pte Ltd.
The registered company address is: 152 Beach Road, #21-01/04 Gateway East, Singapore 189721, Singapore

# Preface

Asia Centre is a think-tank whose Human Rights Programme takes an evidence-based research approach in examining the three main mechanisms that hold the potential to enhance human rights protection in the region. The three mechanisms are National Human Rights Institutions (NHRIs) in Southeast Asian countries, the Association of Southeast Asian Nations (ASEAN) Intergovernmental Commission on Human Rights (AICHR) and the Universal Periodic Review (UPR) of the United Nations' Human Rights Council, which the Centre dubs as the nexus of an emerging human rights architecture in the region.

Asia Centre, through its Human Rights Programme, seeks to advocate for protection provisions and mechanisms in this emerging regional human rights architecture by identifying the protection gaps and engaging with policy makers, academia, civil society, the private sector and other stakeholders to bridge the gap. To this end, Asia Centre undertakes the evidence-based research, convenes expert conferences, undertakes capacity-building trainings and produces publications. The Human Rights Programme aims to produce actionable, policy-oriented research that will serve to enhance the capacity of all stakeholders to advance the protection of human rights in Southeast Asia. The Centre does this by bringing together different stakeholders regularly to foster constructive dialogue and exchange best practices on human rights and other related issues. It fosters and nurtures networks of stakeholders in order to improve engagement with each of the mechanisms over time.

In this book, Asia Centre and the contributors to this volume examine whether these government-sponsored NHRIs are effective in providing protection of human rights in the region. The book demonstrates that while NHRIs constitute a welcome development across Southeast Asia, they have yet to fulfil a strong protection role. This is vital in the context of the protection gap left by other components of the regional human rights architecture, namely the UPR mechanism and the ASEAN Intergovernmental Commission on Human Rights (AICHR). In the *Universal Periodic Review of Southeast Asia: Civil Society Perspectives* (Palgrave Macmillan, 2017), analysis pointed not only to the utility of the UPR as an avenue for regional civil society organization (CSO) engagement, but also to systemic problems with regard to engagement with other stakeholders, the implementation of recommendations by governments, the efficacy of follow-up processes and the UPR's ability to address hard political issues. AICHR, which will be examined in a forthcoming work of the Centre, has a purely promotional mandate and lacks bite as it disseminates the ASEAN Declaration of Human Rights (AHRD)

A vital complement to this regional human rights architecture is the group of NHRIs that lie at the intersection of civil society (national, regional and international) and the state. Six NHRIs have been established in the region, some pre-dating the regional mechanism. They are the Commission on Human Rights in the Philippines (CHRP), Indonesia National Commission on Human Rights (Komnas HAM), Human Rights Commission of Malaysia (Suhakam), National Human Rights Commission of Thailand, Myanmar National Human Rights Commission (MNHRC) and the Provedor for Human Rights and Justice of Timor-Leste (PDHJ). The latter is a special case. As of now, Timor-Leste has yet to be admitted as a full member of ASEAN. In addition, in order to face the regional developments and challenges, these NHRIs, while seeking to improve their national capacities, have also evolved and formalized their network and named it as the Southeast Asia NHRI Forum (SEANF) in 2009. The formalization of SEANF is considered a commitment of the Southeast Asian NHRIs in further strengthening and enhancing their roles in protecting human rights in the region. Beyond Southeast Asia, they are also members in the Asia-Pacific Forum of National Human Rights Institutions (APF) and are part of the Global Alliance of the National Human Rights Institutions (GANHRI), formerly known as the International Coordinating Committee of National Institutions for the Promotion and Protection of Human Rights (ICC). They also contribute stakeholder submissions to the UPR process of the Human Rights Council.

This book emanated from a regional analysis undertaken by Asia Centre and its research network to evaluate the impact of NHRIs on the protection of human rights. Contributors were convened by Asia Centre in the "International Conference on National Human Rights Mechanisms in Southeast Asia: Challenges of Protection" on 13 and 14 July 2017, at Asia Centre in Bangkok. The conference served as a platform for representatives from NHRIs, academics, researchers, students and civil society to explore, through evidence-based research, the potentials, challenges and opportunities of these Southeast Asian NHRIs and their contribution to human rights protection in the region. They questioned the effectiveness of NHRIs in providing protection and explored their protection roles at the national, regional and international levels. The conference addressed such themes as:

- *NHRIs, international human rights systems and networks.* What kind of interaction exists between NHRIs at the international level, for example, with the UPR and the UN? What is the role of GANHRI in the growth and development of the NHRIs worldwide?
- *NHRIs in the national context.* Why did states create NHRIs? What are their mandates, legal bases, powers, functions and compliance with the Paris Principles? What happens to states that do not have an NHRI?
- *NHRIs and regional human rights systems and networks.* Now that the AICHR has been established, what is the relationship between NHRIs and the AICHR? How have the NHRIs responded to the AHRD? To what extent have the regional networks such as the SEANF and the APF helped in terms of advancing the protection role of the NHRIs?
- *NHRIs and human rights protection.* NHRIs' mandates and powers are varied; do they help in securing remedies or compensation? What are their impacts on protecting human rights? Now that NHRIs have engaged with other human rights networks regionally and globally, how have they assisted in dealing with transboundary human rights issues?

The evidence-based research undertaken by the author-practitioners assembled in this book assessed the mandates of NHRIs, their capacity to exercise a quasi-judicial function in pursuit of the protection of human rights, issues that they have addressed and their ability to provide redress and remedies.

Amidst the burgeoning literature on NHRIs globally, works on Southeast Asia needed updating. In addition, this book features rare analysis of Indonesia's national commission and even more rare analysis of Myanmar's national commission by author-practitioner. There is also a review of advocacy efforts for a human rights commission in Singapore that outlines the challenges in countries in Southeast Asia that do not yet have an NHRI. We see this book as both updating and filling gaps in the literature, which will inform theoretical analysis on the capacity of NHRIs to provide protection and thereby advancing international human rights norms in the region.

Asia Centre welcomes collaboration with prospective partners to monitor developments on NHRIs and their protection function within the context of the emerging human rights architecture in the region. In the meantime, Asia Centre will contribute to the discourse and capacity-building initiatives to improve the capacity of NHRIs to undertake their mandates and to develop and enhance national human rights protection systems. Asia Centre will continue with its evidence-based research on NHRIs and the emerging regional human rights architecture moving forward.

Bangkok, Thailand
15 August 2019

James Gomez
Robin Ramcharan

# Acknowledgements

This book was conceived amidst Asia Centre's ongoing work aimed at responding to the changing global human rights landscape and its impact on the region. It involved over a year of conversations with academics, civil society activists, professional staff in international non-governmental organizations, officials from the Association of Southeast Asian Nations (ASEAN) and representatives from the ASEAN Intergovernmental Commission on Human Rights (AICHR), National Human Rights Institutions (NHRIs) and the United Nations about the state of human rights protection in Southeast Asia.

The conversations centred around the role of NHRIs and their effectiveness in enhancing human rights protection. Collectively, the conversations identified a need for national rights commissions to enhance their protection capacities, at a time when democracy and rights seem to be in regression in the region and globally.

One way to understand the gap was to undertake a systematic analysis of the record of six national institutions—hence the need for evidence-based research by author-practitioners to take stock of their track records as revealed in their annual reports, in reports by regional watchdogs and in the UPR process.

Thanks, therefore, are due to the authors who marshalled their experiences into these chapters and who were diligent in revising and editing their submissions within a short time frame. Their insights point not only towards the great potential of NHRIs, but also to their challenges in providing protection in authoritarian social and political contexts.

Thanks are also in order to the team at Asia Centre, Tessa Allebas for her assistance in the editorial work and Patcharee Rattanarong for her administrative support. The Centre is appreciative of its short-term consultants, interns and volunteers, who helped put together the NHRI conference and the subsequent publication.

We are grateful to Gerakbudaya for the publication and distribution of the regional edition of the book and to Palgrave who came onboard for the publication and distribution of the international edition of the book.

We are pleased to bring out this publication at this critical juncture in regional and international affairs when national human rights protection systems hold the key to the advancement of human rights and yet are being severely challenged by the evolving political forces in the region and beyond.

# Contents

# Notes on Contributors

**Kimberly Clair** is Lecturer in Gender Studies at the University of California, Los Angeles. Her dissertation, *The Art of Resistance: Trauma, Gender, and Traditional Performance in Acehnese Communities, 1976–2011*, examines the significance of traditional performance (including dance, music, and theatre) as a trauma resource for survivors of separatist conflict and natural disaster in Aceh, Indonesia.

**Michelle D'cruz** is Regional Consultant with Oxfam International, Nairobi, Kenya. She was previously Programme Coordinator at Asia Centre in Bangkok, Thailand. She served with MARUAH—Working Group for an ASEAN Human Rights Mechanism—Singapore. Michelle holds a Master's in Human Rights from the Institute of Human Rights and Peace Studies, Mahidol University, and an LLB (Hons) from the National University of Singapore.

**Nukila Evanty** is a visiting lecturer at the School of Law, Atma Jaya Catholic University of Jakarta, since 2002; lecturer in the post-graduate programme, Faculty of Law, Mahendradatta University, Bali, since 2005; Director of Rights Foundation; associate researcher at Centre for Strategic and Internaitonal Studies (CSIS) and researcher on issues of social justice, minority, vulnerable and indigenous peoples at ISDS—Institute for Strategic and Development Studies since 2009.

**James Gomez** is Regional Director (Malaysia, Thailand) at Asia Centre. He was previously Regional Director of Amnesty International's Southeast Asia and Pacific Office in Bangkok. He has over 25 years of international experience working for public and private universities, research institutes, think-tanks, inter-governmental organizations and international NGOs. He serves as a technical expert and external consultant to international agencies and universities. He has written extensively on human rights protection in Southeast Asia.

**Henry Koh** Malaysian representative of the Global Fund, is a human rights researcher with a background in international human rights law and mechanisms. Previously he served with Fortify Rights, during which time he wrote this chapter. He was also coordinator of the sub-granting and movement-building strategies of the "Challenging Hate Narratives and Violations of Freedom of Religion and Expression Online in Asia" project with the Association for Progressive Communications.

**Niki Esse de Lang** legal consultant at UN Office on Drugs and Crime (UNODC) Southeast Asia, is a lawyer and human rights advocate from the Netherlands. He served with the UN Regional Office of the High Commissioner for Human Rights (OHCHR) in Bangkok and thereafter as a human rights adviser for the Burma Lawyers' Council (BLC) and a lecturer for the Peace Law Academy. He works with the Karen Human Rights Group (KHRG) as Capacity Building Manager in the Research and Advocacy team.

**Céline Martin** is Program Manager with Destination Justice and has been based alternatively in France and in Cambodia for the past five years. She is a doctoral candidate at Aix-Marseille University (France). Her research is on the protection of human rights in Asia, with a special focus on Southeast Asia. Céline has a Master's in Public International Law and a Master's in International Humanitarian and Human Rights Law from Aix-Marseille University (France).

**Robin Ramcharan** is Executive Director of Asia Centre in Bangkok, and Professor of International Relations at Webster University Thailand. He is also a lecturer for the Department of Political Science and Economics of the Royal Military College of Canada. He has some 25 years of international experience serving in international institutions, the university sector, think-tanks and not-for profit organizations. He holds degrees in international relations and law.

**Inosentius Samsul** is Head of the Draft Law Centre at the Center for Research and Information Services, the Indonesian House of Representatives (Parliament) office, and a lecturer in the Faculty of Law,

University of Indonesia. From 2015 he served as the Head of the Center for Legislative Drafting of the Indonesian House Representatives of the Republic of Indonesia. He holds his Doctor in Law from the University of Indonesia (2003).

**Francesca Paola Traglia** international consultant with the Lutheran World Federation, is a human rights expert with experience working in the United Kingdom, Switzerland, Uganda, Kenya, Colombia and Myanmar. She served in Yangon, Myanmar, with the Lutheran World Federation, managing programmes in the field of humanitarian and development assistance, as well as leading the human rights portfolio for the organization. She holds a Master's of Arts in International Studies and Diplomacy from the University of London—School of Oriental and African Studies and a Bachelor's of Arts in European Studies from the University of London-Royal Holloway College.

**Michael J. V. White** independent legal and policy consultant, is a human rights lawyer and advocate from New Zealand. He has worked as a barrister and solicitor with national human rights institutions and international human rights bodies. In 2015, Michael was appointed an Asia-Pacific Torture Prevention ambassador. He holds a law degree from the University of Auckland, New Zealand, and postgraduate degrees from the University of Auckland and the Australian National University. He has also studied international and comparative law at the Sorbonne University, Paris.

**Isnenningtyas Yulianti** is a researcher at Komnas HAM. She undertook Master's studies in Human Rights and Democration at the Faculty of Politics and Government Studies, Gadjah Mada University. She has been working in the field of economic, social and cultural rights. Her research centres mostly on the rights of minorities, especially persons with disabilities, indigenous peoples and the right to food.

**Domenico Zipoli** is a PhD fellow at the Norwegian Centre for Human Rights (Faculty of Law, University of Oslo) and was a visiting fellow at the Geneva Academy of International Humanitarian Law and Human Rights. He has worked at the Raoul Wallenberg Institute and the European Union's Fundamental Rights Agency. He served with the United Nations Office of the High Commissioner for Human Rights (Human Rights Treaties Division), as well as worked for the Mongolian Human Rights Commission and the Defensoria del Pueblo of Ecuador.

# Abbreviations

| | |
|---|---|
| ACHPR | African Commission on Human and People's Rights |
| ACS | ASEAN SOGIE Caucus |
| ACTIP | ASEAN Convention against Trafficking in Persons |
| ACWC | ASEAN Commission on Women and Children |
| AfHRC | African Human Rights Court |
| AFP | Agence France-Presse |
| AHRC | Asian Human Rights Commission |
| AICHR | ASEAN Intergovernmental Commission on Human Rights |
| ANNI | Asian NGO Networks on National Human Rights Institutions |
| AP | Associated Press |
| APF | Asia Pacific Forum |
| APF-NHRI | Asia Pacific Forum of National Human Rights Institutions |
| ASEAN | Association of Southeast Asian States |
| CADP | Andean Council of Defensorías del Pueblo |
| CAT | Convention against Torture and Other Cruel, Inhuman or Degrading Treatment or Punishment |
| CEDAW | Convention on the Elimination of All Forms of Discrimination Against Women |
| CESCR | Committee on Economic, Social and Cultural Rights |
| CHRP | Commission on Human Rights, Philippines |
| CMW | International Convention on the Protection of the Rights of All Migrant Workers and Members of Their Families |
| CRC | Convention on the Rights of the Child |
| CRPD | Convention on the Rights of Persons with Disabilities |

| | |
|---|---|
| CSOs | Civil Society Organizations |
| DFID | Department for International Development |
| DKBA | Democratic Karen Benevolent Army |
| DPR | House of Representatives |
| EAGs | Ethnic armed groups |
| ECOSOC | Economic and Social Council |
| ECtHR | European Court of Human Rights |
| EN-NHRIs | European Network of NHRIs |
| EMPOWER | Selangor Community Awareness Organization |
| ESCR | Economic, Social and Cultural Rights |
| F-FDTL | Timor Leste Defence Force |
| FIO | Iberoamerican Federation of Ombudsmen |
| FPP | Forest Peoples Programme |
| GANHRI | Global Alliance of National Human Rights Institutions |
| GCs | General Comments |
| GDP | Gross Domestic Product |
| HDI | Human Development Index |
| HIV-AIDS | Human immunodeficiency virus- Acquired Immune Deficiency Syndrome |
| HRC | Human Rights Council |
| HRE | Human Rights Experimentalism |
| HRCT | Human Rights Commission of Thailand |
| HRL | Human Rights Law |
| HRW | Human Rights Watch |
| IACHR | Inter-American Commission on Human Rights |
| ICC | International Coordinating Committee of National Institutions for the Promotion and Protection of Human Rights Subcommittee on Accreditation |
| ICESCR | International Covenant on Economic, Social and Cultural Rights |
| ICCPR | International Covenant on Civil and Political Rights |
| ICJ | International Court of Justice |
| ICPED | International Convention for the Protection of All Persons from Enforced Disappearance |
| ICMW | International Convention on the Protection of the Rights of All Migrant Workers and Members of Their Families |
| IGOs | International Organizations |
| KIA | Kachin Independence Army |
| KIO | Kachin Independence Organization |
| KND | National Disability Commission |
| KOMNAS HAM | National Commission on Human Rights |
| Komnas Perempuan | National Commission on Violence Against Women |

| | |
|---|---|
| KPAI | Komisi Perlindungan Anak Indonesia (Indonesia Commission on Child Protection) |
| KPP-HAM | Commission of Inquiry on Human Rights Violations |
| LANGO | Law on NGO |
| LGBTIQ | Lesbians, Gays, Bisexuals, Transsexuals and Intersex, Queer |
| LOIs | List of Issues |
| LPSK | Witness and Victim Protection Agency |
| LWF | Lutheran World Federation |
| MFA | Ministry of Foreign Affairs |
| MNDAA | Myanmar National Democratic Alliance Army |
| MNHRC | Myanmar National Human Rights Commission |
| MLHR | Ministry of Law and Human Rights |
| NAPHR | National Action Plan on Human Rights |
| NCA | Nationwide Ceasefire Agreement |
| NCPO | The National Council for Peace and Order |
| NGOs | Nongovernmental organizations |
| NHRI | National Human Rights Institutions |
| NHRCT | National Human Rights Commission in Thailand |
| NLD | National League for Democracy |
| OAS | Organization of American States |
| OHCHR | United Nations Office of the High Commissioner for Human Rights |
| OP CRPD | Optional Protocol to the Convention on the Rights of Persons with Disabilities |
| PAP | People's Action Party |
| PDHJ | Ombudsman for Human Rights and Justice |
| PNTL | Timor-Leste National Police |
| PP-PA | Ministry for Women Empowerment and Child Protection |
| PTPPO | Eradication of Human Trafficking Crime |
| PWDs | Persons with Disabilities |
| RECOFTC | Center for People and Forests |
| RWI | Raoul Wallenberg Institute |
| SCA | GANHRI Sub-Committee on Accreditation |
| SEANF | Southeast Asia National Human Rights Institution Forum |
| SEA NHRIs | Southeast Asia National Human Rights Institutions |
| SDGs | Sustainable Development Goals |
| SHRF | Shan Human Rights Foundation |
| SIDA | Sweden International Development Agency |
| SOGIESEC | Sexual Orientation, Gender Identity and Expression of Sex Characteristics |

| | |
|---|---|
| SRS | Sex reassignment surgeries |
| SSPP/SSA-N | Shan State Progressive Party/Shan State Army—North |
| STDs | Sexually transmitted diseases |
| SUHAKAM | Suruhanjaya Hak Asasi Manusia Malaysia (Human Rights Commission of Malaysia) |
| TBs | UN Human Rights Treaty Bodies |
| TNLA | Ta'ang National Liberation Army |
| UDHR | Universal Declaration of Human Rights |
| UN | United Nations |
| UNDP | United Nations Development Programme |
| UNGA | UN General Assembly |
| UNHCR | United Nations High Commissioner for Refugees |
| UNHRC | UN Human Rights Council |
| UPR | Universal Periodic Review |
| WHO | World Health Organization |

# List of Figures

# List of Tables

CHAPTER 1

# Introduction: National Human Rights Institutions in Southeast Asia: Challenges to the Protection of Human Rights

*James Gomez and Robin Ramcharan*

A United Nations (UN) report of a 2003 meeting of National Human Rights Institutions (NHRIs) from 22 commissions noted the centrality and importance of the Paris Principles "and the quasi-jurisdictional powers of national institutions" (United Nations 2004: 15). While safeguarding the respective roles of NHRIs and judiciaries was important, it was highlighted that NHRIs, through sound investigative practices, "can facilitate a greater understanding within the judiciary of international human rights norms to ensure their application in national jurisprudence" (United Nations 2004: 15). In addition, "the advantage of this quasi-judicial mode of complaints-handling is that the procedures are less time consuming, more flexible, informal, non-confrontational, inexpensive and thus more accessible to vulnerable groups, than the courts" (Lindsnaes and Lindholt 2000: 26). The hallmark of a good NHRI is the effective "protection" of human rights, that is, the investigation of complaints by citizens alleging

J. Gomez (✉) • R. Ramcharan
Asia Centre, Bangkok, Thailand
e-mail: james@asiacentre.co.th; robin@asiacentre.co.th



J. Gomez, R. Ramcharan (eds.), *National Human Rights Institutions in Southeast Asia*,
https://doi.org/10.1007/978-981-15-1074-8_1

violations of human rights, the conduct of a quasi-judicial proceedings to determine the validity of the claims and the rendering of decisions or recommendations that aim at securing justice for the victims consistent with international human rights standards and through appropriate remedies.

NHRIs in Southeast Asia are part of a nascent architecture for the protection of human rights that also includes the ASEAN (Association of Southeast Asian Nations) Intergovernmental Commission on Human Rights (AICHR), created in 2010, and the Universal Periodic Review (UPR) of the UN Human Rights Council (HRC) in 2006. The critical question is whether they individually or collectively provide protection of fundamental human rights. On both fronts, the protection function of this emerging human rights architecture appears to be missing and is well documented (Forum Asia 2015; Gomez and Ramcharan 2012, 2017; Morada 2019). AICHR is constrained by its promotional mandate. The UPR, as shown in Gomez and Ramcharan's *The Universal Periodic Review of Southeast Asia*, holds great potential for civil society organizations (CSOs) "to hold up a mirror to their respective governments" (Gomez and Ramcharan 2017: 3). CSOs, who are not participants in AICHR's formal reviews of member states' human rights situations, have engaged enthusiastically with the UPR process, and that trend has continued into the third cycle (2017–2021). However, critiques of the UPR include its ritualism, states' tendency to "note" recommendations they do not like and inadequate mid-term reviews and follow-up processes at the national level.

It is useful to note that while this book focuses on NHRIs in its modern form, some countries in Southeast Asia which have NHRIs have also established Ombudsman offices, for example, Indonesia (2008), Philippines (1987) and Thailand (1997), while Cambodia, which does not have an NHRI, has introduced subnational Ombudsman services in 2017. There is also the Asian Ombudsman Association, where, apart from ASEAN member states Indonesia, Philippines and Thailand, Vietnam's Government Inspectorate (2012) and Malaysia's Public Complaints Bureau (1971), which was designated in 2018 to be an Ombudsman (New Straits Times 2018), are also members (http://www.asianombudsman.com/). Primarily, the Ombudsman is government appointed and examines maladministration by public authorities (see generally Hossain 2000). Human rights violations may arise but this is not the mandate of the Ombudsman. However, many around the world have come to embrace this aspect, as in the case of the Ombudsman in Timor-Leste, which performs the central function of an NHRI.

## NHRI's Protection Role and Southeast Asia

In this context, this collection seeks to determine the potential of NHRIs in Southeast Asia to advance the protection of human rights. Many NHRIs have been established around the world, and since 1987, as discussed by Michael J.V. White in Chap. 1, five out of the ten member states of the ASEAN have established NHRIs. Timor-Leste, which has applied for ASEAN membership, established an Ombudsman for Human Rights and Peace in 2004. The 2007 ASEAN Charter provides for the protection role of NHRIs. Article 16 (1) of the Charter states that its members' "common interest" in the promotion and protection of human rights "shall be achieved through, inter alia, cooperation with one another as well as with relevant ***national***, regional and international institutions/organisations, in accordance with the ASEAN Charter."

The protection role of NHRIs has been widely acclaimed by practitioners and academicians (Ramcharan 2005). They were recognized by the UN Office of the High Commissioner for Human Rights (OHCHR) as pillars of national human rights systems for the promotion and protection of human rights, as playing a crucial role in these endeavors (United Nations 2011), and in advancement of the rule of law. The HRC has encouraged states "to establish effective, independent and pluralistic national institutions" and, where they already exist, "to strengthen them" (United Nations 2013: 2–3). The HRC encouraged national institutions to "play an active role in preventing and combating all violations of human rights" (United Nations 2013: 2–3).

NHRIs, along with Ombudsman offices and other hybrids, have proliferated in the last three decades along with the inexorable march of democracy across the globe since the end of the Cold War and in particular since the World Conference on Human Rights in Vienna in 1993. There are now many such institutions around the world and they take several forms: national commission, national advisory commission, national antidiscrimination commission, an Ombudsman and a "defender of the people" (*defensordel pueblo*) (Cardenas 2004; De Beco 2007). They reflect a particular stage in the evolution of the post-1945 human rights movement, which has gone from norms creation to norms diffusion and now to norm implementation. The first gathering to consider the protection role of

NHRIs took place in 1991, resulting in the well-known Paris Principles adopted by the UN General Assembly in 1993.

Scholarly analysis of the protection roles of NHRIs has featured in many works for the past two decades as NHRIs have proliferated since the 1990s (Cardenas 2003, 2004, 2014; Brems et al. 2013; De Beco and Murray 2015; Goodman 2012; Koo and Ramirez 2009; Mertus 2009; Murray 2007; Reif 2000; Seong 2005). Cardenas has called for the study of their creation and impact. Her work *Chains of Justice: The Global Rise of State Institutions for Human Rights* (2014) offered an explanation of why states would commit to establishing NHRIs, whether they were already compliant domestically with international human rights law or not. The latter scenario is ever more perplexing. She situates the rise of NHRIs in the context of "self-restraining states" in which accountability is provided horizontally across state agencies. NHRIs in this view are created to keep in check other state agencies. Integral to this explanation is a view of the state as a disaggregated entity, as a complex whole and not a unitary actor.

A study by practitioners/CSO body, seeking to go beyond legal and institutional issues, examined "what made NHRIs effective" based on studies of NHRIs in Ghana, Indonesia and Mexico. They noted in particular the issues of relations with other human rights bodies, including CSOs, and accessibility of the most vulnerable in society to the NHRI (ICHRP 2000). They noted further that it was important to go beyond a discussion of standards along the lines of the Paris Principles and to examine public perceptions of what an NHRI is and whether there was social legitimacy of the institution. The crucial measure of the effectiveness of NHRIs, they argued, was whether they were able to respond to the needs of those who were the most at risk of suffering violations. They noted that there is no single, model NHRI for the whole world. They further noted that the Paris Principles are a good and necessary starting point but are not sufficient for a comprehensive examination of the effectiveness of NHRIs.

Studies have been undertaken on NHRIs in different regions of Africa (Murray 2007), Europe (Wouters 2013), Latin America and the Caribbean (Ayeni et al. 2000). Of particular relevance is the critical assessment of Mexico's NHRI made by Human Rights Watch, which noted the body's failure to live up to its promise and in particular its inability to secure remedies and promote reforms to Mexico's dismal human rights record (HRW 2008). Other criticisms included the failure of the body's own procedures and its alleged failure to fully use its mandate and immense resources, despite having qualified investigators. The most damning condemnation was the body's "abandonment" of cases before they were resolved. A study of the difficulties of implementing the Paris Principles in Hong Kong was undertaken by Peterson (Peterson 2004).

Analyses of NHRIs and processes in East and Southeast Asia have been featured in a few works (Burdekin 2007; Cardenas 2004, 2014; Nasu and Saul 2011; and Renshaw 2011). Sonia Cardenas pointed to a number of NHRIs in Asia (India, Indonesia and the Philippines) that emerged due to significant international pressures as well as domestic pressures. National human rights institutions have been established in Australia, Fiji, India, Indonesia, Malaysia, Myanmar, Mongolia, Nepal, New Zealand, Philippines, Republic of Korea, Sri Lanka, Thailand and Timor-Leste. Hugo Stokke has examined the experience of NHRIs in Indonesia, Malaysia and the Philippines against the Paris Principles, noting a persistent issue of the independence of the commissioners cropping up (Stokke 2007). Eldridge has examined the role of NHRIs in forging linkages between governments, civil society and the UN human rights system (Eldridge 2002). Another work by Evans (2004), while noting the NHRI's inability to enforce their decisions, called attention to their constructive role in the promotion and protection of human rights. Evans (2004) has chronicled the record of human rights commissions in relation to religious conflict in the Asia-Pacific region and the possibility of NHRCs contributing to the emergence of a culture of rights. Andrea Durbach, Catherine Renshaw and Andrew Byrnes have attempted to identify the functions that a regional mechanism might play that are distinct from national institutions and regional networks, suggesting that while such mechanisms are important, the protection of human rights still requires the accompanying political will.

Given the emerging works on NHRIs in Asia and in Southeast Asia in particular, this work seeks to contribute to the literature by focusing principally on the Southeast Asian (SEA) countries' NHRIs. Authors collectively probe the quasi-judicial function of the Southeast Asian NHRIs and conclude that where this function was first included, it has either later eroded due to political developments post-establishment or not included in the first place. As a result, NHRIs cannot effectively contribute to the overall "protection" dimension of the human rights architecture emerging in Southeast Asia. Thus, the central thrust across the chapters here is the effectiveness of NHRIs in advancing the protection of human rights. This work examines the state of NHRIs in Southeast Asia.

The conclusion of this work may inform theoretical frameworks aimed at explaining human rights norms diffusion and protection at the domestic level. NHRIs serve to localize human rights norms through their promotion and protection initiatives. Cardenas, as noted above, has argued for the idea of the self-restraining state (Cardenas 2014), though this is not apparent in the current regional regression in democracy and rights. Acharya has noted that localization of norms in Southeast Asia may take place for a variety of reasons ranging from satisfying elite preferences, acknowledging local norms and recognizing resistance by local agents. He posited that domestic political structures are key to understanding localization domestically and regionally. In this argument the varied political systems and authoritarian domestic structures in Southeast Asia limit both the capacity and effectiveness of NHRIs in carrying out their mandates.

This work is grounded in evidence-based research by author-practitioners who are intimately familiar with NHRs. It is based on primary documents inclusive of annual reports by NHRIs, submissions concerning NHRIs under the UN Human Rights Council's Universal Periodic Review, firsthand work with the respective NHRIs by the authors and independent commentators contained in the annual publication of the Asian NGO Networks on National Human Rights Institutions (ANNI) (ANNI Reports 2011, 2012, 2013, 2014, 2015, 2016, 2017, 2018). It takes into account rankings and criteria of the Global Alliance of National Human Rights Institutions (GANHRI), though the focus in this work is not to scrutinize GANHRI's processes or findings but, instead, to examine the NHRIs from the ground up. In this vein, the capacity of such international mechanisms and institutions to affect the behavior of states and to bring about change domestically is well covered in the literature on international institutions over the last few decades. One does not need to revisit this theme here. Suffice it to mention existing analysis such as *International Organisations: Theories and Institutions* (Palgrave Macmillan) and the "Global Institutions Series" of Routledge (see also Amitav 2004).

## Structure of the Book

The chapters assembled here are structured in three parts: Part I examines the regional and universal context in which NHRIs operate, Part II looks at specific case studies of NHRIs and Part III focuses on specific themes such as mental health and land rights of indigenous peoples dealt with by some NHRIs.

Michael J.V. White sets the stage in Chap. 2, with an exploration of the history and development of NHRIs, and examines the role of the Paris Principles. He then considers the institutional and environmental features that are required for NHRIs to work effectively. He argues that NHRIs sit at the crossroads between government and civil society. This enables them to effectively monitor and advocate for improved human rights realization. To perform their tasks effectively, NHRIs need to be autonomous from the state so that they can investigate the state, as well as from NGOs and civil society. It is in the latter aspect where NHRIs have grappled with the dilemma of independence, while at the same time establishing working relationships with both government and NGOs. The independence of these institutions and thus their effectiveness can be fragile and must be vigorously protected by the state, civil society, and members and staff. However, experience shows that few NHRIs are financially and administratively independent of government. White notes that NHRIS must work collaboratively—both bilaterally and through networks—to enhance the understanding of the need for independence and to create greater space for the protection of human rights across the region.

The complementarities between NHRIs and the AICHR are explored by Céline Martin in Chap. 3. She notes that in the absence of a strong regional mechanism, the NHRIs have an important role to play for the promotion and the protection of human rights in the SEA states, assuming that they adhered to the 1993 Paris Principles, which established universal principles for effective NHRIs. She notes, however, that most of the SEA NHRIs do not enforce those principles efficiently or not at all. She identifies possible complementarities between NHRIs and AICHR that can serve to overcome their respective deficiencies through cooperation between these two entities. She explores (1) how, within their own mandates, the SEA existing NHRIs and the AICHR can work together to advance the promotion and protection of human rights in the region; (2) how laws that would establish NHRIs in the remaining countries could be adopted in order to respect the Paris Principles while being strong foundations to the AICHR and (3) how best practices from NHRIs evolving in a different regional environment (OAS, ECtHR, AfHRC) can influence the AICHR to strengthen the relationships between SEA NHRIs.

Another avenue for enhancing the protection function of NHRIs is explored by Domenico Zipoli in Chap. 4. Under a novel governance theory model—human rights experimentalism—he analyses treaty bodies–NHRI interaction as a means of contextualizing global human rights norms. Critiques of the ineffectiveness of the treaty body system, he argues, are to be valued as necessary elements of a properly functioning system. Amongst others, the following two elements are seen as the treaty body system's inherent weaknesses: the apparent ambiguity in standards and the lack of a strong or judicial-type enforcement mechanism. Zipoli notes the complementarity as follows: the TB members together with the UN OHCHR act as orchestrators seeking to influence the behavior of the target, the states' parties to the treaties. In between this bilateral dialectic, the model highlights the fundamental role of the intermediary, UN-affiliated NHRIs and their collective representative body, the GANHRI, which serve as a functional gateway to inform and strive to bridge the aforementioned gap to compliance. By adding an institutional connector between international regulators and the state, orchestration suggests that the classic disconnect and distinction between the international and domestic is to be considered somewhat less draconian.

This intermediary role is not obvious in the case of Myanmar's National Human Rights Commission (MNHRC), whose independence from the state is highly problematic in a country that is in its early phases of a transition to democracy and experiencing ethnic cleansing of the Rohingya minority from Myanmar. Niki Esse de Lang explores the MNHRC in Chap. 5, providing a very rare analysis of this institution. He argues that notwithstanding considerable progress that has been made in recent years, the MNHRC has thus far proven not to have reached a satisfactory level of effectiveness, in that it is not fully in conformity with the Paris Principles. Its ineffectiveness is not only due to its youth, inexperience and lack of political will, but must also be assessed in light of Myanmar's opposition to the creation of effective regional human rights mechanisms, notably the AICHR. This chapter not only analyses the legal framework of the MNHRC and whether or not it conforms with international standards but also its practical work and what it has achieved so far in terms of protection and promotion of human rights. Moreover, it takes a closer look at the creation of AICHR and SEANF and its influence on Myanmar and the MNHRC as well as how the latter two have engaged with these regional bodies.

Francesca Paola Traglia, who worked directly with the MNHRC, nevertheless identifies opportunities for the MNHRC in Chap. 6. She notes that during the 28th Session of the Human Rights Council in March

2015, Myanmar's Deputy Foreign Minister U Thyant Kyaw declared that the MNHRC Law was enacted by the Parliament on 28 March 2014 in order to bring it in compliance with the Paris Principles. This action by the government in 2014 and 2015 showed a clear commitment to move forward on establishing a functioning NHRI in Myanmar; however, despite some improvements, the MNHRC continues to be criticized for a perceived lack of effectiveness in Myanmar (see Aung 2016). She argues that such critiques need to be placed within a larger context of transition and semi-civilian rule, as well as the detailed implications and gaps of "The Myanmar National Human Rights Commission Law." Whereas CSOs insist on a "watchdog role," namely, the state, this remains difficult in emerging democracies and in stages of transition where many human rights challenges are present. The MNHRC can play a crucial role in bridging the divide between civil society and the state and in holding the latter accountable. However, the pace of change for both commission and government needs to match institutional absorptive capacity. Challenges include developing a culture of human rights and democratic governance; navigating plural legal systems; addressing issues related to federalism and governance, constitutional reform, appreciating diversity and addressing the aspirations of ethnic nationalities; ensuring equitable development; and reducing inequalities generated by market reform. Despite the challenges, Myanmar's reforms and advancements since 2011 provide cause for balanced optimism; yet it remains to be seen what the new state councilor's plans are in relation to pushing forward on developing a culture of human rights and democratic governance in Myanmar.

What can the MNHRC learn from the older Komnas Ham, Indonesia's NHRI which was born in similar political circumstances? Analysis of Komnas HAM has been very sparse, featuring in less than five articles over the past two decades. Nukila Evanty analyzes in Chap. 7 the challenges facing Komnas HAM. She notes a negative public perception of this institution because of its slow response to handling of complaints by the public, the lack of responses of the commissioner on the substance of human rights violations reported by the public, neglected reports and problems among the commissioners themselves. Moreover, Komnas HAM has constraints in investigating and monitoring past human rights violations. Recommendations by Komnas HAM are not obeyed. Some long-standing cases under consideration have not yet been resolved, particularly seven (7) cases of past human rights violations: Trisakti incident, Semanggi I and Semanggi II, Talangsari incident, enforced disappearances, mysterious shootings, massacres after the G30S/PKI incident, and the May 1998 riots. She notes obstacles in the implementation of human rights protection in the context of the constitution, some problems and discrepancies between the human rights laws and related laws in connection with the future human rights protection with the new commissioners, the weak power of Komnas HAM and its recommendations.

Inosentius Samsul, in Chap. 9, furthers the analysis of Komnas HAM, which has "more power" in comparison with other national institutions—National Commission on Violence Against Women (Komnas Perempuan) and National Commission on Child Protection (KPAI). Komnas Perempuan and KPAI have different positions with Komnas HAM, although the name is the National Commission. Unlike these, Komnas HAM has more power in terms of position as an independent institution as the NHRI. However, along with the others, he argues that Komnas HAM does not contribute positively to the enforcement of human rights and its image in the public eye has diminished in the New Order period. Komnas HAM still faced various obstacles: human resources are not proportional to the workload and the demands and expectations of the people to get excellent service, and the budget given to Komnas HAM is still limited, and so Komnas HAM cannot perform its functions and duties optimally. His key recommendation is to consolidate, reformulate and better coordinate the authority of Komnas HAM and the other commissions to make them more powerful. He argues for better support from government institutions, financial support and decentralization through the addition of representative offices in the region.

Similar issues affecting the mandates and capacities of other NHRIs in the Philippines, Thailand and Timor-Leste are examined by James Gomez and Robin Ramcharan in Chap. 9. The combined exploration of the three countries' human rights institutions outlines some of their common difficult circumstances even as the authors faced informational and logistical challenges to conducting analysis of these institutions as they faced harsh treatment from their respective states. Nevertheless, Gomez and Ramcharan discuss the mandates, political contexts and protection capacities of the respective NHRIs. In both the Philippines and Thailand, these institutions have come under serious attack by their own governments. In Thailand's case, the very existence of the NHRCT continues to be in doubt, as its commissioners were under severe pressure from the military dictatorship ruling Thailand following the coup of 2014. The NHRCT's status under the 2017 Constitution occasioned alarm over its future existence and its ability to serve the protection of human rights remains a concern after the military-led elections of 2019.

These challenges do not exist in Singapore, where the government has resisted the creation of an NHRI, arguing that it does not need one. James Gomez and Michelle D'cruz, in Chap. 10, analyze the factors that bar the creation of a national institution in Singapore. They note that Singapore's long-standing political structure as a one-party dominant state has often raised the need for a separation of powers. They suggest that Singapore's current political structure continues to act as a hindrance for the establishment of independent institutions such as those related to human rights. Some commentators have proposed that Singapore starts by establishing an Ombudsman. However, the authors caution that there is a risk that such an institution might focus only public service maladministration and not the full suit of human rights issues. Nevertheless, the UPR process has shown that the discourse for establishing an NHRI in Singapore is no longer only domestically situated. It has also attained an international platform. In examining Singapore's one-party state and political structure as hindrance to the establishment of an NHRI, the city-state's experience may well hold true for other countries in the region that do not have an NHRI, such as Brunei, Cambodia, Laos and Vietnam, where similar structures and political cultures may be found.

The depth and breadth of issues that can be tackled by NHRIs in societies that are experiencing, however grudgingly, long-term transitions towards more democratic governance is revealed by Kimberley Clair in Chap. 11. She analyzes the role of Komnas HAM in advancing the rights of people with disabilities, notably those with mental health issues. She discusses Komnas HAM's recent Indonesia foray into the rights of individuals with psychosocial disabilities through new and revised legislation, greater investment in community health organizations, and campaigns aimed to prevent discrimination against persons with severe mental illness. Komnas HAM has investigated human rights violations, recommended amendments to discriminatory laws and policies and produced research on the intersections of mental health and human rights. Nevertheless, protecting the rights of persons with psychosocial disabilities remains a challenge for Komnas HAM due to weak enforcement powers and widespread misconceptions about disabilities and disability rights. Three issues have hampered the institution's mental health advocacy efforts, namely, its inability to enforce legislation; its ambiguous definitions of disability, mental health and human rights; and its uneven, inconsistent approach to mental health advocacy. Moreover, she offers more broadly a critique of Indonesia's Bebas Pasung campaign, which represents a disaggregated approach to mental health and human rights. She suggests that an overemphasis on reporting and identifying cases of *pasung*—the practice of restraining persons with acute mental illness—has discouraged comprehensive discussions of mental health in Indonesian communities.

Likewise, Malaysia's SUHAKAM has tackled sexual orientation, gender identity and expression of sex characteristics (SOGIESEC), which is examined by Henry Koh in Chap. 12. He argues that SUHAKAM has progressed in a positive *albeit* limited manner with regard to the protection of the rights related to sexual orientation, gender identity and expression of sex characteristics (SOGIESC). Overall, however, for a country that has achieved impressive economic development, Malaysia's human rights record has not similarly developed, especially with regard SOGIESC. In comparison with NHRIs in other Southeast Asian nations, Malaysia's NHRI has struggled to take up SOGIESC initiatives due to political and cultural impediments, but SUHAKAM has shown signs of significant improvement in this area.

The thorny issue of land rights of indigenous peoples in Indonesia and its handling by Komnas HAM is assessed by Isnenningtyas Yulianti in Chap. 13. She examines how Komnas HAM handles cases of violations of the ownership rights of indigenous peoples. Komnas HAM does not limit itself to handling cases concerning civil rights and politics itself, but it has also been actively involved in the enforcement of economic, social and cultural rights. In 2016 alone, Komnas HAM had received 2539 cases related to the fulfillment of the rights of economic, social, cultural and society at large. She surveys the handling of cases of land rights of indigenous peoples that has been done by Komnas HAM, including new mechanisms used by Komnas HAM in dealing with land rights for indigenous peoples.

## Conclusion

The establishment of NHRIs has become one of the indicia of a progressive democratic liberal state (Renshaw 2011: 4). However, some have long-warned that many NHRIs are established mainly to appease the international community—"state adaptation"—which has a "paradoxical effect," namely, "most NHRIs remain too weak to protect society from human rights violations at the same time that they create an unprecedented demand for such protection" (Cardenas 2003: 3). At the present time, this appears to be the case with the NHRIs in Southeast Asia, which are all operating in the context of problematic democratic transitions, some less certain than others and in many occasions sliding back to authoritarianism.

The collective assessment offered here is as follows: (1) NHRIs are dependent on the political climate in each state; (2) their quasi-judicial investigative processes are lacking in the follow-through that is necessary for the advancement of justice, not only for the parties in individual cases but more generally for the advancement of human rights consistent with international human rights standards and (3) they do not seem to be capable of securing remedies or advancing this cause for victims of violations of rights.

Gomez and Ramcharan, culling together from the foregoing analyzes, note that NHRI mandates do provide, for the most part, reasonable protection powers on which the NHRIs could build and, if they are willing and enterprising, could expand on. Beyond the mandate to investigate, enabling rules and procedures are in place—such as the ability to call state officials and other types of witnesses to give evidence, immunity and related protections for witnesses, the provision of sanctions for noncompliance, the issuing of recommendations for follow-up action by appropriate authorities—and could easily provide the foundation for a more vigorous protection role. A major problem, however, is the inability and perhaps unwillingness to follow-through.

The record on follow-through is not stellar as NHRIs are simply ignored. Their contribution to providing redress and remedies remains at best aspirational. Effective protection of human rights may serve to advance the rule of law and, in so doing, consolidate young democracies. Moreover, they thrive best in democratic contexts, which have appropriate checks and balances upon governmental authority. The NHRIs in Southeast Asia are products of their individual country's political contexts. As elsewhere, these NHRIs in Southeast Asia generally mirror domestic political developments and demands from the international arena. The record of NHRIs in these areas, in the context of their dependence on the general political climate, can be improved.

Authors in this work take a "normative" position in that they call upon NHRIs to not only fulfill their mandates but also to pursue purposively and to the full extent a quasi-judicial role that is inherent in their functions. A quasi-judicial role is not confined to acting as "friends of the Court" or observing court proceedings. It is inclusive of vigorously exercising investigative powers, making determinations on violations of rights where those do occur, publicly announcing those determinations, indicating the legal reasoning leading to findings of violations and following through with the relevant authorities to pursue redress and remedies for the victims. The 2018 ANNI Report, which surveyed all NHRIs in Southeast Asia, recommended that "NHRIs should be granted adequate powers of investigation and they should have some power to enforce the recommendations that come from those investigations" (ANNI Report 2018: 11).

Despite positive achievements, the actual practice of protection by the NHRIs leaves much to be desired. They reveal that the NHRIs are struggling to perform the protection function effectively. This further reinforces the case for a weak human rights protection architecture in Southeast Asia that is in need of improvement and enhancement. Well-meaning practitioners in NHRIs, who labor valiantly and seek to advance international human rights standards in challenging times, must not take cover behind rules and procedures but must, instead, "push the envelope", so to speak, much the same way that the UN did so in the 1970s and 1980s in order to innovate and create the global human rights protection architecture out of existing law, practice and procedures. This required strong empathy for the victims, conviction, intellectual muscle, legal and professional dexterity and resolute leadership.

Meanwhile, in Southeast Asian countries that do not have NHRIs, Gomez and Ramcharan call for the establishment of NHRIs as they may prove helpful to the governments in navigating the complex national, regional and international human rights ecosystem. However, they should not fall into the same predicament that currently affects NHRIs in Southeast Asia.

## References

Amitav A. 2004. How Ideas Spread: Whose Norms Matter? Norm Localization and Institutional Change in Asian Regionalism," *International Organization*, Vol. 58, No. 2 (Spring), pp. 239–275.

ANNI Report. 2010. *ANNI Report on the Performance and Establishment of National Human Rights Institutions in Asia*. Bangkok: Forum Asia.

———. 2011. *ANNI Report on the Performance and Establishment of National Human Rights Institutions in Asia*. Bangkok: Forum Asia.

———. 2012. *ANNI Report on the Performance and Establishment of National Human Rights Institutions in Asia*. Bangkok: Forum Asia.

———. 2013. *ANNI Report on the Performance and Establishment of National Human Rights Institutions in Asia*. Bangkok: Forum Asia.

———. 2014. *ANNI Report on the Performance and Establishment of National Human Rights Institutions in Asia*. Bangkok: Forum Asia.

———. 2015. *ANNI Report on the Performance and Establishment of National Human Rights Institutions in Asia*. Bangkok: Forum Asia.

———. 2016. *ANNI Report on the Performance and Establishment of National Human Rights Institutions in Asia*. Bangkok: Forum Asia.

———. 2017. *ANNI Report on the Performance and Establishment of National Human Rights Institutions in Asia*. Bangkok: Forum Asia.

———. 2018. *ANNI Report on the Performance and Establishment of National Human Rights Institutions in Asia*. Bangkok: Forum Asia.

Aung Khaing Min and Kuan Joses. 2016. Human Rights Commission comes under fire over record. *Myanmar Times*, 03 February 2016. Available at: http://www.mmtimes.com/index.php/opinion/18786-human-rights-commission-comes-under-fire-over-record.html.

Ayeni, Victor, Reif, Linda, and Thomas, Hayden (eds.). 2000. *Strengthening Ombudsman and Human Rights Institutions in Commonwealth Small and Island States: The Caribbean Experience*. London: Commonwealth Secretariat with The International Ombudsman Institute, Canada.

Brems, E., de Beco, G. and Vandenhole, W. (eds). 2013 *National human rights institutions and economic, social and cultural rights*. Cambridge: Intersentia.

Burdekin, B. 2007. *National Human Rights Institutions in the Asia Pacific Region* Volume 27 of Raoul Wallenberg Institute Human Rights Library, Martinus Nijhoff Publishers.

Cardenas, S. 2003. Emerging Global Actors: the United Nations and National Human Rights Institutions. *Global Governance*, Vol. 9, No. 1, Jan.–Mar. 2003.

———. 2004 *Adaptive states: the proliferation of National Human Rights institutions*. Carr Center for Human Rights Policy Working Paper T-01-04. Available at: http://content.knowledgeplex.org/kp2/cache/kp/24.pdf.

———. 2014. *Chains of justice: the global rise of state institutions for human rights*. Philadelphia: University of Pennsylvania Press.

De Beco, G. 2007. *National Human Rights Institutions in Europe, Cellule de recherché interdisciplinaire en droits de l'homme*, Université catholique de Louvain, Faculté de droit, CRIDHO Working Paper 1.

De Beco, G. and Murray, R. 2015 A commentary on the Paris Principles on national human rights institutions. Cambridge: Cambridge University Press.

Eldridge, P. 2002. Emerging Roles of National Human Rights Institutions in Southeast Asia. *Pacific Review: Peace, Security & Global Change*, Vol. 14, No. 3.

Evans, C. 2004. Human Rights Commissions and Religious Conflict in the Asia-Pacific Region. *International and Comparative Law Quarterly*, Vol. 53, July 2004, pp. 713–729.

Forum Asia. 2015. *The Future of Human Rights in ASEAN Public Call for Independence and Protection Mandates,* A Report on the Performance of the ASEAN Human Rights Mechanism in 2014. Bangkok: Forum Asia.

Gomez, G. and Ramcharan, R. 2012. The Protection of Human Rights in Southeast Asia: Improving the Effectiveness of Civil Society Advocacy. *Asia-Pacific Journal on Human Rights and the Law,* Vol. 2, pp. 27–43.

———. 2017 *The Universal Periodic Review of Southeast Asia: Civil Society Perspectives.* Palgrave.

Goodman, R. et al. (ed.) 2012. *Human rights, state compliance, and social change: assessing national human rights institutions.* Cambridge: Cambridge University Press.

Hossain, K. 2000. Human Rights Commissions and Ombudsman Offices: National Experiences Throughout the World. Martinus Nijhoff.

Human Rights Watch (HRW). 2008. *Mexico's National Human Rights Commission.* February. Vol. 20, No. 1B.

International Council on Human Rights Policy (ICHRP). 2000. *Performance & Legitimacy: National Human Rights Institutions.* ICHRP.

Koo, J.-W. and Ramirez, F. 2009. *National Incorporation of Global Human Rights: Worldwide Expansion of National Human Rights Institutions,* 1966–2004, Social Forces, Vol. 87, No 3, March 2009, pp. 1321–1354.

Lindsnaes, B. and Lindholt, L. 2000. National Human Rights Institutions – Standard setting and achievements," in Lindsnaes et al., *National Human Rights Institutions, Articles and Papers.* Ed. Birgit Lindsnaes, et al., Copenhagen, Danish Human Rights Center.

Mertus, J. 2009. *Human rights matters: local politics and national human rights institutions.* Stanford, CA: Stanford University Press.

Morada, Noel. 2019. ASEAN and Human Protection in Myanmar: From Non-Interference to Non-Indifference? forthcoming. In *Regionalism and Human Protection*, Charles T. Hunt, Noel M. Morada (Eds.), pp. 98–122.

Murray, R. 2007. *The Role of National Human Rights Institutions at the International and Regional Levels: The Experience of Africa/Place.* London: Hart, 2007.

Nasu, H. and Saul, B. (eds.) 2011. *Human rights in the Asia-Pacific region: towards institution building.* London: Routledge.

New Straits Times. 2018. *Malaysia to have its own Ombudsman, replacing Public Complaints Bureau,* 21 September 2018. Available at: https://www.nst.com.my/news/nation/2018/09/413601/malaysia-have-its-own-ombudsman-replacing-public-complaints-bureau.

Peterson, C.J. 2004. The Paris Principles and Human Rights Institutions: Is Hong Kong Slipping Further Away From the Mark?, *Hong Kong Law Journal*, Vol. 33, No. 3, pp. 513–522.

Ramcharan, B. (ed.) 2005. *The Protection Roles of National Human Rights Institutions*. The Hague, Martinus Nijhoff, 2005.

Reif, L. 2000. Building Democratic Institutions: The Role of National Human Rights Institutions in Good Governance and Human Rights Protection. *The Harvard Human Rights Journal* Spring, Vol. 13, No. 1, pp. 1–72.

Renshaw, C. 2011. Testing the Mettle of National Human Rights Institutions: A Case Study of the Human Rights Commission of Malaysia. *Asian Journal of International Law*, 1, pp. 165–198.

Seong, H. (Marcellino). 2005. *National human rights institutions in East Asia: impact of international cooperation on the effectiveness of national human rights institutions*. Genève: Institut universitaire de hautes études internationales, 2005 Diplôme d'études approfondies en relations internationales/IUHEI [265]. Mention Science politique.

Stokke, H. 2007. *Taking the Paris Principles to Asia: A Study of Three Human Rights Commissions in Southeast Asia: Indonesia, Malaysia and the Philippines*. Chr. Michelsen Institute, 2007.

United Nations. 2004. *Effective Functioning of Human Rights Mechanisms: National Institutions and Regional Arrangements. National Institutions for the Promotion and Protection of Human Rights*. Report of the Secretary General. 28 January. E/CN.4/2004/101.

———. 2011. *National Institutions for the Promotion and Protection of Human Rights: Report of the Secretary General*. A/HRC/16/76.

———. 2013. *National Institutions for the Promotion and Protection of Human Rights*, Human Rights Council. A/HRC23/L.15. 7 June 2013.

Wouters, J. 2013. *National human rights institutions in Europe* / [et al.] (eds.) Cambridge: Intersentia.

PART I

# Southeast Asian NHRIs: Regional and Global Perspectives

CHAPTER 2

# National Human Rights Institutions: From Idea to Implementation

*Michael J. V. White*

## Introduction

National human rights institutions (NHRIs) play an increasingly pivotal role in international and national human rights systems. Put simply, NHRIs are national bodies tasked with promoting and protecting human rights. The International Coordinating Committee of National Institutions for the Promotion and Protection of Human Rights[1] Subcommittee on Accreditation has stated (2013: 46):

> [They are] established by States for the specific purpose of advancing and defending human rights at a national level and are acknowledged to be one of the most important means by which States bridge the implementation game between their international human rights obligations and actual enjoyment of human rights on the ground.

[1] Now the "Global Alliance of National Human Rights Institutions."

M. J. V. White (✉)
Independent Legal and Policy Consultant, Wellington, New Zealand


J. Gomez, R. Ramcharan (eds.), *National Human Rights Institutions in Southeast Asia*,
https://doi.org/10.1007/978-981-15-1074-8_2

NHRIs are one of the most important institutional developments of recent years. NHRIs can play a key role in promoting and protecting human rights. They can do so by the unique position they occupy between government, civil society and nongovernmental organisations (NGOs). Their codification in the Paris Principles and endorsement by the United Nations General Assembly in 1993 have changed the human rights landscape globally. The Paris Principles constitute a concrete template for NHRI design, with guidelines covering their independence, jurisdiction, mandate and composition. These principles have had the positive impact of introducing and even strengthening NHRIs. NHRIs can now be found in a wide range of political regimes—from Bahrain to Colombia to Ireland. Their numbers have soured from a handful in 1991 to approximately 120 active NHRIs in 2015. NHRIs are now a mainstay of multilevel human rights governance.

The Asia-Pacific Forum of National Human Rights Institutions has stated that "[s]trong and effective NHRIs help bridge the 'protection gap' between the rights of individuals and the responsibilities of the State by:

- Monitoring the human rights situation in the country and the actions of the State
- Providing advice to the State so that it can meet its international and domestic human rights commitments
- Receiving, investigating and resolving complaints of human rights violations
- Undertaking human rights education programs for all sections of the community
- Engaging with the international human rights community to raise pressing issues and advocate for recommendation that can be made to the State.[2]"

While this may be the case, many challenges remain to ensure that these institutions are strong and effective and have an ongoing positive impact on human rights practices.

This chapter explores the history and development of NHRIs and examines the role of the Paris Principles. It then considers the institutional and environmental features that are required for NHRIs to work effectively.

[2] http://www.asiapacificforum.net/support/what-are-nhris/.

## A Brief History

Modern human rights have their genesis in World War II and the articulation of Roosevelt's four freedoms in the 1941 Atlantic Charter (Roosevelt and Churchill 1941). The Atlantic Charter was an affirmation of "certain common principles in the national policies of their respective countries on which they based their hopes for a better future for the world" (ibid.). It emphasised freedoms for all the men in all the lands. Nelson Mandela had noted that while one of the purposes of the 1941 Charter was clearly to mobilise support for the Allies among nonaligned countries and colonies, it had a much wider impact, reaffirming faith in the dignity of each human being and propagating a host of democratic principles (1994: 83–84).

The following year in 1942, the Declaration of the United Nations was adopted by 25 countries declaring a commitment to the principles of the Atlantic Charter (United Nations 1942). The preamble of the Declaration states (ibid.):

> that complete victory over their enemies is essential to defend life, liberty, independence and religious freedom, and to preserve **human rights** and justice in their own lands as well as in other lands, and that they are now engaged in a common struggle against savage and brutal forces seeking to subjugate the world.

The 1942 Declaration of the United Nations formed the basis for the United Nations Charter, the Universal Declaration of Human Rights and all subsequent international human rights covenants and conventions. The international human rights framework that emerged is premised on the centrality of the role of states and their governments in protecting human rights. In line with this emphasis, the importance of establishing independent national machinery explicitly devoted to the enforcement and improvement of human rights became rapidly apparent. Human rights involve the relationship between individuals and the state. Accordingly, the practical task of protecting human rights is a national one. The emergence of democratic rule in many countries post–World War II highlighted to importance of democratic institutions in safeguarding the legal foundations upon which human rights are based. It became rapidly apparent that the effective enjoyment of human rights calls for the establishment of national infrastructures.

The importance of national institutions was first considered by the Economic and Social Council (ECOSOC) in 1946 where member states were invited to consider establishing information groups or local human rights committees (1946). Although there was some diplomatic debates and occasional resolutions that acknowledged the importance of national institutions (ECOSOC 1960), it was not until some 30 years later that progress was made to strengthen such institutions. In 1978, the Commission on Human Rights—the predecessor of the United Nations Human Rights Council—organised a seminar which resulted in draft guidelines for the structure and functioning of national institutions. The United Nations General Assembly subsequently endorsed these guidelines (1978: 1).[3] The guidelines suggested that national institutions should:

1. "Act as a source of human rights information for the Government and people of the country
2. Assist in educating public opinion and promoting awareness and respect for human rights
3. Consider, deliberate upon, and make recommendations regarding any particular state of affairs that may exist nationally, and the Government may wish to refer to them
4. Advise on any questions regarding human rights matters referred to them by the Government
5. Study and keep under review the status of legislation, judicial decisions and administrative arrangements for the promotions of human rights, and to prepare and submit reports on these matters to the appropriate authorities
6. Perform any other function which the Government may wish to assign to them in connection with the duties of that State under those international agreements in the field of human rights to which it is a party" (OHCHR 1993: 3).

The Office of the High Commissioner for Human Rights notes in relation to structure that the guidelines recommended that national institutions should:

1. "Be so designed as to reflect the composition, wide cross-sections of the nation, thereby bringing all parts of that population into the decision-making process regarding human rights

[3] The General Assembly also requested that the Secretary-General submit a detailed report on NHRIs.

2. Function regularly, and that immediate access to them should be available to any member of the public or any public authority
3. In appropriate cases, have local or regional advisory organs to assist them in discharging their functions" (ibid.: 4).

While this was a significant step forward, it should be noted that the guidelines referred to national institutions in a general way which included government agencies and public organisations concerned with human rights. The idea of independence was still in its infancy.

The first NHRIs had emerged during the late 1970s and early 1980s. However, up until 1991 there had been little interaction or collaboration between the small numbers.[4] In September that year, the first International Workshop on National Institutions for the Promotion and Protection of Human Rights took place in Paris. At this workshop, the principles relating to the status of national institutions ("the Paris Principles") were developed. The Paris Principles provide a benchmark—a set of minimum requirements—for NHRIs.

While the impetus for the creation of NHRIs was continuing to grow, perhaps the watershed moment was the 1993 World Conference on Human Rights in Vienna. At the Conference, NHRIs compliant with the Paris Principles were, for the first time, formally recognised as important actors in the promotion and protection of human rights. Their establishment and strengthening were formally encouraged (1993: 36). That same year the Paris Principles were adopted by the United Nations General Assembly by resolution 48/134 of 20 December.

Since then, the establishment and strengthening of NHRIs in compliance with the Paris Principles have been central concerns of the United Nations and other international actors. The Human Rights Council has regularly passed resolutions relating to NHRIs, and Treaty Monitoring

[4] It is unclear exactly how many institutions existed prior to 1990. This is because it is difficult to be certain about the type and number of institutions in Africa at the time. For all other regions there were only eight:

- three in Asia-Pacific (New Zealand, Australia and the Philippines)
- three in the Americas (Canada, Mexico and Guatemala)
- two in Europe (France and Denmark)

In Africa there were 3 institutions which could possibly be added to the tally taking the total to 11 (Benin, Togo and Morocco).

Bodies often include recommendations for establishing or strengthening NHRIs in their Concluding Observations.

The Paris Principles are the basis for engaging in the international human rights system. NHRIs, through their Global Alliance, undertake a peer review of new NHRIs and periodic reviews of existing NHRIs to assess their compliance with the Paris Principles. Those found to be fully compliant ("A" status NHRIs) have strong rights of participation in international human rights forums, including the Human Rights Council, with the Special Procedures and the Universal Periodic Review, and the Treaty Monitoring Bodies.

## Creating Minimum Standards

The Paris Principles detail minimum standards of independence from government (through establishment via constitutional or legislative text, financial autonomy, appointment processes) and pluralism—both in the composition of the NHRI and the appointment of its members. The principles further require that an NHRI should be given as broad a mandate as possible.

### *Independence*

The appreciation of the importance of independence has developed overtime. Today independence is considered the cornerstone of an NHRI. It is one of the elements which enable them to navigate the unique position they occupy, between government, civil society and NGOs.

There are broadly four levels of independence: independence of the institution, independence of its office holders, operational independence and financial independence or autonomy. In order to protect the independence of the institution, the Paris Principles require that a national institution have its mandate "clearly set forth in a constitutional or legislative text" (United Nations General Assembly 1993). By creating and setting out the powers and mandates of an NHRI constitutionally or legislatively, the NHRI is given a degree of formal independence and is less vulnerable to influence or interference than if established by an executive order. Best practice is imbedding the establishment of an NHRI in constitutional provisions rather than ordinary legislation. However, this may not always be possible depending on a state's constitutional framework. One example of an NHRI being established by constitutional provisions in the Asia-Pacific region is Timor-Leste's Office of the Provedor for Human Rights and Justice. The Provedor's office is established under section 27 of the Constitution, which states:

> [T]he Ombudsman shall be an independent organ in charge to examine and seek to settle citizens' complaints against public bodies, certify the conformity of the acts with the law, prevent and initiate the whole process to remedy injustice ... [t]he activity the Ombudsman shall be independent from any means of grace and legal remedies as laid down in the Constitution and the law.

The office of the Provedor's independence is further reinforced by Law No. 7/2004 setting up the office. Article 5 provides that "the Office shall operate as an independent statutory body and shall not be subject to the direction, control or influence of any person or authority."

By contrast, in the case of the New Zealand Human Rights Commission, it is established as an "independent Crown entity" pursuant to the Crown entities Act 2004, an ordinary piece of legislation.

In addition to structural independence, the Paris Principles acknowledge the very real need to maintain the independence of office holders if an NHRI is going to be effective in discharging its mandate. This is primarily achieved in two main ways:

1. Ensuring a stable mandate for office holders
2. Ensuring a transparent process of appointment and dismissal

Looking across the region, independence of office holders is generally enhanced by making full-time appointments with a duration of at least three years. In some states, civil society is involved in the appointment process. This can further enhance independence. It also helps address the Paris Principles requirement of Pluralism. The Human Rights Commission of Thailand is one such example, requiring a selection committee comprising a diverse range of members, including judges, academics, the chairman of the Law Council and representatives from private human rights organisations. In addition to the mandate and process of appointment, the appointees themselves are important to a body's independence. The Commonwealth Secretariat has noted (2001: 29):

> Whatever the appointment process, the crucial requirement for appointees is that they are demonstrably politically neutral and persons of high integrity

> and standing. Without these characteristics, the office is unlikely to gain the confidence of the public.

Operational independency requires an NHRI to be able to appoint its own staff and manage its resources and work programme free of government interference. One indicator of operational independence is the ability of an NHRI to undertake investigations. Such powers can include the ability to require production of documents, witnesses and so on. For example, Part 5 of the New Zealand Human Rights Act 1993 enables a human rights commissioner to apply to the courts for an order requiring the production of documents or requiring a person to give evidence in an inquiry. It should be noted that it is unusual for such powers to be used. Former Australian Human Rights Commissioner, Chris Sidoti, explains the reason for this as follows (Spencer 2002):

> If there were no powers, those with information essential to the effective functioning of a national human rights institution could withhold the information without fear of the consequences. The institution would be stymied in its work, unable to obtain the information it requires and so unable to form any conclusions about the matter under investigation. But, where the powers exist, those with information have no incentive to withhold it and will almost always provide it without any compulsion—because they know that they can be compelled if they refuse to tender it voluntarily.

Finally, an NHRI must have full financial autonomy—their budget should not be subject to interference by the executive or any other branch of government. NHRIs should be able to determine their strategic priorities and activities and have enough resources to carry out their functions effectively. Full financial and administrative autonomy can be difficult to achieve and maintain.

### *Pluralism*

Pluralism is a recognition that there are many different groups active in a state, and NHRIs need to accommodate and recognise these differences—including languages, cultures, religion and so on. The importance of this diversity is expressly recognised in the Paris Principles which requires both members and staff of an NHRI to be drawn from a broad cross-section of society, ensuring multiplicity of opinion (United Nations General Assembly 1993).

In societies divided among ethnic, political and/or religious grounds, the criterion of pluralist representation becomes even more significant. Without diversity, there is a danger that the NHRI and its work will not be viewed with public confidence, therefore damaging its credibility and legitimacy.

### *Structure*

The Paris Principles do not proscribe a structure or framework. The 1993 Vienna Declaration on Human Rights states that "it is the right of each State to choose the framework which is best suited to its particular needs at the national level" (United Nations World Conference on Human Rights 1993: 36). NHRIs can take many forms. The International Coordinating Committee of National Institutions for the Promotion and Protection of Human Rights Subcommittee on Accreditation has identified the following structural models (2013: 47):

- Commissions
- Ombudsman institutes
- Hybrid institutions
- Consultative and advisory bodies
- Research institutes
- Civil rights protectors
- Public defenders
- Parliamentary advocates

Interestingly however, to date, NHRIs across the Asia-Pacific region have, in the main, been cast in a similar mould. Of the 24 national institutions across the region, 19 are human rights commissions (Fig. 2.1).

### *Broad Mandate*

The Paris Principles confirm that "a national institution shall be given as broad a mandate as possible" (United Nations General Assembly 1993). While there is scope within the idea of "a broad mandate" for creating bespoke institutions to align with specific environments and frameworks, the principles do set out a non-exhaustive list of functions that NHRIs should have (ibid.):

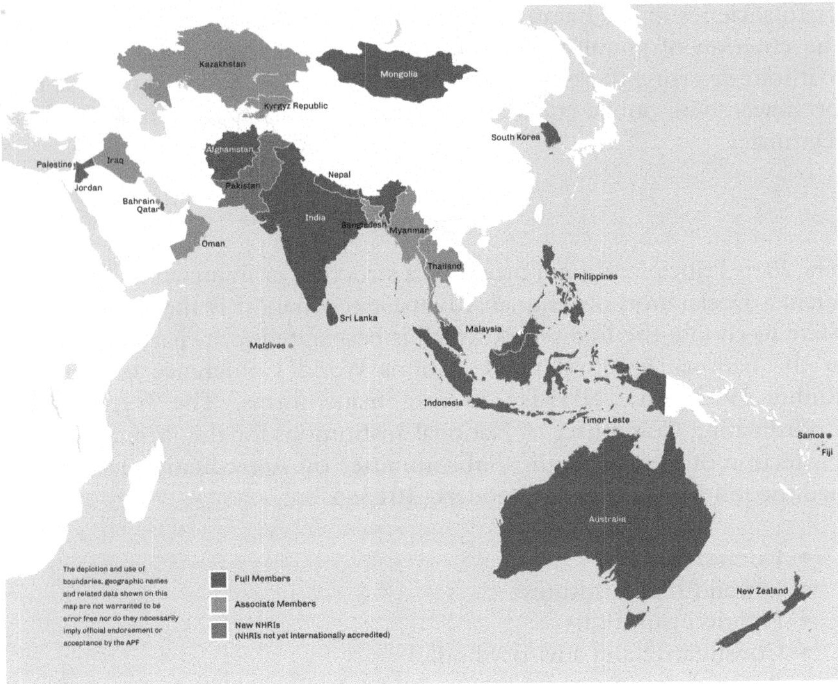


**Fig. 2.1** Number of NHRIs across the region. (Source: Asia-Pacific Forum of National Human Rights Institutions)

- monitor the implementation of human rights obligations of the state party and report annually (at least);
- report and make recommendations to the government, either at the government's request or on its own volition, on human rights matters, including on legislation and administrative provisions, the violation of human rights, the overall human rights situation in the country and initiatives to improve the human rights situation;
- promote harmonisation of national law and practice with international human rights standards;
- encourage ratification of human rights treaties;
- contribute to reports that states parties are required to submit to the United Nations treaty bodies on the implementation of human rights treaties;
- cooperate with regional and United Nations human rights bodies as well as with human rights bodies of other states;

- assist in the formulation of human rights education programmes; and
- raise public awareness about human rights and efforts to combat discrimination.

When we look across the region, the functions of NHRIs generally align with the functions set out in the Paris Principles. Burdekin concluded in his assessment of NHRIs in the Asia-Pacific region that their functions cover a range of activities, such as (Burdekin and Naum 2007):

1. advising government and parliament on issues related to legislation or administrative practices, or proposed legislation, or policies or programmes within their jurisdiction;
2. educating the public and members of the executive (police, prison officials, the military) and the judiciary about human rights and disseminating information about human rights;
3. monitoring compliance by government, government agencies and the private sector on international human rights treaty obligations;
4. promoting the ratification of human rights treaties and advising on the development of new international human rights instruments;
5. contributing to government reports to international treaty bodies and following up and disseminating reports by the treaty bodies;
6. cooperating with the United Nations, other NHRIs and national and international NGOs;
7. inspecting custodial facilities and places of detention;
8. receiving and investigating complaints of human rights violations, conciliating such complaints or providing other remedies;
9. compelling the attendance of witnesses and production of documents where necessary to conduct effective enquiries or investigations and taking evidence on oath or affirmation; and
10. conducting national enquiries into systemic violations of human rights.

## Being an Effective NHRI—Beyond the Paris Principles?

The Paris Principles clearly create the platform for an NHRI to effectively operate. However, in some circumstances, complying fully with the formal criteria in the Paris Principles may not be possible in the short- to medium term. In these cases what makes an effective institution?

The International Council on Human Rights Policy report Performance and Legitimacy: NHRIs noted that many NHRIs that formally respected the Paris Principles were not particularly effective in guaranteeing human rights. Others—less numerous—failed to comply with the Paris Principles but still achieved reasonable results (2004). This report does not suggest that the Paris Principles are not vital to the successful operation of national institutions. Rather, these institutions have been effective in promoting and protecting human rights despite, not because of their absence. It is, however, interesting to consider these other factors identified by the *Performance and Legitimacy* report (ibid.):

> ***Public legitimacy***
> *National institutions win public or popular legitimacy when they are seen to stand up for the right of the powerless against powerful interests and act fairly in treating issues within their purview. An institution's legitimacy is also always partly rooted in its formal or legal status.*
> ***Accessibility***
> *National institutions should make known what they do, and how they can be contacted, to the general public and non-governmental bodies. Their offices should be accessible. Disadvantaged groups in society should be encouraged to use them.*
> ***Consult and engage with civil society***
> *Civil society organisations, human rights NGOs and community-based groups, can be effective links between national institutions and individuals or groups who are politically, socially or economically marginalised. Civil Society's involvement is particularly important in the creation of NHRIs.*[5]
> ***Strategic focus***
> *Programmes should focus on issues of immediate daily concern and be relevant to the public and to public bodies.*
> ***Develop effective international links***
> *NHRIs can become a key meeting point where national human rights enforcement*
> *systems link with international and regional human rights bodies. NHRI networks can provide support and guidance—they can assist strengthening independence and reinforce public legitimacy.*[6]

[5] "If you give birth to a human rights commission in a climate of ignorance and lack of understanding, potential hostility and suspicion, this will prove to be problematic; people will not understand the role of such a commission."

[6] For example, the role of GANHRI and the APF.

## Establishing NHRIs in the Asia-Pacific Region

Having considered what NHRIs are, where they come from and broadly what they do, it is useful to close by coming full circle and consider why a state would want to establish an NHRI?

One proposition is that NHRIs are created largely to satisfy international audiences. They are a relatively low-cost way of improving a state's international reputation. The International Council on Human Rights Policy has suggested there are essentially three reasons for the establishment of an NHRI (ibid.):

1. To facilitate transition from conflict (democratisation): South Africa, Philippines, Spain and so on
2. To consolidate and improve human rights protections: Australia, Canada, New Zealand and so on
3. To respond to allegations of serious human rights abuses: Mexico, Togo, Nigeria

In addition to these reasons, Renshaw, Byrnes and Durbach suggest three factors contributing "to the national momentum towards the establishment of NHRIs in the Pacific" (2010):

1. Recognition that rights are at present inadequately protected and that there is a need for further measures to promote and protect human rights.
2. There is a need for ongoing dialogue about human rights and culture. NHRI could play a role in shepherding this dialogue informed by international norms but situated within the state and close to the people.
3. Sovereignty remains a principal concern for nations of the Pacific. Regionalism is seen as a supplement to national efforts.

These factors may apply equally to the wider Asia-Pacific/Asia region.

At the time of writing, 24 NHRIs had been established across the region in very different and sometimes challenging environments. The effectiveness of these institutions is often perceived to rest upon their independence. Even where established in accordance with the Paris principles, the problem remains of how to maintain the required independence of an institution which is established by law and financed by national government, and whose members are appointed—to a greater or lesser degree—by those governments. This is an ongoing challenge.

Another concern often raised in relation to NHRIs in the region is that they only have recommendatory powers. While some NHRIs have "quasi-judicial" powers in relation to obtaining evidence, they are not judicial bodies. Generally, they operate by way of recommendations, proceed far less formally than courts and frequently resolve complaints by mediation or conciliation. Some NHRIs do have the power to make "orders," "determinations" or findings in some instances. However, enforcement of these can be more problematic.

## Concluding Remarks

NHRIs sit at the crossroads between government and civil society. This is their point of difference and what enables them to effectively monitor and advocate for improved human rights realisation.

As mentioned earlier, to do so effectively requires NHRIs to be autonomous from the state so that they can investigate the state as well as other actors committing human rights abuses. They must also be independent from NGOs and civil society. It is here where NHRIs often must grapple with the uncomfortable dilemma of how to be independent, while at the same time establishing working relationships with both government and NGOs. The NHRI bears the responsibility to ensure that they are not merely an extension of the government, but an independent oversight agency willing to speak out against their appointers if necessary.

The independence of these institutions and thus their effectiveness can be fragile and must be vigorously protected by the state, civil society, and members and staff. For example, experience shows that few NHRIs are financially and administratively independent of government. This creates ongoing tension with the need for NHRIs to maintain independence.

As more and more NHRIs are established throughout the region, it is important to understand what independence and legitimacy might look like in different country contexts. NHRIs must work collaboratively—both bilaterally and through networks—to enhance the understanding of the need for independence and to assist institutions strengthen their independence where there are gaps. Creating the space for robust national institutions to operate will ultimately improve the protection of rights across the region.

## References

Burdekin, Brian, & Naum, Jason. 2007. *National human rights institutions in the Asia-Pacific region*. Leiden; Boston: Martinus Nijhoff Publishers

Commonwealth Secretariat. 2001. *National Human Rights Institutions: Best Practice*.

ECOSOC. 1946. *Resolution 2/9 of 21 June*.

———. 1960. *Resolution 772B(XXX)* of 25 July.

International Council on Human Rights Policy. 2004. *Performance & Legitimacy: National Human Rights Institutions*, Geneva.

Mandela, N. 1994. *Long Walk to Freedom: The Autobiography of Nelson Mandela*.

Office of the High Commissioner for Human Rights (OHCHR). 1993. *Fact Sheet No. 19, National Institutions for the Promotion and Protection of Human Rights*.

Renshaw, C, Byrnes, A, Durbach, A. 2010. Human Rights Protection in the Pacific: The Emerging Role of National Human Rights Institutions in the Region, *New Zealand Journal of Public International Law*, Vol. 8, No. 1.

Roosevelt, F.D., & Churchill, W.S. 1941. *Atlantic Charter*, Newfoundland.

Spencer, S. 2002. *Access to Information Powers* (Unpublished paper presented at the Scottish Executive Conference, Establishing our Rights, Roles for Scotland's Human Rights Commission, Edinburgh, Scot., 17 Feb. 2002).

The International Coordinating Committee of National Institutions for the Promotion and Protection of Human Rights' Subcommittee on Accreditation. 2013. *Report and Recommendations of the Session of the Sub-Committee on Accreditation (SCA) Geneva 13–16 May 2013*. Accessed 10 August 2017 at: http://nhri.ohchr.org/EN/AboutUs/GANHRIAccreditation/Documents/Report%20May%202013-Consolidated-English.pdf.

United Nations. 1942. *The Declaration by United Nations*, Washington.

United Nations General Assembly. 1978. *A/Res/33/46* of 14 December.

———. 1993. *Principles relating to the Status of National Institutions (The Paris Principles) adopted by resolution 48/134* of 20 December.

United Nations World Conference on Human Rights. 1993. *Vienna Declaration and Programme of Action a/conf.157/23*, Vienna.

CHAPTER 3

# National Human Rights Institutions in Southeast Asian States: The Necessary Foundation for an Efficient ASEAN Intergovernmental Commission on Human Rights

*Céline Martin*

## Introduction

In the absence of a strong regional mechanism, national human rights institutions (NHRIs) have an important role to play for the promotion and protection of human rights in Southeast Asian (SEA) states, where those NHRIs are in conformity with the 1993 Paris Principles (United Nations 1993). Those principles include independence both in their funding and in their operations, with the possibility of conducting inquiries based on individual communications. According to the Global Alliance on NHRIs (GANHRI), which is mandated by the United Nations (UN) to grade and give accreditation to NHRIs ("Global Alliance of the National Human Rights Institutions" 2017), most of the SEA NHRIs do not enforce those principles at an efficient level, or not at all. Given the lack of

C. Martin (✉)
Aix-Marseille University, Marseille, France
e-mail: celine@destinationjustice.org



J. Gomez, R. Ramcharan (eds.), *National Human Rights Institutions in Southeast Asia*,
https://doi.org/10.1007/978-981-15-1074-8_3

independence of the SEA NHRIs and the inefficiency of the ASEAN Intergovernmental Commission on Human Rights (AICHR), it is natural to examine the complementarity of NHRIs and the AICHR in their roles, both at the national and the regional levels. The literature on this topic is sparse and this chapter contributes to filling that void. Indeed, it argues that such complementarity is a fortuitous possibility should NHRIs and the AICHR take their cooperation to the next level.

This chapter explores (1) how, within their own mandates, the existing SEA NHRIs and the AICHR can work together to advance the promotion and protection of human rights in the region; (2) how laws that would establish NHRIs in the remaining countries could be adopted in order to respect the Paris Principles while being strong foundations to the AICHR; and (3) how best practices from NHRIs evolving in a different regional environment (OAS [Organization of American States], ECtHR [European Court of Human Rights], AfHRC [African Human Rights Court]) can influence the AICHR to strengthen the relationships between SEA NHRIs.

## NHRI and the Protection Gap

Twenty years ago, the Tehran Framework, adopted during the yearly OHCHR regional workshop for Asia-Pacific, laid out four pillars for the advancement of human rights, one of which was the idea that NHRIs are the most solid foundation at the national level to build an efficient regional human rights mechanism (Baik 2012: 194). The UN has recognised that NHRIs can operate as bridges between the international human rights norms and mechanisms and the national ones, their quasi-jurisdictional powers allowing them to have a more efficient protective role than regional mechanisms; at least this is the case in Southeast Asia. The region has a young, non-binding and heavily criticised regional human rights mechanism, the AICHR, that was adopted in 2009 by the ten ASEAN states. The AICHR, being stripped of several prerogatives (such as receiving individual complaints and making consequent investigations, etc.), has not done much over the past eight years to improve the protection of human rights in an effective manner in Southeast Asia. Moreover, only five of the ten ASEAN states, and Timor-Leste,[1] have an

[1] Timor-Leste is due to join ASEAN in 2017 and is currently an observer within the AICHR mechanism.

NHRI and half of them do not comply entirely with the 1993 Paris Principles (GANHRI 2016). Other members have so far resisted creating an NHRI.

While the SEA region is currently facing a general backlash on human rights protection, and in the absence of a strong regional mechanism, it is opportune to investigate how, or if, NHRIs could (re)enforce the protective role of the AICHR. This chapter therefore explores (1) how, within their own mandates, the SEA existing NHRIs and the AICHR can work together to advance the promotion and protection of human rights in the region; (2) how laws that would establish NHRIs in the remaining countries (Brunei-Darussalam, Cambodia, Laos, Singapore and Vietnam) could be adopted in order to respect the Paris Principles while having strong foundations to the AICHR; and (3) how best practices from NHRIs evolving in a different regional environment (Organization of American States (OAS), European Court of Human Rights (ECtHR), or the African Human Rights Court (AfHRC)) can influence the AICHR to strengthen the relationships between SEA NHRIs.

## Nascent Cooperation Between Existing NHRIs and AICHR

In 2004, the four existing human rights commissions in Southeast Asia, namely, KOMNAS HAM, SUHAKAM, CHRP and NHRCT, "decided to come together as a united force to help fast track the establishment of an ASEAN human rights mechanism" (SEANF 2017). It later led to the creation of a forum that took the name of Southeast Asia National Human Rights Institution Forum (SEANF) in 2009. In 2010, the Provedor of Timor-Leste joined as the fifth member, and in 2012, the MHRC became the sixth member of SEANF. Thirteen years ago, this "united force" was the first expression of cooperation between the SEA NHRIs and the later established AICHR and shows a long-lasting regional interest in enhancing regional promotion and protection of human rights.

In 2007, to strengthen their relationships, the then four members adopted a Declaration of Cooperation that encouraged the Southeast Asian NHRIs to "do whatever possible to carry out jointly, either on bilateral or multilateral basis, programmes and activities in areas of human rights identified and agreed upon at the meetings" (SEANF 2007). It also mandated SEANF members and the AICHR to gradually develop regional strategies to better promote and protect human rights in the region. All members therefore agreed to advise their own government on the necessary steps to establish an ASEAN human rights mechanism complying with the ASEAN Charter (SEANF 2007).

Despite the willingness of the Southeast Asian NHRIs to engage with the AICHR, no real achievement was made between 2009 and 2014. This changed when the AICHR changed its view on NHRIs and decided to hold "a long-requested meeting with the NHRI representatives on 29 April 2014 during the Consultation with Stakeholders on the Contribution to the Review of the Terms of Reference (TOR) in Jakarta" (Wahyuningrum 2014). During this meeting, civil society organisations (CSOs) presented a report on AICHR's work, highlighting points where the Commission underperformed. Their first point focused on its failure to establish an institutionalised relationship with stakeholders including NHRIs (SAPA Task Force on ASEAN and Human Rights 2014). It led the AICHR to adopt guidelines on its relations with the CSOs, from which NHRIs are considered part of (AICHR 2015). Those guidelines adopted in 2015 allow CSOs to apply for a consultative status with the AICHR, although the procedure has been deemed controversial as lacking transparency (ICJ 2016). After two rounds of a long process, no NHRI has been awarded such status or—to this date—has been known to have even applied (AICHR 2017a). As of today, it is not clear whether this status would reinforce the already well-established cooperation between NHRIs and the AICHR. Indeed, based on section 18 of the Guidelines, the CSOs awarded with a consultative status can be consulted by the AICHR for consultation, seminar, workshop, regular reporting/briefing, implementation of specific studies, project implementer or any other format determined by the AICHR (AICHR 2015). Rather than a two-way cooperation and interaction, the formula shows that the AICHR intends to remain in control of the issues treated. Moreover, the section 19 provides that "[o]fficial transmission of documents from CSOs and institutions shall be submitted to the ASEAN Secretariat who will circulate to the AICHR Representatives" (AICHR 2015). Therefore, the AICHR is stripped by the ASEAN of the possibility to receive *unwanted* communications.

Until today, SEANF NHRI members keep "seeking a regular mode of engagement with the ASEAN, AICHR, ACWC, and related human rights bodies in Asia" (Khine Khine Win 2016), by organising and participating to activities gathering the subregional human rights body(ies), officials and CSOs. For instance, last March, SUHAKAM jointly organised with the AICHR, the first-ever *AICHR Judicial Colloquium on the Sharing of Good Practices regarding International Human Rights Law* in Kuala Lumpur (AICHR 2017b). Strengthening the relationship and cooperation between NHRIs and the AICHR through the SEANF is primordial, but we may emphasis on the need for both the existing Southeast Asian NHRIs (whether within the SEANF or outside of it) and the AICHR to assist the other five countries of the subregion to adopt a national human rights body falling under the scope of the 1993 Paris Principles.

## Lessons Learnt: Best Practices from NHRIs Evolving in Different Regional Contexts

As of 24 January 2017, the GANHRI Sub-Committee on Accreditation (SCA) has accredited 117 NHRIs throughout the world: 74 of which with an *A* status (full compliance with the Paris Principles), 33 with a *B* status (not full compliance) and 10 with a *C* status (non-compliance) (GANHRI 2017b). Most of those NHRIs evolve in different national and regional context and have built through the year's different relationships with regional human rights bodies. This section examines briefly NHRI's interactions within the European, the Latin American and African mechanisms while trying to draw best practices that could be applied in Southeast Asia. Those best practices are all related to NHRIs' prerogatives to participate in the respective judicial systems. Indeed, it is worth recalling that among those prerogatives, and depending on the format of the NHRI, "some NHRIs have the power to bring matters to court if their decisions are not adhered to; an NHRI should be prepared to use this power also with respect to participation. An NHRI should consider intervening in court cases touching upon participation as friend of the court (*amicus curiae*) to ensure that the relevant human rights provisions are considered by the courts" (Ulrik Spliid 2013; Inter-Parliamentary Union 1994).

### *NHRIs in Europe*

Several European regional organisations have acknowledged and promoted the establishment of strong and independent NHRIs in the European countries.[2] This section focuses on the relations between

[2] In 2007, building on ongoing work across its programmes, OSCE's ODIHR established a focal point for human rights defenders and NHRIs which closely monitors the situation of

NHRIs, the European Network of NHRIs (ENNHRI)[3] and the ECtHR. Indeed, the Council of Europe "emphasised the NHRIs' cooperative role. European NHRIs, for instance, have played an active part in the process of the reform of the ECtHR" (European Union Agency for Fundamental Rights 2012).

With a view to reinforcing the cooperation between the ECtHR and NHRIs, the 2012 Brighton Declaration issued during the High Level Conference on the Future of the ECtHR provided that "the States Parties are determined to work in partnership with the Court to achieve this, drawing also on the important work of the Committee of Ministers and the Parliamentary Assembly of the Council of Europe as well as the Commissioner for Human Rights and the other institutions and bodies of the Council of Europe,[4] and working in a spirit of co-operation with civil society and National Human Rights Institutions" (High Level Conference on the Future of the and European Court of Human Rights 2012). The Declaration therefore acknowledged the role of European NHRIs in the ECtHR's[5] proceedings. Nonetheless, European NHRIs have been able to intervene as a third party through the procedure of the *amicus curiae*,

human rights defenders and NHRIs in the OSCE region and promotes and protects their interests (see http://www.osce.org/odihr). Similarly, the Council of Europe and its Commissioner for Human Rights have also highlighted the need for states to have Paris Principles–compliant NHRIs in place (see http://www.coe.int/en/web/commissioner/co-operation-with-national-human-rights-structures?desktop=true).

[3] ENNHRI enhances the promotion and protection of human rights across the wider Europe region by bringing together NHRIs to work on a wide range of human rights issues and supporting their development. ENNHRI has a membership of 41 NHRIs from across wider Europe, including Ombudsmen institutions, human rights commissions and institutes: see http://ennhri.org/Promoting-and-protecting-human-rights-across-wider-Europe.

[4] The Council of Europe (CoE) is an international organisation whose stated aim is to uphold human rights, democracy, rule of law in Europe and promote European culture. Founded in 1949, it has nowadays 47 member states: see http://www.coe.int/en/web/portal/home.

[5] For instance, intervention by Des Hogan on behalf of the European Group of NHRIs, High-Level Conference on the Future of the ECtHR, Interlaken, 18–19 February 2010, available at: https://www.bj.admin.ch/dam/data/bj/staat/menschenrechte/emrk/ber-ministerkonf-fe.pdf and intervention by Beate Rudolf, on behalf of the European Group of NHRIs, High-Level Conference on the Future of the ECtHR, Izmir, 26–27 April 2011, available at: https://www.ihrec.ie/download/doc/izmir_oral_statement_european_group_of_national_human_rights_institutions.doc.

both alone[6] or as a group. Indeed, NHRIs have become increasingly interested in joining the proceedings of the ECtHR and their ability to do so has been recognised in the new under Article 36§2 of the ECHR (Rajska and Rudzińska-Bluszcz 2016). After several successful interventions by NHRIs alone, the European Network has been able to submit *amici curiae* briefs as an organisation before the ECtHR. What later became the ENNHRI intervened for the first time in 2008, in the case *DD v. Lithuania* which is considered "the first such application as a third-party, in other words not as a party to the proceedings, by a European NHRI before this regional court" (European Union Agency for Fundamental Rights 2012). In August 2011, the European Group made its second intervention before the ECtHR in *Gauer v. France*, focusing its submission on the international standards on protecting women and girls with an intellectual disability from intrusive procedures such as sterilisation (ENNHRI 2011). The European NHRIs have also a role to play in the execution of the ECtHR level as they can "have a role in the implementation of the judgments of the European Court both at the European and national level" (de Beco 2010). NHRIs can indeed provide information to the Council of Ministers of the CoE in charge of the execution of the judgement, or/and they can monitor its implementation at the national level by giving recommendations to the state authorities on the best measures to take. The European NHRIs are therefore at the heart of the promotion and protection of human rights, and a true partner of the ECtHR as "they can form bridges between both national and international human rights systems" (de Beco 2010).

### *NHRIs in the Americas*

This section addresses only the NHRIs in the Latin American context and not the Americas as a whole since the United States and Canada chose to stay out of the mechanisms in relation to human rights and NHRIs. Indeed, the region has a dense array of regional platforms, among them the Organisation of American States[7] and its independent mechanism for

[6] See, for example, the intervention of the Northern Ireland Human Rights Commission in *Shanagan v. UK* or the Polish Helsingki Foundation for Human Rights' intervention in *Staroszczyk v. Poland* (no. 59519/00, 22 March 2007).

[7] The organization was established in order to achieve among its member states "an order of peace and justice, to promote their solidarity, to strengthen their collaboration, and to defend their sovereignty, their territorial integrity, and their independence." Today, the OAS

the promotion and protection of human rights, the Inter-American Commission on Human Rights (IACHR)[8] and the Court. OAS showed early on an interest in NHRIs with a declaration calling for their establishment in all member states in 1997 (NHRI Torture prevention & response 2012). Since then, the OAS has continuously promoted the role of these institutions, which are taking the form of Ombudsman (*Defensor del pueblo*) in most of Latin American states, and has sought to ensure their human rights promotion and protection roles domestically. Similar to the European and Southeast Asian NHRIs, the Iberoamerican Federation of Ombudsmen (FIO)[9] has coordinated the work of the all NHRIs in the Americas since its creation in 1995, independent from the FIO but working in cooperation with it are subregional peer networks such as the Andean Council of Defensorías del Pueblo (CADP)[10] created in 1998, which includes the NHRIs of Bolivia, Colombia, Ecuador, Peru, Venezuela and Panama (NHRI Torture prevention & response 2012). However, contrary to Europe or SEA, *all* countries in Latin America have at least one NHRI; indeed, they often have several national and local ones. Most of those institutions were created in the early 1990s (except for Uruguay, Chile and Brazil created in the 2010s), and have therefore long experience of handling the promotion and protection of human rights in a changing context. Similar to the ECtHR, the Iberoamerican has intervened in proceedings of the IACHR through the procedure of *amicus curiae*. The Peruvian Defensor del Pueblo[11] is known for its numerous interventions, and the Court extensively relies on its *amici curiae*, as well as other documents such as reports submitted as evidence before the Court. NHRIs can also assist the Court in the implementation of its judgments. Nationally, the Latin American Ombudsmen have also powers before the courts to

brings together all 35 independent states of the Americas and constitutes the main political, juridical and social governmental forum in the Hemisphere: see http://www.oas.org/en/about/member_states.asp.

[8] The IACHR is a principal and autonomous organ of the Organization of American States ("OAS"). It is composed of seven independent members who serve in a personal capacity. Created by the OAS in 1959 and together with the Inter-American Court of Human Rights ("the Court" or "the I/A Court H.R.), installed in 1979, the Commission is one of the institutions within the inter-American system for the protection of human rights ("IAHRS"). See http://www.oas.org/en/iachr/mandate/what.asp.

[9] See: http://www.portalfio.org/.

[10] See: http://www.defensoria.gob.bo/sp/noticias_proc.asp?Seleccion=359.

[11] See the *Five Pensioners Case*, 23 February 2003, no°98 (2003), IACHR; or, *Barrios Altos Case*, 3 September 2001, no. 83 (2001), IACHR.

effectively protect the human rights and are known to effectively assist the public in gaining access to the judiciary (Reif 2004).

### *NHRIs in Africa*

Aside from being members of networks such as the Network of African National Human Rights Institutions (NANHRI),[12] African NHRIs have historically engaged with the African Commission on Human and People's Rights (ACHPR) by attending sessions aimed at assisting the ACHPR in the protection and promotion of human rights. Indeed, following a decision in 1998 (IHRDA 2015), NHRIs can become affiliated with the Commission thanks to a mechanism like the GANHRI-SCA's accreditation mechanism based on the 1993 Paris Principles (NANHRI 2016a, b). As of 2016, there were 27 NHRIs with *Affiliate* status at the ACHPR, 18 of which received an accreditation *A* (NANHRI 2016a, b). A recent report by UNDP and NANHRI, *Study on the State of National Human Rights Institutions in Africa*, focuses on six key areas of NHRIs: establishment and oversight, independence, financing, capacity, stakeholder engagement, and rights-based service delivery and development. Outside of NANHRI, some African NHRIs have also concluded bilateral agreements which comprise exchange of knowledge, information and best practices, as well as technical support. The case studies conducted by UNDP and NANHRI show "that recently established NHRIs that benefit from peer support, during their inception periods, perform better in terms of capacity and effectiveness" (UNDP and NANHRI 2016: 73). A UNDP representative acknowledged that "the recognition of the need for effective NHRIs as well as the general changes in the African political and social landscape, and growing international advocacy, have greatly increased the profile of human rights issues in Africa" (UNDP 2016). The study, which concludes that NHRIs play an essential role in a country towards the advancement of the human rights agenda, good governance and sustain-

[12] African NHRIs first gathered in Yaoundé (Cameroon) in February 1996 and adopted the *Yaoundé Declaration* establishing a Coordinating Committee of African National Institutions for the promotion and protection of Human Rights tasked with assisting in the coordination of African NHRIs' activities and enhancing their visibility. In October 2007, they formally created the Network of African National Human Rights Institutions (NANHRI) to replace the Coordinating Committee. There are 44 (out of the 47 NHRIs present on the African continent) members. See http://www.nanhri.org/members/.

able development, also drew key findings (UNDP 2016) that could be applied to the SEA NHRIs too. Among them are:

- It is important to strengthen the human rights-based approach.
- NHRIs should be strengthened to become flag bearers of such an approach among relevant government agencies.
- NHRIs have human and financial constraints and need greater capacity.
- Governments are encouraged to provide appropriate political will for the legal, financial and operational autonomy of NHRIs.
- Governments should work closely with NHRIs in order to address emerging human rights issues.

The effectiveness of NHRIs in Africa has been criticised and lessons can be drawn from this as well. An examination of NHRIs' interactions with the regional human rights mechanisms reveals that NHRIs "are not making serious efforts to engage the Commission" (IHRDA 2015). Indeed, according to the African Activity Reports from the 52nd to 56th Ordinary Sessions, respectively 24, 32, 42, 18 and 43 NHRIs attended the sessions, while over the same period, an average of 5 NHRIs issued statements (IHRDA 2015).

Similarly, NHRIs' engagement with the Court is poor (Reif 2004: 252) as none of them has yet intervened in the proceedings due to a general lack of information (on whether one of their nationals has submitted a complaint, on the proceedings before the Court, on whether their country recognised the Court, etc.) (IHRDA 2015). Moreover, it seems that the African NHRIs interpret their mandates narrowly and deem themselves non-competent to assist the Court and/or the Commission in the implementation of the decisions.

### *Lessons*

After looking at how NHRIs interact with their regional human rights mechanisms in Europe and Americas, we concluded that most of all NHRIs operate with the following scheme:

- NHRIs, before engaging with the regional mechanism (Commission or Court), have gained a strong position at home, with effective prerogatives of reporting, assisting the public to access and gain justice and intervening as a third party when necessary.

- NHRIs first intervene alone before action by the regional human rights mechanism, which then proceeds, first, before the commission and then before to the Court.
- NHRIs, operating under a regional network, also succeed in gaining access to the regional mechanism and are deemed more powerful in their action as such.
- NHRIs are valued as a strong ally by the regional mechanism and have become a partner both at the regional and the national levels.

If we look at the African situation, we acknowledge that while there are NHRIs in forty-seven out of the fifty-four countries on the continent, much remains to be done in terms of the quality of the relationships between the regional human rights mechanisms and NHRIs, when there is one. The overall situation is therefore closer to the one in Southeast Asia even through the political and human rights contexts are different. In response to the scepticism of NHRIs, analysts have argued that "dualism or monism as a prevailing system does not count much so long as states have agreed to be bound by international treaties as a matter of principle" (Dinokopila 2010). Therefore, to curb NHRIs' engagement with the regional mechanisms and to reinforce their capacities, NANHRI issued (in 2016) two reports. The first one is a set of *Guidelines on the Role of NHRIs in Monitoring Implementation of Recommendations of the African Commission on Human and People's Rights and Judgements of the African Court on Human and People's Rights* while a second one is a *Mapping Survey of the Complaint Handling Systems of African National Human Rights Institutions.*

In considering Southeast Asian NHRIs, it must be recalled that when the European and Latin American NHRIs were created in those regions, the regional human rights mechanisms already existed and was fully functioning. NHRIs have therefore been integrated to an already existing mechanism. In Southeast Asia, this is not yet the case, so part of problematic for the existing NHRIs is to apply the above scheme while assisting the AICHR in creating a binding mechanism too. The second part of the problematic would be to assist the other SEA countries in adopting NHRIs in the coming years that would already integrate those best practices.

## Setting New NHRIs in SEA as Strong Foundations for the AICHR

National human rights institutions, when established in the rights circumstances and in accordance with the 1993 Paris Principles, can play a significant role in promoting and protecting the human rights and fundamental freedoms set forth in the Universal Declaration of Human Rights and international human rights treaties (OHCHR-Cambodia 2006). Whatever their forms, NHRIs are intended to complement state organs responsible for ensuring that human rights are protected and observed, and they can also provide an important bridge between government and civil society (OHCHR-Cambodia 2006). With the partial success of the already existing NHRIs in the region, it feels important to remind how setting new NHRIs in the remaining Southeast Asian countries could reinforce and push further the development of the AICHR and a binding mechanism. By drawing from the above good practices combined with the Paris Principles, we would like to make sure that NHRIs would be created in Brunei-Darussalam, Cambodia, Laos, Vietnam or Singapore based on those principles and are equipped to last in time. And, so they do not meet the faith of the NHRC of Thailand or Myanmar which have been downgraded to a *B* accreditation due to their lack of independence while Indonesia was re-upgraded to an accreditation *A* at the end of 2016 thanks to its efforts (GANHRI 2017a). Their existence in SEA, and their mandate and activities, "have been described as an '*unhappy marriage*' between national human rights institutions and national governments" (Phan 2012).

As mentioned, an NHRI can be created under one of four models: a human rights commission, an advisory committee, an Ombudsman or a human rights institute. We have previously seen that, in general, the African and West European countries have preferred a hybrid form of commission and committee, while Latin American countries prefer the Ombudsman model. Scholars identified the human rights commission model, predominant in Commonwealth countries, as the classic type of NHRI since it is the model that is the closet from the one articulated in the Paris Principles (Dam 2007). According to those principles, a commission carries out a wide range of functions, including advising the government on human rights issues, monitoring implementation of human rights laws and carrying out awareness-raising and training activities in the area of human rights, and depending on the countries, can be granted quasi-judicial investigatory authority (United Nations 1993). Scholars have also identified another model based on the National Consultative Commission of Human Rights of France and therefore referred to as the *French model* (Dam 2007). This model emphasised the *advisory* role of the body in building bridges between civil society and the government rather than focusing on investigation and monitoring. To sum up, "while institutions developed under the human rights commission model act as quasi-judicial watchdogs on the activities of the state in human rights matters, the French emphasis is on supplementing the activities of the state in pursuing research and awareness" (Dam 2007). Rather than conforming to a unique model, in the 1980s and '90s, the idea of adopting an NHRI with a hybrid form between the Ombudsman and commission emerged in the Americas and Eastern Europe. This hybrid Ombudsman/commission is often mandated "not just to monitor the legality and fairness of public administration but also to promote and protect human rights in the public sector" while been equipped also with "strong investigative powers and the authority to monitor compliance" (Dam 2007). Southeast Asian states have so far privileged the French model of commission, except for Timor-Leste, which has established an Ombudsman, but we might acknowledge, based on the Latin American NHRIs' experiences that the hybrid form of Ombudsman and commission might suit better when it comes to supporting the development of regional mechanism.

Efforts from CSOs have been observed in the remaining Southeast Asian countries to push for the establishment of independent NHRI. In this regard, the Asia Pacific Forum noted that it has responded to "requests for advice from governments and civil society on the role, function, establishment and accreditation of NHRIs […] includ[ing] Cambodia, Laos, and Vietnam" (Asia Pacific Forum 2017). However, it has also emerged that, even though being backed up by neighbouring states through UPR recommendations, those efforts were not materialised yet. For instance, Singapore, who continuously argues that human rights are Western values, received such recommendations from Timor-Leste, Indonesia or even Malaysia and cannot therefore dismiss the relevance of establishing an NHRI (Kuah 2016). Brunei and Laos have both declined the recommendations made to them on adopting an NHRI, and despite CSOs' request, nothing has yet been done to establish such an institution (The Brunei Project 2016; FIDH 2015). In Cambodia, the first efforts to establish an NHRI go back twenty years and have recently received some support by the executive following the Second UPR. However, the backlash that followed the adoption of the Law on NGO (LANGO) in 2015 has put a stop to the efforts of establishing an NHRI (ADHOC 2015). In Vietnam, after a 2011 report from UNDP titled *Building a National Human Rights Institution A study for the Ministry of Foreign Affairs of the People's Republic of Vietnam*, and since the 2013 Constitutional reform, the government has shown some willingness to establish an NHRI (Vu and Tran 2016), but it has yet come to life.

It has been recognised that enacting a law establishing an NHRI can take time as consultation is needed among all stakeholders as well as the necessity of securing funding on a long-term basis to insure the institution's continuous independence. In its report to the Ministry of Foreign Affairs of the People's Republic of Viet Nam, UNDP highlighted a simple thirteen-step process that might be worth knowing:

- Step 1 Establishment committee
- Step 2 Mandate and functions of the institute
- Step 3 Landscape of human rights challenges
- Step 4 Consultation of stakeholders
- Step 5 Draft structural model
- Step 6 Establishment of a board of trustees/of the commission
- Step 7 Recruitment of the board of directors
- Step 8 Draft strategic plan
- Step 9 Refining the structure: organisation and processes
- Step 10 Recruitment of staff
- Step 11 Funding
- Step 12 Establishment of an international network
- Step 13 The path towards accreditation with the ICC

Cambodia and Vietnam have already achieved some of those steps and can count on the support of the APF, SEANF and UN agencies. However, no support by AICHR has been publicly made while it has been proven in other regional context that mutual support between NHRIs and a regional human right mechanism can only reinforce both. The presence of well-grounded NHRIs in the remaining SEA countries will reinforce the practice of human rights at the national level to only benefit the regional level.

## Conclusion

It has been admitted by several stakeholders that "[t]he work of SEANF member-NHRIs on receiving and investigating complaints from victims of human rights violations, monitoring human rights program implementation, investigating situations, carrying out field visits and offering remedies can support the work of AICHR at the subregional level" (Wahyuningrum 2014). Beyond SEANF's commitment to the protection and promotion of human rights at the subregional level, the reinforcement of the work of the AICHR will come from the rationalisation of human rights practice and from the realisation that it is beneficial for all branches of the tree. NHRIs have proven, through the years and despite various contexts, being one of the most reliable institutions to practice human rights at the national level, protecting people's rights as well as institutions. Therefore, through the concordant efforts of all stakeholders, from existing NHRIs, governments working towards the establishment of an NHRI, the AICHR itself, regional and international NHRIs networks, as well as CSOs, there is a hope for the development of a stronger regional mechanism. The only unknown component is how much time will be needed.

## References

ADHOC. 2015. Cambodia: Symbolic Institutions Are No Substitute. https://www.forum-asia.org/uploads/wp/2015/09/2-Cambodia-FINAL-03-Aug-2015.pdf.

AICHR. 2015. *Guidelines on the AICHR's Relations with Civil Society Organisations.* https://www.google.com.kh/url?sa=t&rct=j&q=&esrc=s&source=web&cd=1&cad=rja&uact=8&ved=0ahUKEwjMvJiwvdHUAhWBtJQKHT5ACVoQFgglMAA&url=http%3A%2F%2Faichr.org%2F%3Fdl_name%3DGuidelines_On_The_AICHRS_Relations_With__CSOs.pdf&usg=AFQjCNGPKXGxHGc1qKw_YVCop_3UUSQ1-g.

———. 2017a. News Archive. http://aichr.org/News/.

———. 2017b. AICHR Judicial Colloquium on the Sharing of Good Practices Regarding International Human Rights Law. March 13. http://aichr.org/ai1ec_event/aichr-judicial-colloquium-on-the-sharing-of-good-practices-regarding-international-human-rights-law/?instance_id=351&doing_wp_cron=1489098338.6069040298461914062500.

Asia Pacific Forum. 2017. Supporting the Establishment of National Human Rights Institutions. http://www.asiapacificforum.net/support/establishment-of-nhris/.

Baik, Tae-Ung. 2012. *Emerging Regional Human Rights Systems in Asia.* Cambridge; New York: Cambridge University Press.

de Beco, Gauthier. 2010. Role of National Human Rights Institutions in the Implementation of the Judgements of the European Court of Human Rights.

http://www.bristol.ac.uk/media-library/sites/law/migrated/documents/gauthierdebecopres.pdf.

Dam, Shubhankar. 2007. Lessons from National Human Rights Institutions Around the World for State and Local Human Rights Commissions in the United States, Human Rights Commissions and Criminal Justice, 5 (August). http://www.constitutionalvalues.org/pdf/docs/Dam%2C%20Lessons%20from%20National%20Human%20Rights%20Commissions%20Around%20the%20World.pdf.

Dinokopila, Bonolo R. 2010. Beyond Paper Based Affiliate Status: National Human Rights Institutions and the African Commission on Human and People's Rights. *African Human Rights Law Journal*. http://www.scielo.org.za/scielo.php?script=sci_arttext&pid=S1996-20962010000100003.

ENNHRI. 2011. Amicus Curae in Gauer and Others v. France. https://www.ihrec.ie/download/pdf/gauer_ors_v_france_in_french.pdf.

European Union Agency for Fundamental Rights. 2012. *Handbook on the Establishment and Accreditation of National Human Rights Institutions in the European Union*. Luxembourg: Publications Office of the European Union. https://www.google.com.kh/url?sa=t&rct=j&q=&esrc=s&source=web&cd=7&cad=rja&uact=8&ved=0ahUKEwjtnJ-i29HUAhXLnJQKHcU-BscQFghaMAY&url=http%3A%2F%2Ffra.europa.eu%2Fsites%2Fdefault%2Ffiles%2Ffra-2012_nhri-handbook_en.pdf&usg=AFQjCNF2NphM_p4kpXfqbA-zndHIqyixt0Q.

FIDH. 2015. Laos: Government Mocks UN Human Rights Review. *Worldwide Movement for Human Rights*. June 30. https://www.fidh.org/en/region/asia/laos/laos-government-mocks-un-human-rights-review.

GANHRI. 2016. National Human Rights Institutions and United Nations Treaty Bodies. http://nhri.ohchr.org/EN/IHRS/TreatyBodies/Annual%20Meeting%20of%20Chairpersons%20of%20Human%20Rights%20Tre/GANHRI%20background%20paper%20FINAL.pdf.

———. 2017a. Directory of Institutions – Asia Pacific. http://nhri.ohchr.org/EN/Contact/NHRIs/Pages/Asia-Pacific.aspx.

———. 2017b. Sub-Committee on Accreditation (SCA). http://nhri.ohchr.org/EN/AboutUs/GANHRIAccreditation/Pages/default.aspx.

Global Alliance of the National Human Rights Institutions. 2017. Accessed March 17. http://nhri.ohchr.org/EN/AboutUs/Pages/History.aspx.

High Level Conference on the Future of the, and European Court of Human Rights. 2012. *Brighton Declaration*. http://www.echr.coe.int/Documents/2012_Brighton_FinalDeclaration_ENG.pdf.

ICJ. 2016. ICJ Urges AICHR to Adopt Transparent Accreditation Procedure, June 6. https://www.icj.org/icj-urges-aichr-to-adopt-transparent-accreditation-procedure/.

IHRDA. 2015. FactSheet: NANHRI and the African Court & African Commission. http://www.ihrda.org/wp-content/uploads/2015/11/Fact_Sheet_NANHRI_African_Court_African_Commission.pdf.

Inter-Parliamentary Union. 1994. *Strengthening National Structures, Institutions and Organisations of Society Which Play a Role in Promoting and Safeguarding Human Rights.* http://www.ipu.org/conf-e/92-1.htm.

Khine Khine Win. 2016. Southeast Asia National Human Rights Institution Forum (SEANF). *Global New Light Of Myanmar*, June 9. http://www.globalnewlightofmyanmar.com/southeast-asia-national-human-rights-institution-forum-seanf/.

Kuah, A. 2016. Singapore Needs Independent Human Rights Commission. Text. *The Straits Times.* February 3. http://www.straitstimes.com/forum/letters-on-the-web/singapore-needs-independent-human-rights-commission.

NANHRI. 2016a. *Guidelines on the Role of NHRIs in Monitoring Implementation of Recommendations of the African Commission on Human and Peoples' Rights and Judgments of the African Court on Human and Peoples.* Published by The Network of African National Human Rights Institutions. Available at https://www.nanhri.org/wp-content/uploads/2016/10/draft-13-English-Version.pdf.

———. 2016b. *A Mapping Survey of the Complaint Handling Systems of African National Human Rights Institutions.* Published by The Network of African National Human Rights Institutions. Available at https://www.nanhri.org/wp-content/uploads/2016/10/English-Mapping-Survey-Final.pdf.

NHRI Torture prevention & response. 2012. Latin America – NHRI. http://nhritortureprevention.org/nhris/latin-america/.

OHCHR-Cambodia. 2006. *Paris Principles on National Human Rights Institutions.* Vol. Preface.

Phan, Hao Duy. 2012. *A Selective Approach to Establishing a Human Rights Mechanism in Southeast Asia: The Case for a Southeast Asian Court of Human Rights.* Martinus Nijhoff Publishers.

Rajska, Dagmara, and Zuzanna Rudzińska-Bluszcz. 2016. *Ombudsperson Institutions in Europe: Their Role as Third Party Interveners before the Echr and Their Initiatives before the Council of Europe.* Key.

Reif, Linda C. 2004. *The Ombudsman, Good Governance and the International Human Rights System.* Leiden, The Netherlands: Koninklijke Brill NV.

SAPA Task Force on ASEAN and Human Rights. 2014. Submission to the AICHR Regional Consultation with Civil Society on the Review of the AICHR TOR « FORUM-ASIA. https://www.forum-asia.org/?p=16979.

SEANF. 2007. Declarations: ASEAN NHRIs Forged Cooperation Agreement. http://seanf.asia/index.php/home/declarations.

———. 2017. South East Asia NHRI Forum. http://seanf.asia/index.php/about-us/89-south-east-asia-nhri-forum.

The Brunei Project. 2016. The Important Role Played by National Human Rights Institutions. June 10. https://www.facebook.com/thebruneiproject/posts/1609719802651514.

Ulrik Spliid. 2013. NHRIs and Public Participation. Issue Paper. The Danish Institute for Human Rights. https://www.humanrights.dk/files/media/billeder/udgivelser/nhris20and20public20participation.pdf.

UNDP. 2016. National Human Rights Bodies Playing Key Role in Advancing Africa's Rights Agenda, Says Study. December 16. http://www.africa.undp.org/content/rba/en/home/presscenter/articles/2016/12/14/national-human-rights-bodies-playing-key-role-in-advancing-africa-s-rights-agenda-says-study.html.

UNDP, and NANHRI. 2016. Study on the State of National Human Rights Institutions (NHRIs) in Africa. http://www.nanhri.org/wp-content/uploads/2016/11/State-of-Africa-NHRIs-Study-Report-English-v15.pdf.

United Nations. 1993. *Paris Principles on National Human Rights Institutions*. Vol. 48/134. http://www.ohchr.org/EN/ProfessionalInterest/Pages/StatusOfNationalInstitutions.aspx.

Vu, Giao Cong, and Kien Tran. 2016. Constitutional Debate and Development on Human Rights in Vietnam. *Asian Journal of Comparative Law* Vol. 11, No. 2: 235–62. https://doi.org/10.1017/asjcl.2016.27.

Wahyuningrum, Yuyun. 2014. AICHR After Five Years: Progress, Challenges and Opportunities. *Focus* 76 (June). http://www.hurights.or.jp/archives/focus/section3/2014/06/aichr-after-five-years-progress-challenges-and-opportunities.html.

CHAPTER 4

# National Human Rights Institutions and the United Nations Human Rights Treaty Body System: A Rebuttal to the Skeptics

*Domenico Zipoli*

## Introduction

This chapter argues that the "ineffectiveness critique" of the United Nations Human Rights Treaty Body system insufficiently factors in the essential role of National Human Rights Institutions (NHRIs). NHRIs are necessary elements of a properly functioning human rights protection system, and this shall be verified through the application of one specific theoretical structure, namely, Human Rights Experimentalism (HRE). It is through HRE's five-stage reasoning that the fundamental role played by NHRIs will be outlined.

A critical analysis of the UN Human Rights Treaty Body system essentially focuses on the persistent disjuncture between international human rights standards, on the one hand, and practice in domestic jurisdictions, on the other, often referred to as the human rights "compliance gap." A

D. Zipoli (✉)
Norwegian Centre for Human Rights, Faculty of Law, University of Oslo, Oslo, Norway
e-mail: domenico.zipoli@nchr.uio.no



J. Gomez, R. Ramcharan (eds.), *National Human Rights Institutions in Southeast Asia*,
https://doi.org/10.1007/978-981-15-1074-8_4

recurrent trend both among academic and policy environments has been to subject UN Human Rights Treaty Bodies (TBs) to what may be generally referred to as the "ineffectiveness critique" (Moyn 2012; Posner 2014), conventionally branding the system as weak top-down and a-contextualized (Hathaway 2002: 2020; Dai 2013: 95). Among others, the following two elements are the system's inherent weaknesses: the apparent ambiguity in standards and the lack of a strong or judicial-type enforcement mechanism.

By first reviewing aspects of such critical scholarship, the chapter wishes to highlight that recent impact studies do not sufficiently reflect on the role of domestic non-state actors in bringing about human rights policy change following treaty ratification (Dai 2013: 95–96).[1] This chapter wishes to situate the engagement of NHRIs within such narrative, framing the TB–NHRI interaction within the procedural structure of HRE. One specific example of Southeast Asian NHRI, the Indonesian Human Rights Commission (Komnas HAM), and its participation in the CCPR reporting cycle will be offered as an exemplary case study showcasing HRE application to TB–NHRI engagement. It is through this relatively novel governance theory that the abovementioned criticisms are to be valued as necessary elements of a properly functioning system, reliant on the iterative and mutually constitutive relationship between the global norm and local contextualization. The analysis will above all focus on the ICCPR and ICESCR, two examples of earlier UN human rights treaties whose provisions do not explicitly allow for stakeholder involvement.[2] If the HRE structure results are applicable to such earlier treaties, one may assume overall application throughout the TB system.

## UN Human Rights Treaty Impact Assessments—The Fuel for Skepticism

It is nearly 50 years since the first UN human rights treaty entered into force.[3] The number of TBs which the UN human rights system is endowed with has now grown to a total of ten, with active discussions on expanding

[1] Reliance on domestic actors is particularly crucial for international human rights, given the absence of an international enforcement mechanism and weak institutions.

[2] The latest human rights treaties specifically mention stakeholder involvement, including NHRIs (CRPD, Art. 33 and OPCAT Art. 17).

[3] The International Convention on the Elimination of All Forms of Racial Discrimination (ICERD) entered into force on 4 January 1969.

this number further. This growth of the TB system has on the one hand increased worldwide human rights monitoring capacity, while on the other it has caused the system's overall complexity to bring about structural challenges to its effectiveness (risk of substantive overlap, contradiction, lack of coordination and a fragmentation of the human rights protection system as a whole). To obviate these ensuing challenges, the UN has taken several initiatives, the most recent of which (2014) aims to streamline and harmonize the work of the ten Geneva-based committees. Apart from structural challenges, performance evaluations of UN human rights treaties have been offering a rather bleak picture. Two different sets of assessments may be discerned, both of which use the act of formal treaty commitment (ratification) as the yardstick for evaluating domestic human rights implementation.

The first category of TB performance evaluations covers a selection of (if not all) TBs within the same investigative effort. Taking six of the major human rights conventions, Emilie Hafner-Burton and Kyoteru Tsuitsui (2005: 1373–1411) find that ratification is significantly associated with an increase in state repression. Oona Hathaway (2002: 1935) discusses the apparent limits of treaties in reducing human rights violations, highlighting that "the poor reporting record merely reflects the main weakness of the treaty body regime—States lack incentives to police their compliance with Treaty Body procedure (reporting) and Treaty Body recommendations." On the lack of incentives for states to comply, Anne Bayefski (2001) also finds that "states may selectively provide requested information, present information in a way that obscures the situation on the ground, or ignore concerns or questions posed by the treaty body." She also points to low TB awareness, especially among those individuals and groups most affected by treaty violations as TB processes are mainly conducted far from domestic scrutiny (media and nongovernmental organizations [NGOs]). In his often-cited study on human rights treaty impact, Eric Neumayer (2005) evinces that treaty ratification may be associated with worse personal integrity rights, have a negative impact on civil rights and may even lead to an overall worsening of human rights in defined circumstances, for instance within autocracies without free civil society.

The second category relates to *treaty-specific* impact studies, highlighting the necessary specificity of each human rights treaty's functioning. The ICCPR has been subject to the highest amount of research on the impact of treaty ratification and we hereby offer just several selected examples. By initially asking herself whether the ICCPR makes a difference in human rights behavior, Linda Camp Keith (1999) finds no relationship between ICCPR ratification and human rights practices. Yonatan Lupu (2013) finds no significant impact—negative or positive—of CCPR ratification on physical integrity rights guarantees. Wade Cole's (2015) investigation leads to similar findings, as no significant aggregate between ICCPR ratification and physical integrity or empowerment rights was identified. A negative relationship between ratification and rights performance was found by Heather Smith–Cannoy (2012), whose analysis associates' ratification with worse human rights performance over time. Similarly, Daniel Hill (2010) finds that ICCPR ratification is associated with a small but significant decrease in physical integrity protections.

The above review suggests that whether analysis is generalized or specialized, treaty ratification alone—without the assistance of downstream domestic effects—yields little if any noticeable improvement in human rights guarantees. In other words, treaty ratification does not directly constrain violations. All the above studies have focused their investigative onus on the crystallized point of ratification rather than considering the steps taken before and after ratification. Ratification does not produce reform per se, and this simple caveat is reflected in these studies' partly negative findings on the effectiveness of human rights treaties.

Let us now turn to a specific institutional dialectic which has not been taken into consideration by the above critical assessments. The analysis that follows highlights the vernacular value of NHRIs, a specific domestic actor which is part of state administration but independent from it, defined as "a bridge between international norms and local implementation [...] designed to ensure the state's compliance with its international legal obligations" (Goodman and Pegram 2012: 29).

## UN Human Rights Treaty Bodies—NHRI Interaction and Governance Dynamics

We have started this chapter with a short reflection on the expansion of the UN Human Rights Treaty system. At the same time, NHRIs have also surged in numbers since the initial 1970s' wave of institutional establishment. The 1991 Paris Principles paved the way for what resulted in a fivefold increase of NHRIs worldwide during the 1990s and early 2000s, the total number of accredited NHRIs today amounting to 120. NHRIs vary in institutional structure: Human Rights Commissions, Ombudsmen, Defensores del Pueblo, Procurators for Human Rights and National

Advisory Commissions on Human Rights all have distinct structural and functional peculiarities. But no matter in which form, NHRIs assist and advise states on the implementation of international human rights norms and UN recommendations.

NHRI engagement with the UN human rights system has also been steadily growing, with the Human Rights Council's close cooperation with A-status NHRIs enshrined in its very foundation (GA resolution 60/251 and HRC resolution 5/1). Further progress has been made to enhance the participation of NHRIs in the context of the UPR. With the broadening of their contribution opportunities, as per the outcome of the review of the Council in 2011 and through resolution 16/21,[4] NHRIs are now involved in all UPR stages. Beyond the UPR, the close interaction between NHRIs and the Council is also exemplified by their contributions to Special Procedures. For example, national institutions help monitor and encourage the local implementation of the recommendations of Special Rapporteurs on thematic issues. In December 2015 the UN General Assembly's Third Committee, in a ground-breaking GA Resolution 70/173,[5] had called on all relevant UN processes and mechanisms to enhance the participation and contributions of Paris Principles–compliant NHRIs to their work. And notwithstanding specific reference to increasing TB-NHRI interaction,[6] the actual extent and dynamics related to such specific cooperation is, however, somewhat less clear-cut. The binary, growing complexity common to both TBs and NHRIs is just one of the shared traits:

- Both of a quasi-judicial nature (soft institutions)[7]
- Both not subsidiary bodies (ideally, independent)
- Both supervising states' implementation of international standards (soft mechanisms of enforcement)

[4] Available at http://www.ohchr.org/Documents/HRBodies/HRCouncil/RegularSession/Session23/TF/A-HRC-RES-16-21_en.doc.

[5] GA Res. 70/173 (Third Committee), National Institutions for the Promotion and Protection of Human Rights, A/RES/70/163 (17 December 2015).

[6] "The General Assembly: [...] 17. Invites the human rights treaty bodies, within their respective mandates and in accordance with the treaties establishing these mechanisms, to provide for ways to ensure the effective and enhanced participation by national human rights institutions compliant with the Paris Principles at all relevant stages of their work."

[7] A specific range of "processes and practices that have a normative/regulatory dimension, but that do not operate primarily through the conventional mechanisms of command-and-control-type legal institutions" (De Burca and Scott 2007).

TB–NHRI interaction is not an innovative call for institutional dialogue. The *Marrakech Statement on strengthening the relationship between NHRIs and the human rights treaty bodies system* (10 June 2010)[8] and the *Conclusions of the International Roundtable on the Role of National Human Rights Institutions and Treaty Bodies* (Berlin, 23 and 24 November 2006)[9] are two clear examples that international policy has indeed proceeded, at least on paper, in this direction. Furthermore, two standardized mechanisms of NHRI-TB interaction already exist, namely National Preventive Mechanisms[10] and National Monitoring Mechanisms.[11] Both mechanisms have often found their domestic institutional space within existing NHRIs.

From a *governance perspective*, the classic principal-agent model, whereby states delegate specific mandate and powers to international organizations (IGOs, in the case at hand, the OHCHR), has been challenged by the growing number of state and non-state actors involved in the transmission belt between the global and domestic arenas. In addition, this two-agent system has been found to hold inherent structural faults, among others the unaccountability in relation to "false positives" (Simmons 2009), that is states which commit to UN human rights treaties without the intention of complying. New institutional agents are able to play important roles in the channeling, translation and application of international norms by operating in novel spaces of interaction, at bilateral, multilateral, regional and trans-governmental levels. Outside of direct state control, they are also perfectly placed to act as domestic overseers of state action vis-à-vis their international commitments. And while IGOs continue to play the fundamental role of norm creation and global coordination, the growing regime complexity has resulted in a shift away from exclusive state party–UN dialectics, adding additional layers of non-state and private authority.

In order for this overgrowth of human rights governance levels to be clearly outlined and structured, international relations theorists have recently introduced the concept of *orchestration* (Abbot and Snidal 2009), a distinct form of institutional management architecture to collaboration,

[8] Available at http://www2.ohchr.org/english/bodies/HRTD/docs/MarrakeshStatement_en.doc.

[9] Available at http://www.osce.org/odihr/26111?download=true.

[10] OPCAT, Art. 3.

[11] CRPD, Art. 33.2.

delegation and hierarchy. This method, useful to keep in mind during this chapter's argumentation, stems from the need to bypass state consent in a governance framework which has recently turned more ambitious and open-ended than ever before. In short, orchestration occurs when (1) the *Orchestrator* (IGO) seeks to influence behavior of the *Target* (state) via *Intermediaries*, and (2) the *Orchestrator* lacks authoritative control over the *Intermediaries*, which, in turn, lack the ability to compel compliance of the *Target* (Pegram 2015).

If we are to apply this structure to TB governance in relation to NHRIs, the model is adjusted accordingly: the TB members together with the United Nations Office of the High Commissioner for Human Rights (OHCHR) act as *Orchestrators* seeking to influence the behavior of the *Target*, the states parties to the treaties. In between this bilateral dialectic, the model highlights the fundamental role of the *Intermediary*, in our case UN-affiliated NHRIs and their collective representative body, the Global Alliance of National Human Rights Institutions (GANHRI). It is the context-specific knowledge of and independence from the state which make NHRIs a functional gateway to inform and strive to bridge the gap to compliance. This three-legged institutional environment (Orchestrator–Intermediary–Target) is particularly suited to the legal nature of the international human rights treaty system, based on both hard law (treaties, conventions and protocols) and soft law (recommendations, declarations, principles and guidelines) instruments. Amongst this varied mix of legal standings, NHRIs have gradually been vested with increased margins of independent and effective action outside of the state's authority, thus breaking the traditional (and criticized) two-agent (state party–UN) system. By adding an institutional connector between international regulators and the state, orchestration suggests that the classic disconnect and distinction between the international and domestic is to be considered somewhat less draconian.

## Human Rights Experimentalism—A Lens for Rebuttal

This chapter argues that a relatively novel governance approach is perfectly suited to rebut critical assessments of TB performance, while at the same time elevating the role of NHRIs as key influencers toward human rights compliance by states. HRE, a human rights–specific strand of Global Experimentalist Governance (Sabel and Zeitlin 2012), is "a theory of multi-level governance that proposes a way in which [human rights] policy can be made and implemented in a multi-level setting" (De Burca 2017: 33) through an iterative and participatory system, among different situated stakeholders and actors, at different levels, across a transnational system. HRE helps the analyst to conceive such varied, multi-actor interdependence within a clear five-stage structure which presents the following features (De Burca et al. 2014: 2):

1. Initial reflection and discussion among stakeholders with a broadly shared perception of a common problem
2. A resulting articulation of a framework understanding with open-ended goals
3. The implementation of these broadly framed goals left to "lower-level" or contextually situated actors who have knowledge of local conditions and considerable discretion to adapt the framework norms to these different contexts
4. A continuous feedback provided from local contexts, allowing for reporting and monitoring across a range of contexts, with outcomes subject to peer review
5. Goals and practices periodically and routinely re-evaluated and, where appropriate, revised considering the results of the peer review and the shared purposes

The essential underpinning of experimentalist governance is thus a shared agreement on broad goals paired with the recognition that such goals will be implemented in variation—from context to context and from state to state. Such implementation is guaranteed by a system of recurrent nonhierarchical review mechanisms, with a prominent role given to stakeholder participation. Knowledge of local conditions is considered a fundamental pivot for a functioning HRE system, thanks to which a stream of continuous feedback flows from the local to the transnational context, aiding the reporting and monitoring necessary for a "most-effective" implementation of the accepted framework norms. The role of NHRIs as participants to the human rights treaty regime is convincingly interpreted by HRE theory. The diverse contexts and capacities related to all state parties to a treaty mean that centrally imposed solutions to collective problems are unworkable. For framework norms to be effectively implemented, they need to be vernacularized through deliberative processes which include both top-down and bottom-up approaches. Paris Principles–compliant NHRIs can play an important role in such processes.

## The UN Human Rights Covenants–NHRI Interaction Through a Human Rights Experimentalist Lens

For clarity, what follows is a chart (Fig. 4.1) exemplifying the reporting life cycle typical of UN human rights treaties. Certain TBs may also initiate individual complaints mechanisms and inquiry procedures, the powers for which often stem from successive Optional Protocols to the treaties. NHRIs may have important roles to play in all TB mechanisms and an experimentalist interpretation allows for a more comprehensive overview of the UN human rights treaties operations, emphasizing the significance of actors which go beyond the bilateral nature of the formally understood engagement between the state and the relevant expert committee.

It is due to the recent and gradual expansion of non-state actor participation within the human rights treaty regime that we now have elements which allow for an interpretation of its operations through an experimentalist lens.

Recent studies have methodically outlined the five experimentalist features within the most recently established regime, the CRPD, which clearly envisages non-state actor participation since its drafting stage and all throughout its operational cycle (De Burca 2010). However, this has

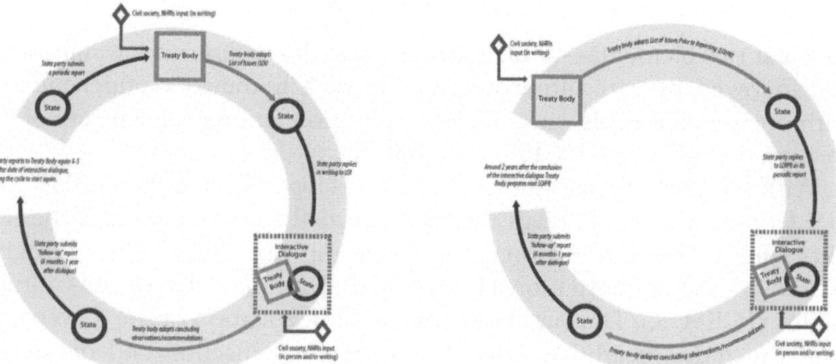


**Fig. 4.1** Reporting life cycles for states parties to the human rights treaties. (Source: C. Broeker, M. O'Flaherty, *Policy Brief—The Outcome of the GA's Treaty Body Strengthening Process*, Universal Rights Group (2014))

not been the case for earlier treaty regimes and the challenge for this chapter is to see whether experimentalism can be applied to the earliest forms of human rights treaties, the two Human Rights Covenants.

The growing participatory dimension, which has so far mainly been associated with civil society actors, will be analyzed by focusing on the role of NHRIs as institutional auxiliaries to the classic engagement between the state and the TB.

Diving into an experimentalist interpretation of the UN Covenants,[12] one can find some experimentalist features more easily represented than others.

Central to experimentalism are three, mutually sustaining characteristics, which elevate the importance of NHRIs (contextually situated actor) within the human rights treaty system:

1. Broad framework goals open to contextualized interpretation for a most effective implementation
2. Broad participation among a nonhierarchical and pluralist set of domestic actors
3. Extensive (and recursive) deliberation

Each of the above characteristics will now be considered in more detail:

### *Broadness and Open-Endedness Toward Contextualized Interpretation*

The first two elements—initial reflection and discussion among stakeholders, followed by a resulting articulation of a framework understanding with open-ended goals—are of easy application among the entirety of the treaties, including the CCPR and CESCR.

With the goal of establishing mechanisms for enforcing the UDHR, the UN Commission on Human Rights proceeded to the drafting of the two Covenants: The International Covenant on Civil and Political Rights (ICCPR) and the International Covenant on Economic, Social and Cultural Rights (ICESCR). During the international negotiation of the Covenants, which included nearly two decades of intense reflection and discussion before reaching a consensus among the 53 different member states of the UN Commission on Human Rights, "it was necessary to accommodate,

[12] For this chapter, the analysis will focus only on the state reporting procedure.

bridge, submerge and conceal deep divisions and differences, especially between democratic-libertarian and socialist-revolutionary states—differences in fundamental conceptions about the relation of society to the individual, about his rights and duties, about priorities and preferences among them" (Henkin 1981: 9). The product of these discussions led to the creation of the two separate treaties, and the history of their drafting led there being distinct differences between them. Contrasting phrasing is one of the most evident, with the ICCPR employing classic and more rigid rights terminology focused on individual rights (e.g. "Every human being has the inherent right to life"—Art 6; "No one shall be held in slavery"—Art 6) while the ICESCR's focus being more on the obligations of the state, characterized by more flexible language (e.g. "The States Parties to the present Covenant recognize the right to work—Art 6). This relatively more obvious open-endedness within the ICESCR articles stemmed from the argument (brought forward by Western states within the Commission) that civil and political rights were *legal rights against the state*, immediately enforceable and absolute, while economic, social and cultural rights were *program rights from the state*, that would take more time to implement through what has been defined as "progressive realization."

Notwithstanding these differences, the result of contradictory pressures and approaches are directly relatable to the first two features of experimentalist governance:

1. At the initial, treaty-making phase, state parties have come together in intergovernmental conferences following a shared understanding that there is a need for stronger legal standards of protection pertaining to the specific range of human rights being discussed.
2. Due to the large number of state parties to these intergovernmental conferences, and the technical necessity of reaching a consensus, both Covenants are characterized by broad and open-ended articulation which requires substantial degrees of interpretation for them to be translated into effective domestic implementation. This flexibility is part and parcel of a system which involves the most disparate set of countries in terms of cultural values, governmental set-ups, stages of development and so forth. The focus on "progressive realization" which ICESCR relies on is perhaps evidence of a more clear-cut intention by the drafters of open-endedness; however, both Covenants clearly do not indicate precise obligations for the State Parties to follow.

Flexibility on how to implement open-ended framework goals is precisely what allows for an extensive participatory approach. NHRIs are part of this approach.

### *Growing Participatory Dimension and Recursivity—The Feedback Loop*

The *third feature* of experimentalist governance relates to the implementation of such open- ended rights through devolution of discretion to local or contextually situated actors. This feature underlines the growing participatory dimension of the human rights treaty system and its value toward a more effective internalization of global human rights standards. Indifferent to which TB and relevant TB mechanism one analyzes, the actors required to act upon them are necessarily locally or contextually situated. In general terms, both the manner of implementation and the actors involved in the process are left to the states parties' discretion, as it is only with contextual knowledge that effective choices can be made.

The *fourth feature*—continuous feedback from local contexts—also puts the participatory dimension at the forefront of the treaty processes, adding a fundamental operative layer within which domestic actors can be involved as effective auxiliaries to compliance: recursivity.

These two experimentalist features are part of both Covenants' operations. Feedback provided by localized actors is channeled through both the HRCttee and CESCR within a system of periodic reporting, arguably the most characteristic monitoring measure of the UN TB system. Signatory states are in fact obliged to periodically report on their compliance with treaty obligations. Such report is then assessed by the two Committees which act in their own capacity as recognized international experts in the field of the specific Treaty's competence. The examination of state reports, which is often referred to as a "constructive dialogue," is of a formally nonbinding nature and involves a non-adversarial review of the information provided by the state, followed by a set of recommendations, also known as Concluding Observations. This institutional "weakness" can be surmounted by relying on, among others, NHRIs' recursive feedback and consequent pressure.

It is within the fourth essential stage of HRE that NHRIs may at best be located as effective influencers of human rights compliance, acting as key actors in bridging the gap between international standards and domestic implementation. NHRIs play a crucial role in the dissemination of

Alternative Reports and ground-level information which aid the Committee's experts toward more up-to-date and contextually informed recommendations directed at state parties. A Paris Principle–compliant and sufficiently empowered NHRI has the potential to "indirectly increase" both the CCPR and CESCR effectiveness (Risse et al. 2013).

Even if both the ICCPR and ICESCR themselves make no explicit mention of NHRI involvement[13] (and appear to hand the norms' implementation, monitoring and reporting entirely to states and their relevant ministries), both Committees have substantiated the role of NHRIs within recent General Comments. While the HRCttee, in its General Comment n. 31, notes that "NHRIs" can contribute "to give effect to the general obligation to investigate allegations of violations promptly, thoroughly and effectively through independent and impartial bodies",[14] the CESCR dedicates General Comment 10 to the role of national human rights institutions in the protection of economic, social and cultural rights.[15]

NHRI involvement in the implementation of the CESCR has witnessed an arguably more explicit recognition during the build up to the GC's adoption. The Limburg Principles[16] are devoid of any reference to NHRIs, partly explainable due to their adoption predating both the Paris Principles and the ultimate international confirmation NHRIs received at the Vienna Conference on Human Rights. A decade later, the Maastricht Guidelines on Violation of ESCR (1998) were adopted, within which NHRIs are specifically mentioned among those actors which "should address violations of economic, social and cultural rights as vigorously as they address violations of civil and political rights".[17] Interestingly and perhaps adding a layer of doubt on CESCR–NHRI interaction, only "NGOs, national governments and international organizations" are mentioned as actors to be involved in the monitoring and documentation of ESCR violations.[18]

[13] Unlike the CRPD, for instance.

[14] UN Human Rights Committee (HRC), General Comment no. 31 [80]. The nature of the general legal obligation imposed on states parties to the Covenant, 26 May 2004, CCPR/C/21/Rev.1/Add.13, para. 15.

[15] UN Committee on Economic, Social and Cultural Rights (CESCR), General Comment No. 10: The role of national human rights institutions in the protection of economic, social and cultural rights, 10 December 1998, E/C.12/1998/25.

[16] Limburg Principles on the Implementation of the International Covenant on Economic, Social and Cultural Rights, E/CN.4/198/17, 8 January 1987.

[17] Maastricht Guidelines on Violations of Economic, Social and Cultural Rights, Maastricht, 22–26 January 1997, sec. 25.

[18] *Ibid.* sec 31.

The seeming disparity of consideration given by the two Committees is, arguably, a matter of formality. NHRIs do, in fact, increasingly contribute to both Committees' operations, and the lack of clarity with respect to HRCtee–NHRI interaction has recently been covered with the adoption of the "[p]aper on the relationship of the Human Rights Committee with national human rights institutions"[19] in which the role of NHRIs in both the reporting procedure and the individual communications procedure under the Optional Protocol has clearly been outlined.

There are several institutional characteristics unique to NHRIs that make them effective as both CCPR and CESCR monitoring agents:

First, NHRIs have an *empowerment advantage*. The "unique position" NHRIs occupy "somewhere between" governments and civil society (Smith 2006: 904), means they can empower domestic stakeholders by bringing them together, thus facilitating the participation of social actors in the process. The presence of an NHRI in the Covenants monitoring process "can provide local and transnational advocacy networks with an important ally inside state bureaucracies and give social groups a channel through which to make their claims for information" (Corkery 2012: 4).

Secondly, NHRIs have an *informational advantage*. Also, in line with the Paris Principles, information gathering powers are substantially more "intrusive" on state departments, sometimes amounting to powers to subpoena information. Such imposition of cooperation between NHRIs and state departments is clearly not comparable to those mechanisms of information gathering typical of civil society organizations. Recalling Dai's theory on domestic constituencies, increasing both the political leverage and informational status of domestic actors is seen as the most effective form of influence of weak international institutions on human rights compliance (Dai 2007, 2013). NHRIs are obvious partners for weak institutions such as the HRCttee and CESCR in influencing state parties toward compliance.

Thirdly, NHRIs have a *temporal advantage*. NHRIs are permanent institutions which can track issues over extended periods to identify trends (subject of course to their institutional capacity). Under the Paris Principles, they are furthermore required to produce an annual report, which is often presented before Parliament. This periodic reporting

[19] UN Human Rights Committee, Paper on the Relationship of the Human Rights Committee with National Human Rights Institutions, CCPR/C/106/3 (13 November 2012).

function perfectly suits an experimentalist governance approach, as the iterative and revisionist approach that the HRCttee and CESCR seem to follow in their periodic reporting procedures can benefit from these yearly human rights–specific parliamentary discussions.

Fourthly, and perhaps most importantly, NHRIs have an *advantage of standing*. A legally defined relationship with the state entails that among those actors which contribute to both CCPR and CESCR compliance, NHRI functions can uniquely feed into the policy cycle at various points. Thus, NHRIs play an important role in "linking the outcomes of monitoring with the development or amendment of policy, to ensure that actions taken by the state to give substance to its international obligations in fact achieve their stated aims." The Paris Principles envisage a "triangular" relationship between the international system–state–NHRI (Carver 2010: 20), an institutional remedy to the "mutual distrust" between the international system and state parties (Rosga and Satterthwaite 2008: 27–28). If NHRIs act as genuinely independent intermediaries in the process, their contextually provided information should authoritatively certify or contest the state's interpretation of its performance under both the ICCPR and ICESCR as well as increase the states' receptiveness of HRCttee and CESCR recommendations if these are substantiated by information gathered, among others, by an official process at the national level.

This triangular relationship is also important in ensuring the implementation of HRCtee and CESCR recommendations, as both international mechanisms so far lack formal follow-up procedures at the national level.

Although "monitoring" as a term is not explicitly mentioned within the Paris Principles, NHRIs do rely on ongoing activities that "systematically use information" to measure the achievement of defined targets and provides feedback on the processes for implementing these targets.[20] Such "monitoring" techniques have been defined as activities that "all NHRIs are to be engaged in" (Carver 2010). During the TB reporting cycle, NHRIs may first provide input during the reporting process both to the Committee, in the form of either alternative reports submission or through private meetings in advance of the official hearings, and to governments themselves, in preparation of the official report. Through these practices, NHRIs are in a position to influence the recommendations by suggesting

[20] High Commissioner for Human Rights, Report of the High Commissioner for Human Rights on Implementation of Economic, Social and Cultural Rights, delivered to the Economic and Social Council, UN Doc. E/2009/90 (8 June 2009).

steps which their respective governments should take to fulfill their obligations, with the invaluable insight into what is, and what indeed is not, achievable within their national context.

After the Committee's adoption of Concluding Observations, a select number of recommendations (usually the most urgent) enter the so-called follow-up procedure, a mechanism put in place to check on the state party's commitments even in between submissions of periodic reports. NHRIs during both follow-up and in-between periodic reports' submissions, more generally, may thus pressurize governments through their peculiar array of institutional actions, including advocacy for legislative reform, facilitating cooperation of domestic actors, actively engaging with the media and (if their specific mandates allow for it) bringing strategic litigation and undergoing national inquiries.

NHRIs' strategic position as monitoring stakeholders enables them to act as both receptors and transmitters within the recursive cycle of CCPR and CESCR activity, as defined through experimentalist theory. Their unique standing also enables NHRIs to translate externally negotiated human rights norms for local audiences. As human rights *intermediaries*, NHRIs can "put global human rights ideas into familiar symbolic terms and use stories of local indignities and violations to give life and power to global movements. [NHRIs] hold a double consciousness, combining both transnational human rights concepts and local ways of thinking about grievances" (Merry 2009: 441–461). While taking the UN human rights instruments as their core frame of reference, NHRIs are what experimentalist theory calls "contextually situated actors who have knowledge of local conditions." With such a unique standing, NHRIs hold significant potential to act as translators between the universal claims of the international rights regime and national idiosyncrasies.

Acting as a bridge between international and domestic spheres of action, as well as being part of the state administration but independently so, NHRIs are perfectly placed to provide direct services to people affected by the gaps identified by the TB mechanism. NHRIs, through their context-specific expertise, are often involved in the publication of guidelines and the establishment of databases which can be invaluable both domestically and in relation to further TB examination. The fourth feature of experimentalism is thus covered by NHRIs as they bring fresh data and new issues from contextualized and situational knowledge, fueling what one may define as "transnational learning."

### *Periodic Re-evaluation and Revision*

Apart from emphasizing the participatory dimension of locally situated actors and their role in providing information, translating and vernacularizing norms from the international to the local, experimentalist governance considers the process of iterative "learning from difference" as an essential element to its theoretical structure. Although initially applied to the European Union's architecture (Sabel and Zeitlin 2008: 271), iteration and revision (De Burca et al. 2014: 2)—the fifth and last experimentalist feature—may also explain how to solve the apparent legitimacy gap of the UN human rights treaty system, where common problems are shared among its participants (the legal norms being set to counter such problems) and the inherent deep, contextually driven, diversity of the participants to the system.

The extent of NHRI involvement within the periodic re-evaluation to which the fifth feature of experimentalism refers to is not as clear-cut as with the preceding two characteristics.

If one looks at the state party-specific reporting cycle of both HRCttee and CESCR, NHRIs can inform both Committees with new data and information, regularly informing both procedures with updates from "the local".[21] In this *country-specific sense*, NHRIs are included in the periodic re-evaluation of domestic goals and practices.

However, if one considers re-evaluation of the *broader framework norms* themselves, NHRIs are considerably less active. Revision may be evinced by the use that both Committees make of General Comments (GCs) in order to update the original, 50-year-old, Covenants. Both the HRCtee and CESCR have utilized GCs (and General Discussion days in preparation of GCs) as an opportunity to update and include issues which had not been taken into consideration at the time of ratification. International NGOs and academic experts have increasingly been involved in the process of drafting GCs, but NHRI participation in these processes has been less constant.[22]

Critics have pointed out that the HRCttee has formulated its GCs within closed meetings and that not all actors involved in the ICCPR system participate in the process, with its internal consensus-driven procedure reflecting the common-denominator of the experts' opinions and

[21] Network of African NHRIs, Network for the Americas, Asia Pacific Forum, European Network of NHRIs.

[22] Research on OHCHR Database website (January 2018).

not much else (Tyagi 2011: 294). With the adoption of the "[p]aper on the relationship of the HRCttee with NHRIs,"[23] it seems to have acted upon these criticisms as it specifically addresses and invites NHRI input on the drafting and use of the Committee's GCs. Only one GC has been adopted since (GC N. 35, replacing GC 10, on the Right to Liberty and Security of Persons (art.9) in 2014[24]) and the HRCttee duly solicited the input of NHRIs, NGOs and academia to submit comments on the draft. Regrettably, the Danish Institute for Human Rights was the only NHRI to submit a comment.

The arguably more explicit provisions related to NHRI involvement in CESCR's operations are recently having a somewhat more satisfactory effect. An analysis of Written Submissions on the latest Draft GC on state obligations under the ICESCR in the context of business activities show six NHRI submissions, which is still a fairly low number in contrast to the vast array of international NGOs and academics involved in the process.[25]

From this preliminary analysis it may be argued that the iterative revisionary dimension has increasingly been present within the Covenants' operations. However, NHRIs have barely been involved in this revisionary process of the framework norms themselves. In both Covenants' GCs submissions and Discussion Days, apart from TB experts (some with a professional NHRI background) and state representatives, it has been mainly international NGOs and experts from academia which have collaborated toward norm revision. It may thus be tentatively argued that for matters of general application, NHRIs tend to be excluded (self-excluded?) with their input being more important during their own state's reporting on treaty compliance. One possible role within this fifth experimentalist feature which may include NHRIs into these revision procedures is input by regional/global NHRI organizations such as the GANHRI, APF,

[23] UN Human Rights Committee, Paper on the Relationship of the Human Rights Committee with National Human Rights Institutions, CCPR/C/106/3 (13 November 2012).

[24] UN Human Rights Committee (HRC), General comment no. 35, Article 9 (Liberty and security of person), CCPR/C/GC/35 (16 December 2014).

[25] NHRI submissions from the Commission on Human Rights of the Philippines, la Defensoria del Pueblo of Ecuador, the Global Alliance of National Institutions for the Promotion and Protection of Human Rights (GANHRI), the National Human Rights Commission of Mexico, the Netherlands Institute for Human Rights and the Northern Ireland Human Rights Commission. Research on OHCHR Database website (January 2018).

NANHRI, ENNHRI and the Network for the Americas. These organizations have the capacity to offer contextually relevant advice built on the shared opinions of many national institutions at once, with a unique experience in terms of bridging the so-called compliance gap between the international and domestic.

## Human Rights Experimentalism and Indonesia—Komnas HAM Engagement

In order to situate the above considerations within the regional focus of the book, what follows is the application of HRE features to one specific Southeast Asian NHRI and its recent engagement with the Human Rights Committee. The choice of applying HRE to the Indonesian context is due to its historically consistent A-status NHRI[26] and its simultaneous accession to both Covenants in 2006.[27] We will divide the Indonesian reporting process to the Human Rights Committee following the three mutual sustaining characteristics central to HRE (*Broadness/Open-Endedness toward contextualized interpretation, Growing Participatory Dimension/Recursivity* and *Periodic Re-evaluation/Revision*). Importantly, each Treaty Body currently engages with NHRIs in different ways. The Human Rights Committee has deliberated its engagement through the issuance of a Paper on the relationship of the Human Rights Committee with national human rights institutions and with regard to the role of NHRIs in the reporting procedure. Tt lists the following stages of recommended engagement:

- Consultations and inputs to the state party report
- Contributions to the list of issues
- Contributions to and during the Committee sessions
- Contributions in follow-up to Concluding Observations
- Contributions under the review procedure (examination in the absence of a state report)

[26] The Indonesian National Commission on Human Rights (Komnas HAM), initially established by Presidential Decree in 1993, had its legal foundation reconstituted after legislation passed the Indonesian House of Representatives (Legislation Number 39 of 1999 Concerning Human Rights). Consistent in its accreditation status under the Sub-Committee on Accreditation procedure, it has received its latest A status grading in March 2017.

[27] Indonesia acceded to both CCPR and CESCR on 23 February 2006.

### *Broadness and Open-Endedness Toward Contextualized Interpretation in the Indonesian Context*

Considering the CCPR reporting cycle following ratification, the first state party report of Indonesia was due on 23 May 2007 and submitted on 19 January 2012. In relation to this initial report of Indonesia, the Human Rights Committee issued its List of Issues (LOIs)[28] for consideration of the state party on 29 April 2013, during the Committee's 107th session. In short, LOIs are transmitted to the state party in advance of the session at which the Treaty Body will consider the State Report and provide a framework for the constructive dialogue with the state party's delegation. It is exactly due to the broad nature of the CCPR articles that contextualized interpretation is possible, in this case applicable to Indonesian domestic policy.

### *Growing Participatory Dimension and Recursivity in the Indonesian Context*

To such LOIs, the state party may submit written responses for consideration of the Committee, and so can civil society and the NHRI in question. Apart from a plethora of civil society submissions,[29] Komnas HAM made a submission in response to the LOIs on 14 June 2013,[30] with Indonesia submitting its replies to the LOIs on 10 July 2013.[31] It is at this stage of the reporting cycle that NHRIs can preliminarily influence, through their own research and policy advice, the work of the Committee and its ensuing recommendations.

[28] Human Rights Committee, List of issues in relation to the initial report of Indonesia (CCPR/C/IDN/1), adopted by the Committee at its 107th session (11–28 March 2013) available at http://tbinternet.ohchr.org/_layouts/treatybodyexternal/Download.aspx?symbolno=CCPR%2fC%2fIDN%2fQ%2f1&Lang=en.

[29] Available at http://tbinternet.ohchr.org/_layouts/treatybodyexternal/SessionDetails1.aspx?SessionID=417&Lang=en.

[30] Comments' of the Indonesian National Human Rights Commission on Indonesia's Compliance with the International Covenant on Civil and Political Rights, 14 June 2013 available at http://tbinternet.ohchr.org/_layouts/treatybodyexternal/Download.aspx?symbolno=INT%2fCCPR%2fIFN%2fIDN%2f14340&Lang=en.

[31] List of issues in relation to the initial report of Indonesia, adopted by the Committee at its 107th session (11–28 March 2013), Addendum, Replies of Indonesia to the list of issues, CCPR/C/IDN/Q/1/Add.1 available at http://tbinternet.ohchr.org/_layouts/treatybodyexternal/Download.aspx?symbolno=CCPR%2fC%2fIDN%2fQ%2f1%2fAdd.1&Lang=en.

It is during the Human Rights Committee's 108th session that the State Report of Indonesia was considered. The constructive dialogue with the Indonesian delegation was held in Geneva on 10 and 11 July 2013. In short, the constructive dialogue consists in the Committee inviting state parties to send a delegation to attend the session at which their report is being considered, in order to allow them to respond to members' questions and provide additional information on their efforts to implement the provisions of the relevant treaty. According to the abovementioned Committee Paper on its relationship with NHRIs, alternative reports and oral presentations are allowed during the constructive dialogue, as well as formal private and closed meetings with the Committee. This is yet another avenue for influence which NHRIs are offered. Komnas HAM did not in this specific instance submit any further alternative report than the one submitted in response to the LOIs. For the purposes of this chapter, however, it is enough to note how Komnas HAM had yet another possibility of informing the Committee, thus starting what HRE defines as extensive and recursive deliberation.

Following the constructive dialogue, the Committee issued its Concluding Observations[32] on 20 August 2013,[33] referring to both positive aspects of a state's implementation of the treaty and areas where the Committee recommends that further action needs to be taken by the state.

Reference to HRE's reliance on participatory deliberation does not end here, however. The Human Rights Committee may issue follow-up recommendations to its Concluding Observations, which it did in the case of Indonesia on 26 July 2013. What this procedure entails[34] is to highlight between two and four recommendations (the "follow-up recommendations") from the Committee's Concluding Observations which require immediate attention because of the level of gravity of the situation. The state party has then one year to reply and amend the highlighted situations. With a one-year delay, Indonesia replied to its follow-up recommendations on 4 March 2015. Its replies were not, however, satisfactory for

[32] Human Rights Committee, Concluding Observations on the initial report of Indonesia, CCPR/C/IDN/CO/1 available at http://tbinternet.ohchr.org/_layouts/treatybodyexternal/Download.aspx?symbolno=CCPR%2fC%2fIDN%2fCO%2f1&Lang=en.

[33] Follow-up to Concluding Observations paras. 8, 10, 12 and 25.

[34] Human Rights Committee, Note by the Human Rights Committee on the procedure for follow-up to Concluding Observations, CCPR/C/108/2, 21 October 2013 available at http://tbinternet.ohchr.org/_layouts/treatybodyexternal/Download.aspx?symbolno=CCPR%2fC%2f108%2f2&Lang=en.

the Committee, which issued a series of follow-up letters specifying the required steps Indonesia had to make in order to fully comply with the previously issued follow-up recommendations.[35] In the absence of a response by Indonesia, the follow-up procedure was discontinued by the Committee on 19 April 2017. Of importance for HRE application to NHRI engagement with the state reporting procedure, third-party submissions are welcome also with respect to follow-up. And although there was no submission from Komnas HAM itself, an example of yet another possibility for national institutions to participate and influence can be seen by the follow-up report submitted by the Indonesian National Commission on Violence against Women (Komnas Perempuan),[36] dated 11 January 2016. Just like HRE postulates, the follow-up procedure and the possibility for third-party engagement are clear indications of the system's reliance on broad participation among a nonhierarchical and pluralist set of domestic actors.

### *Periodic Re-evaluation and Revision—Indonesia*

As mentioned above, NHRIs are included in the periodic re-evaluation of domestic goals and practices merely *from a country-specific sense*. For this reason, re-evaluation of the broader framework norms by Komnas HAM will not be discussed.

The strength of the state reporting procedure lies in its recursivity, with state parties required to periodically submit reports on its implementation of the Convention following a cycle which should last approximately four to five years. As previously mentioned, NHRIs can provide input throughout the cycle, contributing to the state party report, toward LOIs, during Committee sessions as well as contributing to the follow-up procedure. In the case of Indonesia, the state party report for its second reporting cycle was overdue (the established date for submission was 26 July 2017).

[35] Follow-up letters dated 1 April 2015, 1 October 201 and 16 August 2016 available at http://tbinternet.ohchr.org/_layouts/treatybodyexternal/SessionDetails1.aspx?SessionID=623&Lang=en.

[36] Komisi Nasional Anti Kekerasan terhadap Perempuan (National Commission On Violence Against Women—Komnas Perempuan) National Human Rights Institution Independent Follow-up Report on the review of Indonesia Follow-up Report on the implementation of the International Covenant on Civil and Political Rights in Indonesia, available at http://tbinternet.ohchr.org/Treaties/CCPR/Shared%20Documents/IDN/INT_CCPR_NGS_IDN_22689_E.pdf.

Without going into the merits of such delay, it is important to highlight the renewed possibility for Komnas HAM to engage and submit its reports once again throughout this second cycle of reporting, even in the absence of a state report.

## Conclusion

This chapter has attempted to first rebut the critical assessments directed at UN human rights treaties performance. Impact assessments should now step away from ratification effects only and look at the causal mechanisms and conditions underlying human rights treaty impact following the first act of ratification.

Secondly, NHRI interaction with the two Covenants has been interpreted through a Human Rights Experimentalist lens. Within experimentalist features, NHRIs have the potential to play an influential role in successfully integrating and disseminating (in this case both HRCtee and CESCR) recommendations stemming from the reporting cycle into their country's domestic human rights system. Some reservation remains as to how much NHRIs are able or indeed willing to participate outside of their own state's reporting cycle, as can be seen by their relatively low scope of action when called for framework goal re-evaluation (HRE feature 5).

Within the limits of the present chapter, it is hard to outline the various TB-specific idiosyncrasies which relate to NHRI involvement. One may analyze each of the mentioned NHRI–Covenants engagement practices in detail and find means of empirically explaining the direct causation links between them and more effective implementation of the Covenants' action, just as was attempted through the application of HRE to the Indonesian context. It will indeed be part and parcel of this chapter's further development. The ongoing Treaty Body Strengthening Process, initiated by Res. 68/268,[37] has been actively engaged with NHRI involvement, most notably through the High Commissioner for Human Rights report to the Secretary General on TB Strengthening[38] in which she encouraged TBs to institutionalize "aligned models of interaction among

[37] United Nations, GA Resolution 68/268, "Strengthening and Enhancing the Effective Functioning of the Human Rights Treaty Body System," 9 April 2014 (available at http://www.ohchr.org/Documents/HRBodies/TB/HRTD/A-RES-68-268_E.pdf).

[38] Report of the United Nations High Commissioner for Human Rights on the Strengthening of the Human Rights Treaty Bodies, A/66/860 para 4.2.8, p. 66 (2012).

treaty bodies and national human rights institutions […] to harmonize the way the treaty bodies engage with national human rights institutions." Of crucial potential in this regard, Agenda Item 12 of the 2017 Meeting of TB Chairpersons titles "Development of a common treaty body approach to engaging national human rights institutions".[39] It is thus important to substantiate the positive role that NHRIs have in the TB system, and an experimentalist governance framework may help considering future reform.[40]

To conclude, future TB impact assessments should focus on the relationship between human rights treaties and practices on the ground and not on one-shot treatment of ratification as a catalyst for domestic human rights change in and by itself (Cope and Creamer 2016). Incorporation of the treaties' content into domestic policy is in fact to be witnessed in multi-staged, multi-stakeholder processes which span many years, before and after ratification. It is only under certain domestic institutional circumstances that conventions can incentivize facilitation of enhanced human rights protection and NHRIs are perfectly placed to aid toward such endeavor.

## References

Abbot, K. & D. Snidal. 2009. International Regulation without International Government: Improving IO Performance through Orchestration, *Venderbilt Journal of International Law* Vol. 42 No. 2.

Bayefski, A.F. 2001. The Future of UN Treaty Monitoring. Cambridge University Press.

Broeker, C. & M. O'Flaherty. 2014. Policy Brief – *The Outcome of the GA's Treaty Body Strengthening* at http://www.universal-rights.org/wp-content/uploads/2015/02/URG_Policy_Brief_web_spread_hd.pdf.

Camp, L.K. 1999. The United Nations International Covenant on Civil and Political Rights: Does it Make a Difference in Human Rights Behaviour?, *Journal of Peace Research* Vol. 95.

[39] 29th Meeting of Chairpersons (26–30 June 2017, New York), available at: http://www.ohchr.org/Documents/HRBodies/TB/AnnualMeeting/29Meeting/ProvisionalAgenda.docx.

[40] GA Res A/RES/68/268, para 41 decides that by no later than 2020, the General Assembly will undertake a comprehensive review of the effectiveness of measures taken "in order to ensure their sustainability, and, if appropriate, to decide on further action to strengthen and enhance the effective functioning of the human rights treaty body system."

Carver, R. 2010. A New Answer to an Old Question: National Human Rights Institutions and the Domestification of International Law, *Human Rights Law Review* Vol. 11.

Cole, W. 2015. Mind the Gap: State Capacity and the Implementation of Human Rights Treaties, *International Organizations* Vol. 69.

Cope, K.L. and C.D. Creamer. 2016. Disaggregating the Human Rights Treaty Regime, *Virginia Journal of International Law*, Vol. 56, No. 2.

Corkery, A. 2012. *National Human Rights Institutions as Monitors of Economic, Social and Cultural Rights.* Center for Economic and Social Rights Briefing Paper at www.cesr.org.

Dai, X. 2007. *International Institutions and National Policies,* Cambridge University Press.

———. 2013. The Compliance Gap and the Efficacy of International Human Rights Institutions, in T. Risse, S. C. Ropp and K. Sikkink (eds.) *The Persistent Power of Human Rights. From Commitment to Compliance,* Cambridge University Press.

De Burca, G. 2010. The EU in the Negotiation of the UN Disability Convention, *European Law Review* Vol. 35.

———. 2017. Human Rights Experimentalism, *American Journal of International Law* Vol 11, No. 2.

De Burca, G. & J. Scott 2007. Narrowing the Gap: Law and New Approaches to Governance in the European Union, *Colum. Journal of European Law*, 2007, Vol. 13, pp. 13, 3, 513–764.

De Burca, G., R. O. Keohane, and C. Sabel. 2014. Global Experimentalist Governance. *New York University Public Law and Legal Theory Working Papers,* Paper 485.

Eric Neumayer. 2005. Do International Human Rights Treaties Improve Respect for Human Rights? Journal of Conflict Resolution, Vol 49, Issue 6, 2005, 925–953.

Goodman, R. & T. Pegram. 2012. *Human Rights, State Compliance and Social Change – Assessing National Human Rights Institutions*, Cambridge.

Hafner-Burton, E.M. & K. Tsuitsui (2005) Human Rights in a Globalizing World: The Paradox of Empty Promises, *American Journal of Sociology* Vol. 110.

Hathaway, O. A. 2002. Do Human Rights Treaties Make a Difference?, *The Yale Law Journal* Vol. 111.

Henkin, L. 1981. Introduction, *the International Bill of Rights: The Covenant on Civil and Political Rights*, ed. L. Henkin. Columbia University Press.

Hill, D.W. 2010. Estimating the Effects of Human Rights Treaties on State Behavior, *Journal of Political Studies* Vol. 72.

Lupu, Y. 2013. Best Evidence: The Role of Information in Domestic Judicial Enforcement of International Human Rights Agreements, *International Organizations* Vol. 67.

Merry, S. E. 2009. Vernacularization on the Ground: Local Uses of Global Women's Rights in Peru, China, India and the United States, *Global Networks* Vol. 9, 2009, pp. 441–461.

Moyn, S. 2012. *The Last Utopia* Harvard University Press.

Pegram, T. 2015. Global Human Rights Governance and Orchestration: National Human Rights Institutions as Intermediaries, *European Journal of International Relations* Vol. 21, No. 3.

Posner, E. 2014. *The Twilight of International Human Rights Law*. Oxford University Press.

Risse, T, S. C. Ropp and K. Sikkink (eds.) 2013. *The Persistent Power of Human Rights, From Commitment to Compliance*, Cambridge University Press.

Rosga, A and M. L. Satterthwaite. 2008. The Trust in Indicators: Measuring Human Rights, *N.Y.U. Pub. Law & Legal Theory Research* Paper Series, 2008. Working Paper No. 08–59.

Sabel, C. and J Zeitlin. 2008. Learning from Difference: The New Architecture of Experimentalist Governance in the EU, *European Law Journal* Vol. 14.

———. 2012. *Experimentalist Governance in the European Union – Towards a New Architecture*. Oxford: University Press.

Simmons, B. 2009. *Mobilizing Human Rights: International Law in Domestic Politics*. Cambridge University Press.

Smith, A. 2006. The Unique Position of National Human Rights Institutions: A Mixed Blessing?, *Human Rights Quarterly* Vol. 28.

Smith-Cannoy, H.. 2012. *Insincere Commitments: Human Rights treaties, Abusive States and Citizen Activism*, Georgetown University Press.

Tyagi, Y. 2011. *The UN Human Rights Committee – Practice and Procedure*, Cambridge University Press.

PART II

# Protection Challenges in Southeast Asian States

CHAPTER 5

# Assessing the Effectiveness of the Myanmar National Human Rights Commission in the Wider Regional Geo-Political Context

*Niki Esse de Lang*

## Introduction

This chapter argues that, despite considerable progress made in the legal framework of the MNHRC by the adoption of the *MNHRC Law No. 21/2014* (hereafter: *MNHRC Law 2014*) on 28 March 2014, there remain serious legal and political adjustments that have to be made in order for the MNHRC to be in compliance with international standards such as the *Principles relating to the Status of National Institutions for the Promotion and Protection of Human Rights* (hereafter: *Paris Principles 1993*). Most notably, an analysis of the MNHRC's protection and promotion record in recent years has revealed that the MNHRC has not reached a satisfactory level of effectiveness in exercising its mandate. The analysis reveals that this is due to not only a high workload and a lack of capacity but also a lack of political willingness on the part of the MNHRC Commissioners to interfere too much into the domain of powerful actors, such as the Myanmar military. There have also been considerable blunders, which

N. E. de Lang (✉)
UNODC Southeast Asia, Bangkok, Thailand



J. Gomez, R. Ramcharan (eds.), *National Human Rights Institutions in Southeast Asia*,
https://doi.org/10.1007/978-981-15-1074-8_5

could have been avoided, such as keeping the identity of complainants confidential and offer special protection and consideration for victims of human rights abuse.

The MNHRC's lack of effectiveness on the national level is further exacerbated on the regional level where Myanmar and the MNHRC have engaged with the ASEAN Intergovernmental Commission on Human Rights (AICHR) and the different national human rights institutions (NHRIs) in the region, including through South East Asia NHRI Forum (SEANF) and the Asia Pacific Forum for NHRIs (APF). It was found that the first four ASEAN NHRIs from Indonesia, Malaysia, Thailand and the Philippines, the 'ASEAN Four', before MNHRC joined them, have been actively collaborating and promoting for a strong AICHR with strong enforcement powers. However, Myanmar only reluctantly accepted it, after the economically stronger and more democratic states, most of which had NHRIs at that time, supported it. It was also noted that the ASEAN Four, which later formed the SEANF, filled some of the gaps left by AICHR when speaking out on human rights issues in Myanmar, but when the MNHRC joined SEANF, the activism of SEANF towards Myanmar and other ASEAN states diminished.

The analysis in this chapter is based on a qualitative review of primary documents emanating from the MNHRC, such as the MNHRC's 2014 and 2015 annual reports, its official press statements and other materials published on the website and in the government newspaper. The analysis is further supported by reports by the media, civil society organisations, SEANF, the APF, the United Nations and the Special Rapporteur on Myanmar. The chapter purports to contribute to emerging scholarly literature on the MNHRC (De Lang 2012; Liljeblad 2016). It complements this literature by offering insights of an author-practitioner who has first-hand experience working with a local human rights organisation in Myanmar and through that function engaged and met with the MNHRC. The analysis proceeds by first examining the political context of the MNHRC establishment; second, outlining the objectives, duties and powers as well as members' selection process under the 2014 MNHRC Law; third, analysing the effectiveness of the MNHRC in the protection and promotion of human rights; and finally, placing the MNHRC in the regional context. To conclude the chapter, a summary of the progress made, challenges faced and recommendations for improvements will be made.

## The Political Context of the MNHRC Establishment

The MNHRC was formed by presidential decree, *Notification No. 34/2011* (hereafter: *MNHRC Decree 2011*), on 5 September 2011. It then became the fifth NHRI in ASEAN, the other four being from Indonesia, Malaysia, the Philippines and Thailand. Some of the key members, including Chairman U Win Mra and Vice-Chair U Kyaw Tint Swe, were past defenders of Myanmar's human rights record in their former functions as diplomats, and it was feared by different civil society actors, including this author, that they would continue to do so through the MNHRC (De Lang 2012: 8–11; BP & HREIB 2012: 44–46).

Renshaw (2017: 229) argued that 'research on the effectiveness of NHRIs across the Asia-Pacific region' has shown that those 'which are established in the wake of conflict or during political transition experience particular difficulties'. She added that apart from their 'enormous workloads' and 'resource shortages (human, financial, infrastructural)', they face questions of legitimacy from two sets of stakeholders: on one side, civil society groups who 'are inclined to view the new institution with suspicion, as a state-sponsored and ephemeral effort to appease the international community', and on the other side the government, who 'may be skeptical about the wisdom of establishing an institution that has the primary purpose of criticising the government'. She concluded that 'without a functioning relationship with both government and civil society, NHRIs cannot play an effective role in contributing to the new democratic political order' (Renshaw 2017: 229).

Another author, Kabir (2001: 4) argued that NHRIs in Asia can be a 'double-edged sword', with one edge of the sword able to make an actual difference in the protection and promotion of human rights, while the other edge can be used as a tool by governments to protect themselves from international scrutiny by promoting the human rights image of a country on the international and regional levels.

In March 2012, Myanmar's Pyidaungsu Hluttaw (Assembly of the Union, i.e. the Myanmar Parliament) refused to approve the MNHRC's budget because it was created by presidential decree and not in conformity with the *Constitution of the Republic of the Union of Myanmar 2008* (hereafter: *2008 Constitution*). In response, the MNHRC (2012a) issued a public statement in which it affirmed that in order to be an independent institution and comply with the *Paris Principles 1993*, it needs to be established under an act of Parliament. In that public statement the MNHRC (2012a) also announced that:

> Indonesia, Malaysia, the Philippines and Thailand from ASEAN and many countries of the world have established national human rights commissions to promote and protect human rights. [...] According to international reaction, the fact that the MNHRC is the fifth national human rights institution in ASEAN has enhanced the image of the country.

This shows that Myanmar's international and regional reputation is very important for the MNHRC, which supports Kabir's (2001: 4) analogy of an NHRI as a 'double-edged sword', one edge being used as a tool to protect the government from international scrutiny by promoting the human rights image.

Two years later, on 28 March 2014, the MNHRC Law No. 21/2014 (hereafter: MNHRC Law 2014) was adopted by the Pyidaungsu Hluttaw. The adoption of the law can be considered an improvement to the credibility and future sustainability of the MNHRC; however, there are some issues with the law which need to be addressed for the MNHRC to be considered in compliance with international standards such as the Paris Principles.[1]

## Objectives, Duties and Powers, Members' Selection Process and Funding Under the 2014 MNHRC Law

### *Objectives, Duties and Powers*

According to Section 3(b) of the MNHRC Law 2014, one of the main objectives of the MNHRC is 'to create a society where human rights are respected and protected in recognition of the Universal Declaration of Human Rights'. Another objective is 'to effectively promote and protect

[1] The Paris Principles 1993 were adopted by the UN General Assembly in 1993. Six main principles with which NHRIs should comply can be derived from the Paris Principles 1993 (UNDP and OHCHR 2010: 242):

> 1. A broad mandate, based on universal human rights standards; 2. Autonomy from government; 3. Independence guaranteed by statute or constitution; 4. Pluralism including through membership and/or effective cooperation; 5. Adequate resources; and 6. Adequate powers of investigation.

the human rights contained in the international conventions, decisions, regional agreements and declarations related to human rights accepted by the State' (MNHRC Law 2014, Section 3[c]). The earlier MNHRC Decree 2011 merely mentioned the fundamental rights of citizens in the 2008 Constitution, so these references can be considered an improvement; however, something can be said about leaving it up to 'acceptance by the State of human rights norms' whether or not the MNHRC should protect and promote them. Yet, it can still be considered in line with principle 1 of the Paris Principles 1993, which requires '[a] broad mandate, based on universal human rights standards'.

The MNHRC has the duties and powers to recommend to the Myanmar government which international human rights instruments it should become party to; to review proposed laws for consistency with international human rights instruments to which Myanmar is a party of; and to recommend legislation and measures to be adopted for the promotion and protection of human rights to the Parliament through the government (MNHRC Law 2014, Sections 22[b][i]–[ii]). The MNHRC is also mandated to assist the government in its submissions to international human rights instruments to which Myanmar is party (MNHRC Law 2014, Sections 22[b][iii]). None of these duties and powers are new as they were already included in the MNHRC's mandate when it was established by decree (De Lang 2012: 3–4).

The MNHRC also has the mandate 'to coordinate and cooperate with international organizations, regional organizations, national statutory institutions' and 'civil society and non-governmental organizations related to human rights' (MNHRC Law 2014, Section 3[d]). However, Section 22(f) of the MNHRC Law 2014 gives the MNHRC a too wide discretion to choose 'relevant civil society organizations, business organizations, labour organizations, national races organizations, minorities and academic institutions, as appropriate' (emphasis added) which is problematic for principle 4 of the Paris Principles 1993 on pluralism, which requires 'effective cooperation with diverse societal groups' (ICC SCA 2013: 26, as cited in Liljeblad 2016: 440).

The MNHRC already had the mandate to receive complaint letters and to investigate under the MNHRC Decree 2011 but it was not yet mentioned how far these investigative powers would reach. According to Sections 22(c)–(d) of the MNHRC Law 2014, it has the mandate to verify and conduct inquiries as well as visit the scene of human rights violations. The rules of those inquiries and handling of complaints are listed in

Sections 28–40. For example, according to Section 36, the MNHRC is mandated to 'summon in writing any person or office to produce any documents or evidence in their possession or control' except if the release of those documents or evidence would affect the security and defence of the state or if the documents are classified by the departments and organisations of the government. Both limitations are problematic and in contravention of principle 6 of the Paris Principles 1993 on adequate powers of investigation, because limitations in accessing information regarding national security cannot be 'unreasonably or arbitrarily applied and should only be exercised under due process' (OHCHR 2010: [33], as cited in Liljeblad 2016: 435).

The MNHRC cannot inquire into complaints that are already under trial before any court, under appeal or revision or have been finally determined by any court (MNHRC Law 2014, Section 37). Even though this is not in violation of the Paris Principles 1993 and it is generally accepted that NHRIs 'should not sit in appeal or review of the courts' (OHCHR 2010: [193], as cited in Liljeblad 2016: 435), it is still problematic in the current Myanmar context where, according to several reports, the judiciary is notoriously corrupt and inefficient (Crouch 2017: 2, 3; Zue 2015; Fuller 2014). A Myanmar Parliamentary committee even reported that 'a chain of bribery is deeply entrenched throughout the judicial system' (Aung Din 2016).

The MNHRC also has powers to 'inspect [...] the scene of human rights violations and, after notification, prisons, jails, detention centres and public or private places of confinement' (MNHRC Law 2014, Section 22[e]). Further rules on these inspections are provided in Sections 43–45. There is an issue with the MNHRC's ability to make effective inspections as Sections 22(e) and 44(a) require prior notification to the relevant authorities. For such inspections to be effective and prevent any cover up by the authorities, they should be unannounced and without prior notice.

Section 42 of the MNHRC Law 2014 protects complainants and witnesses, and Section 66 gives a further obligation for the MNHRC to ensure the name and identifying information concerning witnesses or other persons under examination are not published or disclosed without the MNHRC's authorisation and it 'may also take other measures for the protection of witnesses'. The wording is rather problematic as the disclosure of the identities of witnesses and other persons under examination is solely at the MNHRC's discretion and does not require consent of the complainants, witnesses and victims themselves. An example in Section

III(f) of this chapter will illustrate how this can lead to unwarranted disclosure of identities and even arrest of complainants.

### *Members and Selection Process*

With regard to the MNHRC's members and selection process, Section 4 of the MNHRC Law 2014 provides that the MNHRC shall consist of 'less than seven and not more than fifteen members'. The President of Myanmar must form a Selection Board comprised of the Chief Justice of the Union; Minister of Home Affairs; Ministry of Social Welfare, Relief and Resettlement; Attorney General of the Union; one representative of the Bar Council; two representatives from the Pyidaungsu Hlutaw; one representative from the Myanmar Women's Affairs Federation; and two representatives from registered NGOs (MNHRC Law 2014, Section 5).

The Attorney General and Chief Justice are both appointed by the President of Myanmar (2008 Constitution, Sections 237 and 299). The Bar Council is chaired by the Attorney General and is not independent of the government (ICJ 2013: 28). The Myanmar Women's Affairs Federation is a so-called government-organised non-governmental organisation (GONGO) which in words of critics was 'run by the wives of the Burmese military junta's top generals' (Naím 2007). Twenty-five per cent of the seats in Myanmar's Parliament, the Pyidaungsu Hlutaw, are reserved for military officers. Therefore, apart from the representatives from the registered NGOs, the Selection Board cannot be said to be truly independent from the Government, nor does the Selection Board reflect a 'pluralist representation of social forces', both factors which are very important for compliance with principles 2–4 of the Paris Principles 1993 on autonomy, independence and pluralism (Liljeblad 2016: 437–438).

Another issue is that currently a lot of NGOs working on human rights in Myanmar operate without government-approved registration, which is still a cumbersome and complicated process requiring the approval from a registration committee. The registration committee for NGOs that want to be registered at the Union level is chaired by the Minister of Home Affairs and can deny registration if the applying organisation might damage the 'rule of law and state security' (Registration of Organisation Law 2014, Section 8).

This Selection Board is mandated to nominate 30 prospective members (MNHRC Law 2014, Sections 6–8) and the President, in coordination with the speakers of the lower and upper house of Parliament, shall then select and appoint suitable members from that list (MNHRC Law 2014, Section 9). The criteria for the prospective members include (a) Myanmar citizenship; (b) not younger than 35 years; (c) integrity and good character as well as independent and impartial; (d) knowledge or experience of human rights, relevant domestic and international laws or good governance and public administration; and (e) commitment to the MNHRC's objectives (MNHRC Law 2014, Section 6). The Selection Board is further required to 'seek to ensure the equitable representation of men and women, and of national races' (MNHRC Law 2014, Section 7[c]).

The current MNHRC is composed of seven male members only and it is unclear of which 'national race' they are (MNHRC 2017a). When the MNHRC was established by MNHRC Decree 2011, it counted 15 members, with 3 female members. After the MNHRC Law 2014 was adopted, the MNHRC was reshuffled to 11 members, with only 6 original members remaining, including Chairperson U Win Mra and the former Secretary, U Sit Myaing, who became Vice-Chairperson. The reshuffled MNHRC only counted two female members and they were among the four MNHRC members who resigned in October 2016 due to a scandal, which will be discussed in Section II of this chapter.

According to the Sub-Committee on Accreditation of the International Coordinating Committee of National Institutions for the Promotion and Protection of Human Rights (hereafter: ICC SCA) in their November 2015 report they 'received conflicting reports regarding whether the most recent selection process was conducted in accordance with the law' and that '[s]everal civil society organisations reported that the recent selection process was not made public' (ICC SCA 2015: 11). One of the former MNHRC members, U Hla Myint, who was involved in the drafting of the *MNHRC Law 2014* and especially the sections on the selection process of new members, criticised the most recent reshuffle and stated to *The Myanmar Times*:

> Did they do the selection by the law? I'm not so sure … I don't know how much they followed the law' (O'Toole 2014).

The fact that the resignations of four MNHRC staff in October 2016 did not lead to their vacated positions to be filled with persons from the list of nominees according to Section 19 of the MNHRC Law 2014 affirms the suspicion that this list of nominees did not yet exist, while it should have been drawn already during the reshuffle in 2014 according to

Sections 6–8. That being said, even if the selection process of the current MNHRC would have been conducted according to the law, it would still have been in contravention of principles 2–4 of the Paris Principles 1993 on autonomy, independence and pluralism as these require that the appointment process is public, transparent and civil society organisations are consulted openly, which has clearly not been the case.

### *Funding*

Section 46 of the MNHRC Law 2014 provides that '[t]he State shall provide the Commission with adequate funding to enable it to effectively discharge the functions assigned to it by this law'. While this seems to be in line with principle 5 of the Paris Principles 1993 regarding adequate resources, the ICC SCA (2015: 12–13) commented that:

> [t]he budget of the NHRC is submitted to the President's Office for approval. Funds are then transferred from this Office on a quarterly basis. The SCA is concerned that this arrangement provides the Executive with substantial control over the NHRC's ability to continue to operate.

## Measuring the Effectiveness of the MNHRC in the Protection and Promotion of Human Rights

The analysis in the previous section has shown that, while there have been considerable improvements in the MNHRC's mandate and powers, on closer inspection, there are also some aspects of the MNHRC Law 2014 which are not in compliance with the Paris Principles 1993. The ICC SCA (2015: 11) recommended to the ICC to accredit the MNHRC with 'B' status which the ICC did on January 2016 (APF 2016). The main reasons for not accrediting the MNHRC with an 'A' status were concerns about its selection and appointment process, its financial independence and lack of female representation and also the lack of interpretation of 'its mandate in a broad, liberal and purposive manner, and promote and protect the human rights of all, including the rights of Rohingya and other minority groups' (ICC SCA 2015: 12).

Liljeblad (2016: 445) argued that the conclusion of the ICC SCA went beyond the text of the *MNHRC Law 2014* or the MNHRC as a body but also went into the sphere of the MNHRC's actions. In the words of Liljeblad 2016: 445):

> The ICC Sub-Committee is reaching out to criticize both the commitment of the MNHRC and the Myanmar state as expressed by their activity levels towards the cause of human rights in their country. [...] The ICC Sub-Committee may be seeking to ensure that the MNHRC and the Myanmar government are fulfilling roles as active promoters of the international system of human rights protection.

In this section the MNHRC's protection and promotion record will be reviewed. A complete display of the MNHRC's activities is outside the scope of the chapter and only some prominent and more recent examples will be brought forward while making a genuine effort for a balanced overview by also bringing forward some positive examples.

### *Land Disputes*

According to the MNHRC's annual reports of 2014 and 2015, land issues make up more than half of all the complaints received (MNHRC 2015a: 14–15; MNHRC 2016a: 19–20). When looking at these annual reports, it is not clear how much ability the MNHRC has, to do something for the complainants, as often the outcome of the MNHRC's recommendation is that the complainant should resort to the judicial process or await the decision of the court (MNHRC 2016a: 21–23). Advice to complainants to resort to the judicial process in Myanmar is not very helpful in the present author's humble opinion and will most likely not lead to a fair outcome as the judiciary in Myanmar is still corrupt and inefficient, as was already pointed out above in Section II(a). Section 34 of the *MNHRC Law 2014* gives the option to 'address the complaint through conciliation' but regarding land issues there is lack of evidence that it is doing so, especially when military actors are involved in the land confiscations.

Another indication that neither the MNHRC nor the Myanmar judiciary are the right avenues for people with grievances regarding land confiscations and land disputes is that there are other mechanisms available, such as the Central Committee on Confiscated Farmlands and Other Lands, which was formed in early 2016 (Htoo Thant 2016) replacing a Parliamentary Land Investigation Commission which operated from August 2012 (Thein et al. 2017: 2). Also, the *National Land Use Policy 2016* instituted a National Land Use Council as well as several decentralised Land Use Committees. Notwithstanding the above, it remains to be seen how effective these other mechanisms will be in addressing Myanmar's major land issues.

### *Conflicts in Kachin State and Shan State*

There are still ongoing internal armed conflicts in Myanmar's border areas, most prominently Kachin State and northern Shan State, where the Myanmar army is conducting campaigns against ethnic armed groups (EAGs) which have not signed the Nationwide Ceasefire Agreement (NCA) such as the Kachin Independence Army (KIA), the Ta'ang National Liberation Army (TNLA), Myanmar National Democratic Alliance Army (MNDAA, also: Kokang Army) and the Shan State Progressive Party/Shan State Army—North (SSPP/SSA-N). This ongoing armed conflict has led to a lot of civilian casualties and displacement as well as severe human rights abuses by the Myanmar military against civilians, including alleged rape and torture (HRW 2012; BP, EM & SEDF 2015: 15–16; TWO 2016). Another problem is the lack of humanitarian access, allegedly blocked by the Myanmar army, to displaced communities (AI 2016).

As early as December 2011, four MNHRC members visited Kachin State, where they interviewed internally displaced persons as well as prisoners. Another visit was conducted in July 2012 during which witnesses were interviewed regarding complaints on human rights violations. As a result, the MNHRC issued a statement on 14 August 2012 to confirm that 'there were certain violations of human rights of the populations of the villages by the armed groups' and 'strongly urged not to violate human rights under any circumstances and to act in accordance with human rights standards' (MNHRC 2012b). In the same statement, the MNHRC confirmed that 'the Tatmadaw [Myanmar army] arrested and interrogated two villagers' and, while not making comments on the interrogation of those suspects for security reasons, recommended that 'torture during the interrogation constitutes violation of human rights and must be avoided' (MNHRC 2012b). In a later statement on 18 January 2013, the MNHRC also urged 'that the question of humanitarian access to the conflict victims and of how safe passage for humanitarian supplies could be guaranteed, be addressed as an urgent matter in the peace dialogue' (MNHRC 2013).

Burma Partnership criticised these two visits and subsequent statements and claimed the MNHRC did not duly investigate allegations of war crimes or crimes against humanity committed by the Myanmar army, while human rights NGOs had evidence to support this claim that (BP 2012: 8). The MNHRC Chairman dismissed allegations of war crimes and crimes against humanity in an earlier interview with the media and added that 'the standard allegation is use of rape as a weapon of war, but our mission was mainly concerned with the humanitarian aspects' (Bernstein 2011).

On 27 February 2015, the MNHRC released a statement on the armed conflict in Laukkai area, Shan State, between the Myanmar army and the Kokang Army/MNDAA. The MNHRC noted 'heavy casualties suffered in the combat area by the populace and combatants of both sides' and urged that 'both sides should take extra care not to inflict undue damage to the lives and belongings of the populace' as well as to avoid 'activities detrimental to the efforts for supply of humanitarian relief' (MNHRC 2015b). However, it does not seem the MNHRC investigated allegations of the Myanmar army using civilians as human shields (RFA 2015) nor allegations of shooting, killing and torture of at least ten ethnic Kokang civilians by the Myanmar army, which was reported by the Shan Human Rights Foundation (SHRF 2015; Lawi Weng 2015).

### *Rakhine/Arakan State and the Rohingya*

One of the criticisms by the ICC SCA towards the MNHRC was that the MNHRC does not interpret 'its mandate in a broad, liberal and purposive manner, and promote and protect the human rights of all, including the rights of Rohingya and other minority groups'. A prominent example is the events in Ducheeratan/Du Chee Yar Tan village, Rakhine/Arakan State, which took place in January 2014. According to the UN High Commissioner for Human Rights, Navi Pillay, her office 'has received credible information that, on 9 January, eight Rohingya Muslim men were attacked and killed in Du Chee Yar Tan village by local Rakhine' and that:

> [a] clash [followed] on 13 January in the same village in which a police sergeant was captured and killed by the Rohingya villagers. Following this, on the same evening at least 40 Rohingya Muslim men, women and children were killed in Du Chee Yar Tan village by police and local Rakhine. (UN News Centre 2014)

In response MNHRC formed an investigation team comprising the MNHRC secretary and three members who visited Sitwe and Maung Taw Township, Rakhine State, and visited Ducheeratan village tract from 30 January to 3 February 2014. In the MNHRC statement of 14 February 2014, it concluded that:

> [t]he news of the killing of 8 Bengalis and 40 Bengalis did not emerge in the Ducheeratan village tract and it is therefore concluded that the said news is unverifiable and unconfirmed. (MNHRC 2014a)

In response the Special Rapporteur on Myanmar, Quintana, announced that 'domestic investigations have failed to satisfactorily address these serious allegations' and if the investigation did not improve 'I will urge the UN Human Rights Council to work with the government of Myanmar to establish a credible investigation' (Lawi Weng 2014).

Another point is that the MNHRC refuses to use the term Rohingya or Rohingya Muslims in its statements and refers to them as Bengalis which is in line with the Myanmar government's consistent policy to not recognise the Rohingya as an ethnic minority but to collectively refer to them as illegal Bengali immigrants from Bangladesh with no right to Myanmar citizenship. This is in violation of the Rohingya's right to self-identification and there is convincing historical evidence that at least a substantial number of Rohingya living in Myanmar are not Bangladeshi immigrants and do not have Bangladeshi citizenship (De Lang 2018). As a result of this treatment by the Myanmar authorities, which is not challenged by the MNHRC, the majority of Rohingya living in Myanmar are rendered effectively stateless.

### *Prison Visits*

The MNHRC has made various prison visits throughout 2014–2016, which is in line with its mandate under Section 43 of the 2014 MNHRC Law. In a presentation given by the MNHRC Chairman in October 2016 during the 21st APF Annual Meeting in Bangkok, Thailand, the Chairman stated that '[t]he most common problem of the prisons was overcrowdedness' and that the MNRHC 'recommended to the authorities to take necessary measures to redress the problem'. According to the MNHRC Chairman, the Ministry of Home Affairs took the recommendation into serious consideration and would take appropriate action. He added that '[t]his is the first time that the Commission has ever been responded positively by the authorities on such a serious matter' (MNHRC 2016b: 12–13). It is worrying, to say the least, that this is the 'first time' the authorities have responded positively.

### *Letpadaung Mine Protest*

During a protest on 22 December 2014 against the Letpadaung mine, the police opened fire on demonstrators, resulting in the death of Daw Khin Win, a 56-year-old lady, and injuring at least ten others (Irrawaddy 2015).

The MNHRC announced on 31 December 2014 that three MNHRC commissioners went to investigate the incident (MNHRC 2014b), and on 14 January 2015 the MNHRC published a detailed press release on the results of their investigation in which it concluded that '[t]he death of Daw Khin Win by gunshot can be construed as an infringement of her right[…] [to life] as stated under Article 3 [of the Universal Declaration of Human Rights]' and that the manslaughter case which was filed at the Salingyi police station 'should be further pursued according to law'. The MNHRC also concluded that there was a 'dereliction in the supervision of the implementation of the [Security] Plan' by the Sagaing Region Police Force and the 'responsible personnel of the [m]onitoring body should be investigated and due action [sic] taken against them' (MNHRC 2015c). While the MNHRC's detailed report and recommendations are commendable, there have been no arrests or further investigations into the death of Daw Khin Win according to a news report by Frontier Myanmar (Sathisan 2016).

### *Protection of Complainants*

On 13 September 2012, Ja Seng Ing, a 14-year-old girl, was killed in Sut Ngai Yang village in Kachin State (Fortify Rights 2015; Ja Seng Ing Truth Finding Committee 2014). A month later her father, Brang Shawng, sent a complaint letter to the MNHRC alleging that his daughter was shot and killed by Myanmar army soldiers (Fortify Rights 2015). Surprisingly, in March 2013 a legal case was initiated by the Myanmar army against Brang Shawng under Article 211 of the Myanmar Penal Code for making 'false charges'. The evidence used against Brang Shawng was an internal Myanmar army investigation which claimed Ja Seng Ing died because of a landmine set by the Kachin Independence Army (Fortify Rights 2015). Brang Shwang was found guilty and given the choice between paying a 50,000 kyat fine (US$50) and serving a six-month prison term, of which he chose the former. According to BP, EM and SEDF (2015: 24):

> Not only did the MNHRC fail to investigate this human rights complaint, they failed to protect the complainant, which resulted in criminal prosecution.

### *Inability to Act in a Case Involving the Military*

In October 2014, a journalist, Aung Kyaw Naing, also known as Ko Par Gyi, was shot and killed while under military custody in Kyaikmayaw

Township, Mon State. He was initially arrested a month earlier on suspicions of belonging to the Democratic Karen Benevolent Army (DKBA) while in reality he was a journalist covering the violent clashes between the DKBA and the Myanmar army (Mizzima 2016; Regan and Stout 2014). The MNHRC investigated the case and released a detailed inquiry report on 2 December 2014, recommending that the Myanmar Police Force should investigate the case 'to the very end' and ensure the case is prosecuted in judicial proceedings (MNHRC 2014c). With regard to the judicial proceedings, the MNHRC (2014c) explicitly recommended that 'this case should be tried in a civil court'.

Despite these recommendations, it was made public in May 2015 by the Myanmar military that on 27 November 2014 two soldiers who were tried in secret for culpable homicide in a military court were acquitted (Mizzima 2016). When the MNHRC was asked if it would take any further steps, Commissioner Nyut Swe responded:

> The Commission has issued two statements on that matter and all our findings have been reflected in those statements. [...] Therefore, we have nothing more to comment. (Artan Mustafa 2015)

### *Failure to Act in the Interest of the Victims*

In September 2016, Myanmar media reported that two girls, Ma San Kay Khaing and Ma Tha Zin, respectively 17 and 16 years of age, were discovered to have worked, as slaves, for five years for a family of tailors in Yangon. According to Swe Win (2016), 'the girls were hidden and kept to work in the tailor shop or in the employer's eighth-floor apartment' and 'they were subject to horrible daily abuse, such as beating, cuts with scissors and burns inflicted on the skin with cigarette buts [sic] and lighters'.

The Myanmar Now reporter, Swe Win, alerted the police, but because they did not act, he alerted the MNHRC. The MNHRC then asked the police to open an investigation which they did. The police report 'advised legal proceedings against the employer and members of his household, if the victims' parents filed an official criminal complaint' (Swe Win 2016). The consent from the parents was important because otherwise the police were not allowed to question the girls and inspect their bodies for physical abuse.

In a meeting at the MNHRC office in Yangon, in the presence the of reporter Swe Win, the MNHRC Commissioner, Zaw Win, discouraged the family of the victims from filing this complaint and advised them to negotiate with the employer and accept compensation. The tailor shop owners were quick to make an offer of 4 million kyats ($3000) and 1 million kyats ($750) for the two girls, respectively—an extremely low amount considering it was also supposed to include the girls' unpaid salary for at least three years. The victims' illiterate parents, not supported by legal counsel, accepted the compensation deal (Swe Win 2016). In a press conference on 20 September 2016, Zaw Win stated:

> The deal was done with the consent of both parties, the employer and the parents of the abused maids. What we did was just organizing their meeting at our office out of kindness since the family members of the girls would be in great trouble if they have to come to Yangon for court trials. (Swe Win 2016)

Swe Win (2016) spoke to a lawyer who informed him that according to the law these type of crimes against minors must be brought before a court: 'This case cannot be settled in such a way. The offenders for this kind of crime cannot even be given bail'. Understandably, many agreed, and the Ministry of Social Welfare, Relief and Resettlement filed a lawsuit against the perpetrators under Section 66(d) of the Myanmar Child Protection Law and the Anti-Human Trafficking Unit of the police filed charges for trafficking and abusing the girls (RFA 2016). Prominent lawyer and legal activist Robert San Aung called the MNHRC's action 'criminal concealment' and 'obstruction of justice' and claimed he would file charges against the MNHRC members involved (RFA 2016). On 6 October 2016, four members of the MNHRC, U Zaw Win, U Nyan Zaw, Dr. Daw Than Nwe and Daw Mya Mya, resigned but both the Myanmar Now reporter Swe Win and lawyer Robert San Aung do not believe that should be the end of it and would like to see accountability of the members who resigned (Shoon Naing 2016).

### *Human Rights Promotion and Education*

Throughout 2014–2016, the MNHRC held several seminars, trainings and workshops: in March 2014 a seminar on the Convention against Torture and Other Cruel, Inhuman or Degrading Treatment or Punishment (CAT) 1984; in August 2014 a training workshop on the International Convention on the Elimination of all forms of Racial

Discrimination (ICERD) 1965; and in March 2015 a workshop was held on a draft law to prevent violence against women (MNHRC 2015a: 31–36; MNHRC 2016a: 14–15). Furthermore, in June 2016, the MNHRC organised a two-day workshop in Nay Pyi Taw on minority rights in collaboration with the OHCHR (MNA 2016a).

A prominent training workshop was also held on the Universal Periodic Review (UPR), in which parliamentarians, government officials and civil society representatives participated, in preparation for Myanmar's then upcoming 2015 UPR (MNHRC 2015a: 37). After Myanmar's UPR, in August 2016, a follow-up workshop on how to implement the UPR recommendations was organised by the MNHRC in collaboration with the Lutheran World Foundation (LWF). Participants included high-level representatives of almost all the ministries, including those of Defence and Home Affairs, several civil society organisations, OHCHR staff and some diplomats (LWF 2016).

In April and September 2015, two workshops were organised by the MNHRC and UN Women on 'UN Security Council Resolution 1325 (UNSCR 1325) on Women, Peace and Security and Related Resolutions' (MNHRC 2015d, e). NGOs were notably absent. After each meeting an outcome statement was published with important recommendations on women's empowerment, promoting women in leadership and governance, quotas for women, raising awareness on gender sensitivity and gender-based violence and the adoption of a law on the prevention of violence against women and girls (MNHRC 2015d, e). The MNHRC and UN Women also organised a workshop on Gender and Security for Upper Officials in December 2015 (MNHRC 2016a: 15).

Starting in 2015, the MNHRC also gave human rights talks, workshops and lectures for officers and staff of Union level ministries and organisations, including military officers, in Nay Pyi Taw (MNHRC 2016a: 15–16). The MNHRC also organised training workshops at the state and region, district and township levels with the aim to disseminate knowledge of human rights to lower-ranking government officials. Some of the topics included in the training workshops were: The Universal Declaration of Human Rights (UDHR) 1948, the nine core human rights treaties, UN human rights mechanisms, NHRIs and the Paris Principles 1993, complaint procedures and the MNHRC Law 2014 (MNHRC 2015a: 38; MNHRC 2016a: 8). In 2016, the MNHRC continued this trend and decided to conduct human rights workshops for prison officials in Yangon and Mandalay regions (MNHRC 2016c).

Throughout 2014–2016, the MNHRC held several human rights talks for the general public and grass-roots-level workshops for local NGOs and CSOs (MNHRC 2015a: 41, 2016a: 9–13, c). In 2015, the MNHRC extended its human rights education activities to secondary and high school students and produced a short documentary on the concept of human rights (MNHRC 2016a: 1, 17–18).

The human rights education activities by the MNHRC to several actors on different hierarchical levels, including the military and other powerful actors such as the police, are very positive. The geographic area seems to be widened as well but it is not clear whether or not human rights education activities are also given to military, border guard forces, police and other authorities that are operating in Rakhine, Kachin, Shan, Kayin, Kayah and other border regions, as those regions have historically been most prone to human rights violations by those actors and in some of those areas civil war and civil strife is still ongoing today.

### *Promotional Activities Relating to Compliance with and Ratification of International Human Rights Treaties*

The MNHRC has made several recommendations relating to Myanmar becoming State Party to international treaties. The MNHRC recommended on 29 January 2014 to President Thein Sein to become State Party to the International Covenant on Economic, Social and Cultural Rights (ICESCR) 1966 and after Myanmar signed this treaty on 16 July 2015, it urged Myanmar to take steps to ratify it (MNHRC 2016a: 6). The MNHRC also recommended to the Myanmar government to sign the ICCPR 1966 (MNHRC 2016c), which unfortunately has not yet ensued.

Furthermore, the MNHRC has translated the UDHR 1948 into Myanmar language and different ethnic minority languages such as Kachin, Mon and Shan and plans for translating it to the remaining ethnic languages[2] (MNHRC 2015a: 11; MNHRC 2016a: 17). It has also translated the International Covenant on Civil and Political Rights (ICCPR) 1966 in Myanmar language but not yet distributed it (MNHRC 2015a: 12).

[2] The present author has already seen a translation of the UDHR by the MNHRC in the S'gaw Karen language.

On 24 March 2015, the MNHRC counselled Myanmar to sign and ratify the Optional Protocol to Convention on the Rights of the Child on the involvement of children in armed conflict 2000, which Myanmar signed on 28 September 2015 (MNHRC 2016a: 6). The MNHRC further recommended in its submission to the CEDAW Committee that the Myanmar government should consider ratification of the Optional Protocol of the Convention on the Elimination of all forms of Discrimination against Women 1999 and to remove its reservation to Article 29 of the Convention on the Elimination of all forms of Discrimination against Women (CEDAW) 1979 (MNHRC 2016d: para. 16). The MNHRC also advocated for Myanmar's ratification of the ASEAN Convention against Trafficking in Persons (ACTIP) 2015 (MNHRC 2016c) which Myanmar did on 21 November 2015 (ASEAN 2015).

Regarding the Child Rights Bill, the MNHRC recommended that it should be adopted speedily and in line with the Convention on the Rights of the Child (CRC) 1989 and the Optional Protocol to the CRC on the sale of children, child prostitution and child pornography 2000, both to which Myanmar is a State Party (MNHRC 2016a: 6, 2015a: 13). Regarding the bill on the Prevention of Violence against Women, the MNHRC advised it should be adopted in line with CEDAW 1979 (MNHRC 2016a: 6, 2015a: 13). Another recommendation was that Myanmar should enact the bill on the Rights of Persons with Disabilities in line with the Convention on the Rights of Persons with Disabilities (CRPD) 2006 to which Myanmar is also a State Party (MNHRC 2015a: 13).

Apart from the above positive examples, there was also an occasion where the MNHRC failed to promote international human rights when commenting on domestic legislation. This was in relation to the widely criticised and condemned discriminatory 'Four Race & Religion Protection Laws',[3] which are in violation of international human rights law (White 2015). According to BP, EM and SEDF (2015: 29–30), the MNHRC Vice-Chair, U Sit Myaing, stated during a meeting with CSOs that these laws 'were in fact in accordance with international treaties such as [CEDAW] and the [CRC]'.

[3]The 'Four Race and Religion Protection Laws' are: *Religious Conversion Law 2015; Buddhist Women's Special Marriage Law 2015*; *Population Control Healthcare Law 2015*; and *Monogamy Law 2015*.

Some examples of how these laws are clearly in violation of international human rights standards are measures giving authorities the right to restrict how often women can give birth and restrictions on religious conversion and the prevention of Buddhist women to marry outside of their faith (Macgregor and Thu Thu Aung 2016). The CEDAW Committee (2016: 15) in its Concluding Observations on Myanmar's state report held that:

> [i]t is concerned, however, at the adoption in 2015 of four so-called "laws on the protection of race and religion", which discriminate against women and girls based on, inter alia, their ethnicity and religion.

The MNHRC submitted its NHRI report to the Universal Periodic Review Second Cycle of Myanmar in November 2015. In the submission, the MNHRC recommends to the Myanmar government to continue cooperating with international human rights mechanisms, both the Special Procedures and the Treaty Bodies (MNHRC 2015f: para. 4). The MNHRC also recommended to the Myanmar Election Commission to ensure free, fair and transparent elections (MNHRC 2015f: para. 8).

In the last paragraph of its submission the MNHRC notes that the Law relating to the Right of Peaceful Assembly and Peaceful Procession 2011 was enacted in 2011 with an amendment in 2014 and 'urges those concerned to abide by the law' and also that 'censorship on press and media publications has [...] been terminated' adding that it 'appeals to the press and media people to uphold the press and media ethics' (MNHRC 2015f: para. 11). It is curious why an NHRI recommends to Myanmar citizens to 'abide by the law' in its stakeholder submission to the UPR where the Myanmar government's human rights record is being reviewed. Also, the claim that media censorship has ended in Myanmar is very premature, as recently Myanmar's press freedom status was determined by Freedom House (2017) as 'not free' and according to a journalist for Frontier Myanmar, Sithu Aung Myint (2017) '[m]edia freedom has not improved in Myanmar under the NLD government'. This has partly to do with the repressive and widely criticised Section 66(d) of the Telecommunications Law 2013 which can lead up to three years' imprisonment of someone who uses any telecommunications network (including the internet, Facebook, Twitter) for 'extorting, coercing, restraining wrongfully, defaming, disturbing, causing undue influence or threatening to [sic] any person'. Mainly the words 'defaming', 'disturbing' and 'causing undue influence' are open to arbitrary interpretation and have been used to limit the freedom of expression (PV 2017; Adams 2017).

Another report was submitted by the MNHRC to the Committee on the Elimination of Discrimination against Women (CEDAW Committee) for the review of Myanmar's 4th and 5th combined report during CEDAW Committee's 64th session. In this submission, the MNHRC made recommendations that Myanmar should 'promulgate a Law on the Prevention and Protection of Violence against Women' (MNHRC 2016d: paras. 8–9). The MNHRC also recommends the establishment of a one stop crisis centre where violence against women victims can seek justice, medical treatment and psychological support (MNHRC 2016d: para. 10). The MNHRC also urged the Myanmar government to work together with national NGOs and the international community to formulate an action plan on UN Security Council Resolution 1325 and related resolutions on Women, Peace and Security (MNHRC 2016d: para. 14).

Unfortunately, a very important point is missing in the MNHRC's submission to the CEDAW Committee, which is to call on the Myanmar government to repeal or at least amend the 'Four Race & Religion Protection Laws' as they are in violation of international standards, including CEDAW, which was confirmed by the CEDAW Committee (2016) itself.

## Myanmar and the MNHRC in the Regional Context

### *The Influence of ASEAN NHRIs on the Establishment of AICHR*

The four member states of ASEAN which had at that time set up independent and effective NHRIs (Malaysia, Indonesia, Thailand and the Philippines) advocated for a strong and liberal ASEAN human rights body to be established under Article 14(1) of the ASEAN Charter 2007 modelled on UN mechanisms (Munro 2011: 1198; ABC 2008). The four member states that were opposed from the beginning were Myanmar, Cambodia, Lao PDR and Vietnam, all states without NHRIs at that time. The 'supporting' states were, at that time, the most democratic in ASEAN, while the 'opposing' states were considered the least democratic states of ASEAN (Munro 2011: 1199).

The AICHR was established on 23 October 2009 during the 15th ASEAN Summit in Cha-am Hua Hin, Thailand in accordance with Article

14(1) of the ASEAN Charter 2007 (AICHR 2012a). It is likely the four NHRIs,[4] at that time commonly referred to as the ASEAN Four, had a considerable influence on their governments for supporting the establishment of an ASEAN human rights body. To illustrate, the ASEAN Four met with the High-Level Task Force on the drafting of the ASEAN Charter on 27 June 2007 and handed them a joint position paper which called for the ASEAN Charter to include provisions on human rights and fundamental freedoms, the importance of the role and establishment of NHRIs and for establishment of an ASEAN human rights mechanism (ASEAN Four 2007a). The ASEAN Four further declared in a joint Declaration of Cooperation that they would 'advis[e] their respective governments to take the necessary steps to establish an appropriate ASEAN human rights mechanism and/or any organ in the ASEAN Charter' (ASEAN Four 2007b).

On 29–30 January 2008, the ASEAN Four agreed to adopt ASEAN NHRI Forum (ANF) as their name. The ANF was consulted in drafting the Terms of Reference for the AICHR on 10–11 September 2008 (ANF 2008), but it seems the ANF was not satisfied with the outcome as they submitted a position paper to the High-Level Panel on 28 August 2009, stating that:

> As a regional human rights body, it lacks independence. Any protection power that it may have is severely circumscribed by its ToR. Its promotional functions are dependent upon political will of member governments. (ANF 2009)

### *Myanmar's Representatives to AICHR and the Influence of AICHR on Myanmar*

The first Myanmar representative was Kyaw Tint Swe, who served two three-year terms from 2009 to 2015 (AICHR 2012b, 2015). He concomitantly served as Vice-Chair for the MNHRC since establishment in 2011 until early 2014 when the MNHRC was reshuffled. As mentioned in Section 1, Kyaw Tint Swe, a career diplomat, was a staunch defender of Myanmar human rights record in the past, especially during his time as

[4] The National Human Rights Commission of Indonesia (KOMNAS HAM), the Human Rights Commission of Malaysia (SUHAKAM), the Commission on Human Rights of the Philippines (CHRP) and the National Human Rights Commission of Thailand (NHRCT).

Myanmar's ambassador and permanent representative to the UN (Lun Min Mang 2016).

The current Myanmar representative to AICHR is U Hla Myint, who has served since 2016 and will continue to do so until 2018. U Hla Myint has worked in different government ministries such as Education, Home Affairs and Foreign Affairs, and several embassies, most recently as Ambassador to Australia from 2008 to 2010 before he served as member of the MNHRC from its inception in 2011 until the reshuffle in early 2014 (AICHR 2016–2018: 12–13).[5] U Hla Myint was one of the MNHRC Commissioners who criticised the 2014 reshuffle of the MNHRC which led to his own dismissal. In an interview with *The Myanmar Times*, he suggested that he was one of the more 'outspoken' members and stated: 'I had disagreement with the other members [...]. Maybe they don't like me' (O'Toole 2014).

When looking at AICHR's actions, or perhaps better formulated 'inactions', about human rights in Myanmar there does not seem to be a willingness by the AICHR to urge Myanmar or the MNHRC to step up its human rights protection. The AICHR has been very quiet on the human rights and humanitarian crisis to which the Rohingya Muslims in Myanmar are victims. Tens of thousands of Rohingya refugees have fled persecution in Myanmar to Bangladesh, Malaysia, Indonesia and Thailand (Lefevre and Kapoor 2015). In a report drafted by regional NGOs on the functioning of AICHR, it was stated that:

> [t]he key concern that remains unchanged since the establishment of both AICHR and ACWC [ASEAN Commission on Women and Children] is [...] the continued silence in responding to human rights violations that occurred in 2015 [...]. For instance, the two commissions practically just stood by amid the sharp increase of refugees and migrants from Myanmar and Bangladesh escaping through the Bay of Bengal and Andaman Sea. [...] A humanitarian crisis unfolded in May 2015, when 5000 refugees and migrants were found stranded at sea and an estimated 370 lost their lives. Inland in Malaysia and Thailand, authorities found mass graves containing the remains of over a hundred persons believed to be human trafficking victims linked to the crisis. (SAPA TFAHR 2016: 1–2)

[5] He should not be confused with namesake U Hla Myint, former Brigadier General in the Myanmar army serving from 1971 until 2002, and who served as Ambassador to Argentina, Brazil and later Japan and from 2011 to 2016 as Mayor of Yangon (Mizzima News 2011; Ye Mon and Myat Nyein Aye 2015).

It is not surprising that the AICHR did not take any measures against Myanmar as the Guidelines on the Operations of AICHR 2012 stipulate in Article 1.5 that decision-making is 'based on consultation and consensus' which effectively gives each representative, including Myanmar's representative to the AICHR, a 'de facto veto power over any decisions, even when they may be supported by a majority of other representatives' (SAPA TFAHR 2013: 10).

### *The ASEAN Four's and SEANF's Activism Towards Myanmar*

In September 2007, the ASEAN Four, together with Timor-Leste's NHRI, the Provedor (Office of the Ombudsman for Human Rights and Justice), during an annual meeting of the Asia Pacific Forum of National Human Rights Institutions (APF) in Sydney urged Myanmar in a joint statement to observe human rights principles when responding to demonstrations (ASEAN Four & Provedor).

In November 2009, the ANF changed their name to South East Asia NHRI Forum due to an objection by the ASEAN Secretariat because they are not an ASEAN body (Collins 2013: 89). This was convenient for the Provedor of Timor-Leste, who joined the club in 2010, as Timor-Leste is not yet an ASEAN member.

During SEANF's Seventh Annual Meeting on 15–16 November 2010, a joint statement was issued which praised the release of Daw Aung San Suu Kyi as 'a partial victory for the long struggle of democracy in Myanmar' but the statement also 'called for the release of other political prisoners as well as sustaining fair and democratic political processes in the country' (SEANF 2010).

In the words of SEANF (2013) the Eighth Annual Meeting of SEANF on 18–19 October 2011 'paved the way for the welcoming of the newly established human rights commission in Myanmar'. Just a little over a week before this, on 10 October 2011, the MNHRC sent an open letter to Myanmar's President Thein Sein, requesting him 'as a reflection of his magnanimity' to grant amnesty and release Myanmar's prisoners of conscience (MNHRC 2011a). The release of these prisoners took place the next day, 11 October 2011, when Myanmar's president granted amnesty to 6359 prisoners (MNHRC 2011b). Because the last statement of SEANF (2010) called for the release of political prisoners this could have been a tactical and carefully planned move by the MNHRC aiming for SEANF membership.

Further discussions on MNHRC's membership of SEANF were held when SEANF visited the MNHRC in June 2012 (MNHRC 2012c). Then on 12–14 September 2012, during the Ninth Annual Meeting of SEANF in Bangkok, Thailand, the MNHRC joined SEANF as its sixth member (SEANF 2013).

It was argued by Collins (2013: 89) that SEANF could be a potential competitor to AICHR as a more robust regional human rights mechanism. However, reality has proven to be different, as SEANF, like the AICHR, is bound by consensus decision-making. So, if new NHRIs from South East Asia join SEANF, especially those less prone to criticise their governments, they will be able to block SEANF's more 'robust' actions.

Since 2012, when the MNHRC joined SEANF, there have not been any public statements by SEANF about human rights in Myanmar, or any other country in ASEAN for that matter, while there have been numerous events, including regional events, which would demand a response from any 'robust' regional human rights mechanism. Examples are the situation of Rohingya in Myanmar, especially the upsurge in violence since 2012; the military *coup d'état* in Thailand in 2014 and subsequent arbitrary arrests and limitations of freedom of speech and the press; the 'war on drugs' in the Philippines, which has led to thousands of deaths; and intimidation, harassment, detention and attacks on rights activists in Cambodia and Vietnam (Corben 2017). Most recently the UN Human Rights Council decided to dispatch an international fact-finding mission to Myanmar 'to establish the facts and circumstances of the alleged recent human rights violations by military and security forces, and abuses, in Myanmar, in Rakhine State' and to extend the mandate of the Special Rapporteur on the situation of human rights in Myanmar (UNIS 2017).

Another factor for SEANF's decreased 'activism' apart from the MNHRC joining the club can be linked to the fact that since 2013, Thailand's NHRI, the NHRCT, has not been performing well. It was initially warned by the ICC SCA in October 2014 for no longer following the Paris Principles and giving it one year to improve. After that did not happen, the NHRCT was downgraded from an 'A status' NHRI to a 'B status' in November 2015 (GANHRI 2017a: 9; Draper and Kamnua 2016).

### *The MNHCR in SEANF and APF*

SEANF has been organising annual regional conferences on 'Human Rights and Agribusiness in Southeast Asia' in collaboration with the Forest

Peoples Programme (FPP) and various national NGO partners since 2011. In 2014 it was the MNHRC's turn, when it hosted the Fourth Regional Conference on Human Rights and Agribusiness in Southeast Asia from 4 to 6 November 2014, together with the FPP and the Center for People and Forests (RECOFTC). The conference included a wide range of participants, including the SEANF members and CSOs from most ASEAN countries. As an outcome of the conference, a joint statement was adopted by the participants expressing, inter alia, the need for improved adoption of NHRI's recommendations by governments, the need for an ASEAN Human Rights Court and national level complaints and redress mechanisms (Yangon Statement 2014: 3). This statement can be considered quite progressive and was most likely heavily influenced by wishes of the CSOs present at the conference.

The MNHRC was Chair of SEANF from 29 to 30 September 2015 until 26–27 September 2016, when the Chairmanship was handed over to the CHRP for 2017 (MNA 2016b). During the time that the MNHRC assumed Chairmanship, it organised two technical working group meetings and two special meetings (MNHRC 2016b: 10). The technical working group meetings were held in Yangon on 27–28 January and 2–3 June 2016, respectively, and items discussed during those meetings were SEANF's permanent secretariat, developments in GANHRI, the Sustainable Development Goals, the rights of older persons and the ASEAN Convention against Trafficking in Persons 2015 (Khine Khine Win 2016; MNHRC 2016e, f). One of the special meetings was held on 1 June 2016, and the strategic plan for 2017–2022 was discussed there (MNHRC 2016f). The other special meeting was the 13th annual meeting on 26–27 September 2016, during which SEANF issued a statement on the rights of older persons (MNA 2016b). In the same year, the MNHRC gave comments and recommendations on the Older Persons Bill to Myanmar's Parliament (MNHRC 2016b: 8).

The APF is the Asia-Pacific regional NHRI forum, with 24 NHRI members from the Asia Pacific region, including all the SEANF members. The MNHRC applied for membership of APF in October 2012 (APF 2012a) and on 5 November 2012, during the 17th Annual Meeting of the APF in Jordan, the MNHRC was admitted to the APF as associate member, pending its application to the ICC for membership (APF 2012b). Associate members cannot nominate a senior representative as voting councillor on the APF Forum Council, which is the decision-making body of the APF (APF 2017a, b). The APF noted, in its assessment of the

MNHRC application, several concerns related to the MNHRC's establishment by decree, the absence of a clear selection and dismissal process, many (government) seconded staff and the lack of financial independence (APF 2012a). The APF has supported the MNHRC in drafting the new MNHRC law (APF 2012a, 2017c).

## Conclusion

The preceding analysis, while recognising the improvements made, denotes that the MNHRC is not yet fully in compliance with the Paris Principles. For the MNHRC to be recognised with an 'A' status by the GANHRI Sub-Committee, it must go beyond amending the text of the MNHRC Law 2014 and interpret 'its mandate in a broad, liberal and purposive manner' and make sure that its actions 'promote and protect the human rights of all, including the rights of Rohingya and other minority groups' (ICC SCA 2015: 12).

The MHRC's approach to its work thus far reveals that, apart from a few positive examples, its protection record is not up to standards. There is surely a very high caseload which can be partly to blame for the MNHRC not being able to address each individual case in detail and pursue it to the very end. However, it seems that in some of the above cases, there is also a certain unwillingness or inability to pry too much into the Myanmar government's affairs, especially the military's, sphere of operations and control. In this regard, Special Rapporteur on Myanmar, Yanghee Lee, in her report to the UN General Assembly, urged the Commission 'to act as an independent and objective human rights advocate and not to shy away from issues deemed sensitive to the Government' (Yanghee Lee 2016: 4).

It is understandable that the MNHRC does not have the power to enforce its recommendations; however, it could employ its unique position between civil society and the government to bridge the gap that exists between the two. The cases mentioned above show that the MNHRC interprets its protection mandate as completed after issuing a report or public statement on the matter. However, thus far it has failed to pursue a case further, to the point where justice is served or fair redress for the victims is achieved. These are the true indicators of effective protection of human rights.

The promotion record was found to be fairly positive with some examples of the MNHRC organising important conferences, meetings and workshops where meaningful discussions were held. The human rights education activities by the MNHRC for several actors on different hierarchical levels, including the military, police and other powerful actors, are also commendable. The geographic coverage seems to have widened as well but it would be good to hear more about human rights education activities to military, border guard forces, police and other authorities that are operating in Rakhine, Kachin, Shan, Kayin, Kayah and other border regions, as those regions have historically been most prone to human rights violations by those actors.

With regard to promoting the ratification of international human rights treaties, the MNHRC has made some efforts, but it could do more, namely, convincing the Myanmar government to ratify important core treaties such as the ICCPR 1966, CAT 1984, ICERD 1965, International Convention on the Protection of the Rights of All Migrant Workers and Members of Their Families (ICMW) 1990 and International Convention for the Protection of All Persons from Enforced Disappearance (ICPED) 2006.

The MNHRC has also given recommendations to the Myanmar government to enact certain laws speedily and in compliance with international treaties, but unfortunately, not all of these efforts were positive or effective. When it came to the 'Four Race and Religion Protection Laws', which is clearly discriminatory based on gender and religion, the MNHRC has failed to criticise and call for their amendment or annulment.

In the last section, the engagement of the MNHRC and Myanmar on the regional level was assessed. It was shown that while the ASEAN Four, before MNHRC joined the club, have been actively promoting for a strong AICHR with strong enforcement powers, less democratic states, such as for example Myanmar were not so keen for AICHR to be established and only reluctantly accepted it, after the economically stronger and more democratic states, most of which had NHRIs at that time, supported it. It was concluded that due to the de facto veto power of the AICHR members, the AICHR has been very quiet on the human rights and humanitarian crisis to which the Rohingya Muslims in Myanmar are victim. Furthermore, it was noted that the ASEAN Four, which later formed ANF and then SEANF, initially seemed to fill some gaps left by AICHR when speaking out on human rights issues in Myanmar. One author even argued SEANF could be a potential competitor to AICHR as a more robust human rights body. However, this potential was short lived, because, after the MNHRC became a SEANF member in 2012, the activism of SEANF towards Myanmar and other ASEAN states diminished, even though there were indeed plenty of (regional) human rights issues. The reason for this was given that, like the AICHR, the SEANF can only act by consensus, when all of its members agree.

Throughout the chapter, ample evidence and angles have been discussed that lead to the unfortunate conclusion that the MNHRC, including its work on the regional level, is not fully effective in the promotion and protection of human rights in Myanmar. Judging from its actions, its main overarching purpose is to promote Myanmar's human rights image in the international plane and protect the government from outside scrutiny. One of the key steps that need to be taken towards becoming more effective is ensuring the selection process of the MNHRC's members is revised in accordance with the Paris Principles, especially on the autonomy, independence and pluralism. An increased involvement of civil society actors in this process is extremely important. Another important step which would be very beneficial would be giving the MNHRC enforcement powers to ensure it can follow up on its recommendations, which currently seem to fall on deaf ears without any consequences.

## References

ABC Radio Australia. 2008. ASEAN human rights body to rely on 'peer pressure *ABC Radio Australia*, 22 July (updated on 19 December 2011). Available at: http://www.radioaustralia.net.au/news/stories/200807/s2310241.htm.

Adams, B. 2017. Re: Section 66(d) of the Telecommunications Law, *Human Rights Watch*, 10 May. Available at: https://www.hrw.org/sites/default/files/supporting_resources/hrw_letter_on_66d_20170510.pdf.

Amnesty International (AI). 2016. *Myanmar: Lift restrictions immediately on humanitarian aid*, 20 October. Available at: https://www.amnesty.org/en/latest/news/2016/10/myanmar-lift-restrictions-immediately-on-humanitarian-aid/.

Artan M. 2015. Cases proceed silently in Myanmar journalist's 2014 killing *International Press Institute (IPI)*, 28 May. Available at: https://ipi.media/cases-proceed-silently-in-myanmar-journalists-2014-killing.

ASEAN Intergovernmental Commission on Human Rights (AICHR). 2012a. About. Available at: http://aichr.org/about/.

———. 2012b. AICHR Representatives Brief Curriculum Vitae, AICHR Representatives 2009–2012, 2 October. Available at: http://aichr.org/?dl_name=AICHR_Representatives_Brief_CV.pdf.

———. 2015. AICHR Representatives 2013–2015, 3 October. Available at: http://aichr.org/?dl_name=AICHR_Representatives_2013-2015_as_of_3_October_2015.pdf.

ASEAN NHRI Forum (ANF). 2008. ASEAN NHRIs Vision of an ASEAN Human Rights Body, 11 September. Available at: http://seanf.asia/index.php/home/joint-statements/15-asean-nhris-vision-of-an-asean-human-rights-body.

———. 2009 Position Paper Concerning the Political Declaration on the ASEAN Intergovernmental Commission on Human Rights (AICHR), 28 August. Availableat:http://seanf.asia/index.php/home/joint-statements/47-position-paper-on-aichr5.

Asia Pacific Forum of National Human Rights Institutions (APF). 2012a. *Application for Membership – Myanmar National Human Rights Commission*, 5 October. Available at: http://www.asiapacificforum.net/media/resource_file/Myanmar_NHRC_Application_for_APF_Membership_Supporting_Documents.pdf.

———. 2012b. '17th APF Annual Meeting, 2012', 5 November. Available at: http://www.asiapacificforum.net/events/apf-17/.

———. 2016. *ICC releases accreditation report*, 28 Jan 2016. Available at: http://www.asiapacificforum.net/news/icc-releases-accreditation-report.

———. 2017a. *Our members*. Available at: http://www.asiapacificforum.net/members.

———. 2017b. *APF Forum Council*. Available at: http://www.asiapacificforum.net/about/governance/forum-council/.

———. 2017c. *Providing Advice and Expertise*. Available at: http://www.asiapacificforum.net/about/providing-advice/.

Aung Din. 2016. Myanmar's Old Judiciary a Challenge to the New Era of Governance, *cogitASIA*, 5 January. Available at: https://www.cogitasia.com/myanmars-old-judiciary-a-challenge-to-the-new-era-of-governance/.

Bernstein, D. 2011. Burma's President Orders Ceasefire in Kachin State, *Voice of America*, 14 December. Available at: http://www.voanews.com/a/burmas-president-orders-ceasefire-in-kachin-state-135582003/168275.html.

Burma Partnership (BP). 2012. Burma's NHRC: An Empty Gesture, 10 January. Available at: http://www.burmapartnership.org/wp-content/uploads/2011/10/Burmas-NHRC-Updated-Jan-2012.pdf.

Burma Partnership (BP) and Human Rights Education Institute of Burma (HREIB). 2012. Burma: Curb Your Enthusiasm. Analysis of the Establishment of the New Myanmar National Human Rights Commission, in Asian Forum for Human Rights and Development (FORUM-ASIA) (ed), *2012 ANNI Report on the Performance and Establishment of National Human Rights Institutions in Asia*, Bangkok, pp. 39–66. Available at: http://www.forum-asia.org/uploads/books/2012/nov/05033_ANNI%202012.pdf.

Burma Partnership (BP), Equality Myanmar (EM) and Smile Education and Development Foundation (SEDF). 2015. Burma: All Shook Up', in Asian Forum for Human Rights and Development (FORUM-ASIA) (ed), *2015*

*ANNI Report on the Performance and Establishment of National Human Rights Institutions in Asia*, Bangkok, pp. 13–34. Available at: https://www.forum-asia.org/uploads/wp/2015/09/ANNI_Report_2015.pdf.

Collins, A. 2013. *Building a People-Oriented Security Community the ASEAN way*, London (UK) & New York (USA): Routledge.

Committee on the Elimination of Discrimination against Women (CEDAW Committee). 2016. Concluding observations on the combined fourth and fifth periodic reports of Myanmar, 25 July, UN Doc CEDAW/C/MMR/CO/4-5.

Corben, R. 2017 HRW: Deteriorating Outlook for Human Rights in SE Asia, *Voice of America*, 13 January. Available at: http://www.voanews.com/a/human-rights-watch-southeast-asia/3674978.html.

Crouch, M. 2017. The Judiciary in Myanmar, in A. Simpson, N. Farrelly and I. Holliday (eds), *Routledge Handbook of Contemporary Myanmar*, New York: Routledge (forthcoming).

De Lang, N.E. 2012. The Establishment and Development of the Myanmar National Human Rights Commission and its Conformity with International Standards, *Asia-Pacific Journal on Human Rights and the Law*, Vol. 13, No. 1, pp 1–41.

———. 2018 'Rohingya and other Muslims in Myanmar', in F. De Varennes and C.M. Gardiner (eds), *Routledge Handbook of Human Rights in Asia*, New York: Routledge (forthcoming).

Draper, J. and Kamnua, P. 2016 Downgrading of Thai human rights body a wake-up call *The Nation*, 4 February. Available at: http://www.nationmultimedia.com/news/opinion/aec/30278458.

Fortify Rights. 2015. Myanmar: Overturn Wrongful Conviction of Brang Shawng', *Press Release*, 18 February. Available at: http://www.fortifyrights.org/publication-20150218.html.

Freedom House. 2017. Freedom of the Press 2017, Myanmar Profile. Available at: https://freedomhouse.org/report/freedom-press/2017/Myanmar.

Fuller, T. 2014. Myanmar's Opening Up Hasn't Loosened Graft in Courts, *The New York Times*, 24 October. Available at: https://www.nytimes.com/2014/10/25/world/asia/myanmars-opening-up-hasnt-loosened-graft-in-courts.html?_r=0.

Global Alliance of National Human Rights Institutions (GANHRI). 2017a. About us: GANHRI Sub-Committee on Accreditation (SCA)', viewed 22 June 2017. Available at: http://nhri.ohchr.org/EN/AboutUs/GANHRIAccreditation/Pages/default.aspx.

———. 2017b. Chart of the Status of National Institutions, 26 May. Available at: http://www.ohchr.org/Documents/Countries/NHRI/Chart_Status_NIs.pdf.

Htoo Thant. 2016. Committee for solving land disputes accused of conflict of interest, *The Myanmar Times*, 28 September. Available at: http://www.

mmtimes.com/index.php/national-news/nay-pyi-taw/22765-committee-for-solving-land-disputes-accused-of-conflict-of-interest.html.

Human Rights Watch (HRW). 2012. Untold Miseries, Wartime Abuses and Forced Displacement in Kachin State', March 2012. Available at: https://www.hrw.org/sites/default/files/reports/burma0312ForUpload_1_0.pdf.

International Commission of Jurists (ICJ). 2013. Right to Counsel: The Independence of Lawyers in Myanmar'. Available at: http://www.burmalibrary.org/docs16/ICJ-MYANMAR-Right-to-Counsel-en-red.pdf.

International Coordinating Committee of National Institutions for the Promotion and Protection of Human Rights Sub-Committee on Accreditation (ICC SCA). 2013. General Observations as adopted in Geneva in May 2013. Available at: http://nhri.ohchr.org/EN/AboutUs/Governance/Documents/ICC%20SCA%20General%20Observations.pdf.

———. 2015. Report and Recommendations of the Session of the Sub-Committee on Accreditation, 20 November. Available at: http://nhri.ohchr.org/EN/AboutUs/GANHRIAccreditation/Documents/SCA%20FINAL%20REPORT%20-%20NOVEMBER%202015-English.pdf.

Ja Seng Ing Truth Finding Committee. 2014. Who Killed Ja Seng Ing?, 6 December. Available at: http://www.burmapartnership.org/wp-content/uploads/2014/12/REPORT_Who-Killed-JSI_6.Dec_.14.pdf.

Kabir, AHM. 2001. Establishing National Human Rights Commissions in South Asia: A Critical Analysis of the Processes and the Prospects, *Asia-Pacific Journal on Human Rights and the Law*, Vol. 2, No. 1, pp. 1–53.

Khine Khine Win. 2016. Southeast Asia National Human Rights Institution Forum (SEANF) *The Global New Light of Myanmar*, 9 June. Available at: http://www.globalnewlightofmyanmar.com/southeast-asia-national-human-rights-institution-forum-seanf/.

Lawi Weng. 2014. Govt Investigation 'Failed' to Address Alleged Rohingya Killings: UN Envoy, *The Irrawaddy*, 20 February. Available at: https://www.irrawaddy.com/news/burma/govt-investigation-failed-address-alleged-rohingya-killings-un-envoy.html.

———. 2015. Burma Army Shot, Tortured Kokang Civilians During Conflict: Rights Group, *The Irrawaddy*, 5 March. Available at: https://www.irrawaddy.com/news/burma/burma-army-shot-tortured-kokang-civilians-during-conflict-rights-group.html.

Lee, Y. 2016. Report of the Special Rapporteur on the situation of human rights in Myanmar, 29 August, UN Doc A/71/361.

Lefevre, A.S. and Kapoor, K. 2015. SE Asia vows to rescue 'boat people'; Myanmar seizes migrant vessel *Reuters*, 29 May. Available at: http://www.reuters.com/article/us-asia-migrants-us-idUSKBN0OE05T20150529.

Liljeblad, J. 2016. The 2014 Enabling Law of the Myanmar National Human Rights Commission and the UN Paris Principles: A Critical Evaluation', *Journal of East Asia and International Law*, Vol. 9, No. 2, pp. 427–447.

Lun Min Mang. 2016. Former regime defender to be state counsellor's minister, *Myanmar Times,* 12 May. Available at: http://www.mmtimes.com/index.php/national-news/20249-former-regime-defender-to-be-state-counsellor-s-minister.html.

Lutheran World Foundation (LWF). 2016. LWF Myanmar behind "milestone" meeting on human rights, 15 August. Available at: https://www.lutheranworld.org/news/lwf-myanmar-behind-milestone-meeting-human-rights.

Macgregor, F. and Thu Thu Aung. 2016. New govt to defend 'race and religion' laws at UN meeting, *Myanmar Times,* 6 July. Available at: http://www.mmtimes.com/index.php/national-news/21218-new-govt-to-defend-race-and-religion-laws-at-un-meeting.html.

Mizzima News. 2011. Retired ambassador Hla Myint likely to replace Rangoon Mayor, *Mizzima News,* 9 March. Available at: https://web.archive.org/web/20110501002409/http://www.mizzima.com/news/inside-burma/4987-retired-ambassador-hla-myint-likely-to-replace-rangoon-mayor.html.

———. 2016. 'Myanmar shelves investigation into journalist killing', *Mizzima News,* 6 April. Available at: http://www.mizzima.com/news-domestic/myanmar-shelves-investigation-journalist-killing.

Munro, J. 2011. The relationship between the origins and regime design of the ASEAN Intergovernmental Commission on Human Rights (AICHR), *The International Journal of Human Rights,* Vol. 15, No. 8, pp. 1185–1214.

Myanmar National Human Rights Commission (MNHRC). 2011a. Request submitted in open letter by members of the Myanmar National Human Rights Commission to the President of the Republic of the Union of Myanmar, 10 October. Available at: http://www.mnhrc.org.mm/en/statements-2/request-submitted-in-open-letter-by-members-of-the-myanmar-national-human-rights-commission-to-the-president-of-the-republic-of-the-union-of-myanmar/.

———. 2011b. Open Letter to the President of the Republic of the Union of Myanmar by the Myanmar National Human Rights Commission, 12 November. Available at: http://www.burmapartnership.org/2011/11/myanmar-national-human-rights-commissions-open-letter-to-president-thein-sein/.

———. 2012a. Statement of the Myanmar National Human Rights Commission on its establishment and its current status of functioning, *Statement No. 2/2012,* 27 March, p. 16. Available at: http://mnhrc.org.mm/en/statements-2/the-statement-of-the-myanmar-national-human-rights-commission-on-its-establishment-and-its-current-status-of-functioning-statement-no-22012/.

———. 2012b. Statement of the Myanmar National Human Rights Commission on its trip to the Kachin State, *Statement No. 5/2012,* 14 August. Available at: http://www.mnhrc.org.mm/en/statements-2/statement-of-the-myanmar-national-human-rights-commission-on-its-trip-to-the-kachin-state-52012/.

———. 2012c. Statement of the Myanmar National Human Rights Commission (MNHRC) concerning its membership in the South East Asia NHRIs Forum (SEANF), *Statement No. 6/2012*, 17 September. Available at: http://www.mnhrc.org.mm/en/statement-of-the-myanmar-national-human-rights-commission-mnhrc-concerning-its-membership-in-the-south-east-asia-nhris-forum-seanf-no-6-2012/.
———. 2013. Statement of the Myanmar National Human Rights Commission on humanitarian assistance for the conflict victims of the Kachin State, *Statement No (1/2013)*, 18 January. Available at: http://www.mnhrc.org.mm/en/statement-of-the-myanmar-national-human-rights-commission-on-humanitarian-assistance-for-the-conflict-victims-of-the-kachin-state-statement-no-1-2013/.
———. 2014a. Statement of the MNHRC on the findings of the Commission Team from its investigation of the incident at the Ducheeratan village, *Statement No. (2/2014)*, 17 February. Available at: http://www.mnhrc.org.mm/en/2014/02/statement-of-the-mnhrc-regarding-the-findings-of-the-commission-team-from-its-investigation-of-the-incident-at-the-ducheeratan-village-tract-statement-no-22014/.
———. 2014b. The inquiry report of the Myanmar National Human Rights Commission into the death of Ko Aung Naing (a) Ko Aung Kyaw Naing (a) Ko Par Gyi, 2 December. Available at: http://www.mnhrc.org.mm/en/2014/12/the-inquiry-report-of-the-myanmar-national-human-rights-commission-into-the-death-of-ko-aung-naing-a-ko-aung-kyaw-naing-a-ko-par-gyi.
———. 2014c. Myanmar National Human Rights Commission to investigate the incidents at Letpadaungtaung Copper Mine Project, 31 December. Available at: http://www.mnhrc.org.mm/en/2014/12/myanmar-national-human-rights-commission-to-investigate-the-incidents-at-letpadaungtaung-copper-mine-project/.
———. 2015a. Press Release by the Myanmar National Human Rights Commission on the Armed Conflict in Laukkai Area, *Statement No. (2/2015)*, 27 February. Available at: http://www.mnhrc.org.mm/en/2015/02/press-release-by-the-myanmar-national-human-rights-commission-on-the-armed-conflict-in-laukkaing-area
———. 2015b. Outcome Statement of senior officials Workshop on UN Security Council Resolution 1325 on Women, Peace and Security and Related Resolutions', 28 April. Available at: http://mnhrc.org.mm/en/statements-2/outcome-statement-of-senior-officials-workshop-on-un-security-council-resolution-1325-on-women-peace-and-security-and-related-resolutions/.
———. 2015c. 2014 Annual Report, 2 June. Available at: http://www.mnhrc.org.mm/app/uploads/2015/09/2014-Annual-Report-English-Version-1.pdf.

———. 2015d. Letters sent to the Thai Foreign Ministry and Thai National Human Rights Commission, 5 November. Available at: http://www.mnhrc.org.mm/en/2015/11/.

———. 2015e. Press statement on the inquiry of riots of 22nd December 2014 at Latpadaungtaung Copper Mine Project in Salingyi Township', *Statement No. (1/2015)*, 15 January. Available at: http://www.mnhrc.org.mm/en/2015/01/myanmar-national-human-rights-commission-press-statement-on-the-inquiry-of-riots-of-22nd-december-2014-at-latpadaungtaung-copper-mine-project-in-salingyi-township/.

———. 2015f. Letter from the Chairperson of MNHRC to the Chairperson of NHRI Thailand with regards to the case of two Myanmar workers sentenced to death for murder, 28 December. Available at: http://www.mnhrc.org.mm/en/2015/12/.

———. 2016a. South East Asia National Human Rights Institutions Forum Technical Working Group Meeting (TWG 1/2016), 27 January. Available at: http://www.mnhrc.org.mm/en/2016/01/south-east-asia-national-human-rights-institutions-forum-technical-working-group-meeting-twg-12016/.

———. 2016b. A Report to the United Nations Committee on the Elimination of Discrimination against Women on the Implementation of the Convention on the Elimination of All Forms of Discrimination against Women (CEDAW) in Myanmar, June. Available at: http://tbinternet.ohchr.org/Treaties/CEDAW/Shared%20Documents/MMR/INT_CEDAW_IFN_MMR_24177_E.pdf.

———. 2016c. South East Asia National Human Rights Institution Forum (SEANF) Technical Working Group Meeting (2/2016) convened', 2 June. Available at: http://www.mnhrc.org.mm/en/2016/06/south-east-asia-national-human-rights-institution-forum-seanf-technical-working-group-meeting-22016-convened/.

———. 2016d. 2015 Annual Report, 10 June. Available at: http://www.mnhrc.org.mm/app/uploads/2017/05/2015-Annual-Report-Eng-19-12-2016.pdf.

———. 2016e. Presentation given to the 21st APF Annual Meeting; Bangkok, Thailand; October 2016. [PowerPoint slides]. Retrieved from http://www.asiapacificforum.net/resources/work-myanmar-nhrc-apf21/.

———. 2016f. Statement by Myanmar National Human Rights Commission on the occasion of the International Human Rights Day which falls on the 10th of December 2016, *Statement No. 15/ 2016*, 10 December. Available at: http://www.mnhrc.org.mm/en/statement-by-myanmar-national-human-rights-commission-on-the-occasion-of-the-international-human-rights-day-which-falls-on-the-10th-of-december-2016-no-15-2016.

———. 2017a. About: Commissioners, viewed 21 June 2017. Available at: http://www.mnhrc.org.mm/en/about/commissioners/.

———. 2017b. Relation with other NHRIs', viewed on 29 June 2017. Available at: http://mnhrc.org.mm/en/relation-with-other-nhris-2/.

Myanmar News Agency (MNA). 2016a. Workshop on Minority Rights held in Nay Pyi Taw' *The Global New Light of Myanmar*, 14 June. Available at: http://www.globalnewlightofmyanmar.com/workshop-on-minority-rights-held-in-nay-pyi-taw.

———. 2016b. SEANF holds 13th Annual Meeting *The Global New Light of Myanmar*, 27 September. Available at: http://www.globalnewlightofmyanmar.com/seanf-holds-13th-annual-meeting/.

Naím, M. 2007. Democracy's Dangerous Impostors, *The Washington Post*, 21 April. Available at: http://www.washingtonpost.com/wp-dyn/content/article/2007/04/20/AR2007042001594.html.

O'Toole, B. 2014. Rights body shake-up under fire, *The Myanmar Times*, 29 September. Available at: http://www.mmtimes.com/index.php/national-news/11803-rights-body-shake-up-under-fire.html.

Progressive Voice (PV). 2017. 66(D) Must Go *Progressive Voice Blog Posts*, 14 June. Available at: http://progressivevoicemyanmar.org/2017/06/14/66d-must-go/.

Radio Free Asia (RFA). 2015. Fighting Intensifies in Myanmar's Kokang Region Amid Allegations of Rights Violations, *Radio Free Asia*, 2 March. Available at: http://www.rfa.org/english/news/myanmar/violations-03022015153044.html.

———. 2016. Myanmar President's Office Investigates Maid-Abuse Case, *Radio Free Asia*, 22 September. Available at: http://www.rfa.org/english/news/myanmar/myanmar-presidents-office-investigates-maid-abuse-case-09222016160550.html.

Regan, H. and Stout, D. 2014. A Reporter's Death Shows Just How Little Burma Has Changed, *Time*, 4 November. Available at: http://time.com/3550460/burma-myanmar-military-journalist-killing-aung-kyaw-naing.

Registration of Organization Law (2014, Pyidaungsu Hluttaw Law No. 31) 1376, New Moon of Thadingyut 7th day (July 18, 2014).

Renshaw, C. 2017. Human Rights under the New Regime, in A. Harding and Khin Khin Oo (eds), *Constitutionalism and Legal Change in Myanmar*, Oxford [UK]; Portland, OR: Hart Publishing, pp. 215–234.

Sathisan, V. 2016. Letpadaung, Daw Khin Win and impunity, *Frontier Myanmar*, 14 November. Available at: http://frontiermyanmar.net/en/letpadaung-daw-khin-win-and-impunity.

Shan Human Rights Foundation (SHRF). 2015. Situation Update: Shooting, killing and torture of civilians by Burma Army during Kokang conflict, 4 March. Available at: http://www.shanhumanrights.org/index.php/news-updates/205-shooting-killing-and-torture-of-civilians-by-burma-army-during-kokang-conflict.

Shoon Naing. 2016. Four national human rights commissioners resign over child domestic workers scandal, *Myanmar Times*, 7 October. Available at: http://

www.mmtimes.com/index.php/national-news/yangon/22961-four-national-human-rights-commissioners-resign-over-child-domestic-workers-scandal.html.

Sithu Aung Myint. 2017. Questioning the government's commitment to media freedom *Frontier Myanmar*, 26 February. Available at: http://frontiermyanmar.net/en/questioning-the-governments-commitment-to-media-freedom.

Solidarity for ASEAN People's Advocacies Task Force on ASEAN and Human Rights (SAPA TFAHR). 2016. Breaking the Silence and Unlocking Barriers for Human Rights Protection in ASEAN: A report on the performance of the ASEAN Human Rights Mechanisms in 2015, Asian Forum for Human Rights and Development (FORUM-ASIA), Bangkok. Available at: https://www.forum-asia.org/uploads/wp/2016/10/Breaking-The-Silence-AICHR-Performance-Report-2015.pdf.

Solidarity for Asian People's Advocacy Task Force on ASEAN and Human Rights (SAPA TFAHR). 2013. Still Window-Dressing: A Performance Report on the Third Year of the ASEAN Intergovernmental Commission on Human Rights (AICHR) 2011–2012, Asian Forum for Human Rights and Development (FORUM-ASIA), Bangkok. Available at: http://www.forum-asia.org/uploads/publications/2013/June/Still-Window-Dressing-final-ready-for-print.pdf.

South East Asia National Human Rights Institutions Forum (SEANF). 2010. SEANF Supports Release of Aung San Suu Kyi, 16 November. Available at: http://seanf.asia/index.php/home/news/64-seanf-supports-release-of-aung-san-suu-kyi.

———. 2013. About us: South East Asia NHRI Forum. Available at: http://seanf.asia/index.php/about-us/89-south-east-asia-nhri-forum.

Swe Win. 2016. Teenage maids escape slavery, torture at Yangon tailor shop, *Myanmar Now*, 19 September. Available at: http://www.myanmar-now.org/news/i/?id=dd805b77-b869-46a1-9c1a-610e4ceb9057.

Ta'ang Women's Organization (TWO). 2016. Trained to Torture, Systematic war crimes by the Burma Army in Ta'ang areas of northern Shan State (March 2011–March 2016). Available at: http://en.palaungwomen.com/reports/Trained%20to%20Torture%20-%20English_for%20Web.pdf.

The Irrawaddy. 2015. Memorial Held for Slain Letpadaung Protester in Sagaing, *The Irrawaddy News*, 23 December. Available at: https://www.irrawaddy.com/news/burma/memorial-held-for-slain-letpadaung-protester-in-sagaing.html.

The National Human Rights Commission of Indonesia (KOMNAS HAM), the Human Rights Commission of Malaysia (SUHAKAM), the Commission on Human Rights of the Philippines (CHRP) and the National Human Rights Commission of Thailand (NHRCT) (ASEAN Four). 2007a. ASEAN NHRIs Appeal for Provision in the ASEAN Charter, 28 June. Available at: http://

seanf.asia/index.php/home/joint-statements/12-asean-nhris-appeal-for-provision-in-the-asean-charter.

———. 2007b. Declaration of Cooperation, 28 June. Available at: http://www.aseanhrmech.org/downloads/NHRI%20Declaration%20of%20Cooperation.pdf.

San Thein, Pyae Sone and Diepart, J-C. 2017. Transparency under Scrutiny. Information disclosure by the Parliamentary Land Investigation Commission in Myanmar. *MRLG Case Study Series #1*. Vientiane: Mekong Region Land Governance. Available at: http://www.burmalibrary.org/docs23/MRLG-2017-02-Case-study-Parliamentary-Land-Investigation-MMR-red.pdf.

United Nations (UN) News Centre. 2014. Top UN officials call for probe into latest violence in Myanmar's Rakhine state, 23 January. Available at: http://www.un.org/apps/news/story.asp?NewsID=46987.

United Nations Development Programme (UNDP) and Office of the High Commissioner for Human Rights (OHCHR). 2010. UNDP-OHCHR Toolkit for collaboration with National Human Rights Institutions, December. Available at: http://www.ohchr.org/Documents/Countries/NHRI/1950-UNDP-UHCHR-Toolkit-LR.pdf.

United Nations Information Service (UNIS). 2017. Human Rights Council decides to dispatch a fact-finding mission to Myanmar to establish facts on violations, especially in Rakhine State, *United Nations Office of the High Commissioner for Human Rights,* 24 March. Available at: http://www.ohchr.org/EN/NewsEvents/Pages/DisplayNews.aspx?NewsID=21443&LangID=E.

United Nations Office of the High Commissioner for Human Rights (OHCHR). 2010. National Human Rights Institutions: History, Principles, Roles and Responsibilities' *Professional Training Series No. 4 (Rev.1)*. Available at: http://www.ohchr.org/Documents/Publications/PTS-4Rev1-NHRI_en.pdf.

*Yangon Statement on Human Rights and Agribusiness in Southeast Asia*. 2014. 6 November. Available at: http://www.forestpeoples.org/sites/fpp/files/news/2014/11/Yangon%20Statement%20on%20Human%20Rights%20and%20Agribusiness%20in%20Southeast%20Asia.pdf.

Ye Mon and Myat Nyein Aye. 2015. Government unveils Yangon development plan, *Myanmar Times,* 11 June. Available at: http://www.mmtimes.com/index.php/national-news/yangon/14977-government-unveils-yangon-development-plan.html.

Zue Zue. 2015. Burma's Judicial System Deeply Corrupt, Parliament Told, *The Irrawaddy*, 9 December. Available at: https://www.irrawaddy.com/news/burma/102553.html.

CHAPTER 6

# From Transition to Government Accountability: Opportunities for the Myanmar National Human Rights Commission

*Francesca Paola Traglia*

## Introduction

During the 28th Session of the Human Rights Council in March 2015, Myanmar's Deputy Foreign Minister U Thyant Kyaw declared, "In order to be more compliant with the Paris Principles, the Myanmar National Human Rights Commission Law was enacted by the Parliament on 28 March 2014" (Human Rights Council, 28th Session). This action by the government already back in 2011 and 2014 shows a clear commitment to move forward in establishing functioning NHRIs in Myanmar; however, despite some improvements, the MNHRC continues to be criticized for a perceived lack of effectiveness in Myanmar (Myanmar Times 2016).

This chapter argues that an assessment of the MNHRC against such critiques needs to be placed within a larger context of transition and semi-civilian rule, as well as the detailed implications and gaps of The Myanmar National Human Rights Commission Law. Often CSOs insist that NHRIs should take a "watchdog" role on the state; however, in emerging

F. P. Traglia (✉)
Lutheran World Federation, Geneva, Switzerland



J. Gomez, R. Ramcharan (eds.), *National Human Rights Institutions in Southeast Asia*,
https://doi.org/10.1007/978-981-15-1074-8_6

democracies and in stages of transition where many are the challenges governments face in advancing human rights, NHRIs can play a crucial role in bridging the divide between civil society and the state. What opportunities are there for the MNHRC under the new semi-civilian government? The MNHRC has great potential to play an effective role in assisting civil society in holding the government accountable for human rights commitments as well as providing useful guidance to government on necessary policy reform for improving the human rights situation in Myanmar.

This analysis is made using primary documents and from firsthand experience of the author in advising, guiding and facilitating the work of the MNHRC in Myanmar while working for an international NGO. There has been virtually no systematic analysis of the MNHRC, except for work done by this author, de Lang (also in this volume) and Lijleblad (2017a, b).

This chapter proceeds first with an examination of the political context of democratic transition in Myanmar. Thereafter, the Mandate is highlighted as a key area to be understood considering its limitations and opportunities for improvements. Public opinion and the main critiques against MNHRC's efficiency and effectiveness are outlined for the author to subsequently illustrate the opportunities that will help improve the work, efficiency and effectiveness of the Commission. The latter should be taken as recommendations to aid MNHRC spearhead the government in taking a leap into a new era of enhanced human rights protection in Myanmar.

## The Myanmar Context

### *Transition and Its Implications*

The context in Myanmar has changed dramatically since 2008, when the country was hit by a devastating cyclone (Nargis), during which time an amended controversial constitution (2008) was passed in Parliament. The elections in November 2010—though widely seen as falling significantly short of international standards—started a remarkable process of change in the country. Key points include the convening of a largely civilian parliament in April 2011, which has since enacted a series of economic and political reforms; the signing of ceasefire agreements with all but one of the ethnic armed groups in early 2012, followed by ongoing talks surrounding a nationwide ceasefire agreement; and by-elections in April 2012 that saw Aung San Suu Kyi's National League for Democracy win 42 out of 44 seats (DFID 2014). Aung San Suu Kyi herself took her seat as an MP in parliament in May 2012.

Fundamental challenges remain. In a region containing some of the fastest-growing economies in the world, Myanmar remains one of the poorest countries in Asia. Data about poverty in Myanmar is difficult to obtain and most of it is unreliable, but there is evidence of widespread poverty and vulnerability. Its Human Development Index rank of 149/186 (UNDP) is the lowest in the region.

Sustained armed conflict has caused widespread displacement since 2011, when the long-standing ceasefire broke down, according to the Special Rapporteur (Lee 2017). In Shan and Kachin States, unacceptable reports of serious human rights violations allegedly committed by several parties to the conflict including the Tatmadaw and ethnic armed groups have continued to arise. The Tatmadaw, or some elements of it, conduct themselves in violation of human rights. Some of these cases are reported but cannot be verified for lack of access. This figure includes over 50,000 believed to be living in KIO controlled areas and over 20,000 people living in the homes of host families. Subsequent information suggests there could now be more than 120,000 since heavy fighting broke out again, sporadically between September 2013 and April 2014. In addition, an estimated half a million people are also still internally displaced in eastern Myanmar and some 128,000 people (UNHCR) continue to live in refugee camps in Thailand (DFID 2014).

In addition, inter-communal violence between the predominantly Muslim Rohingya and the predominantly Buddhist Rakhine, and discriminatory policies toward Muslim populations, have led to a segregation of many communities and a deteriorating humanitarian situation in Rakhine State. Outbreaks of inter-communal violence—mostly anti-Muslim in its nature—have spread to other parts of the country.

The NLD government, after the welcomed landslide victory in 2015 and taking power in early 2016, has failed to become a beacon of hope, failing to fulfill expectations of its own people and that of the wider international community.

Ethnic conflicts have drastically escalated in the past year; the October 2016 attacks in Northern Rakhine prompted an army crackdown and critics as well as an OHCHR Report of victims' testimonies that fled to Bangladesh say that it may amount to crimes against humanity (Guardian 2016). More and more, an increase in online defamation cases, resulting from the controversial Telecommunications Act, is placing strains on the freedom of speech in the country. Aung San Suu Kyi and her government have not stepped forward in any meaningful way to address the latter not showing an interest to engage/improve the situation.

In relation to engagement with international human rights mechanisms, one can notice, as a practitioner, a reluctance to move forward on accepted recommendations both from the UPR and the from CEDAW reviews that took place, respectively, in 2015 and 2016, with claims that it was the previous government's reports and commitments. The lack of interest in engaging in a meaningful way with civil society and the Myanmar National Human Rights Commission leaves waves of confusion, making it difficult for stakeholders to devise successful strategies for engagement with the current government in order to advance human rights in Myanmar.

Myanmar is in rapid political and economic transition, with a triple-reform agenda focused on democratic governance and rule of law; national unity and peace via reconciliation with political parties and ethnic armed organizations. This difficult transition is also characterized by market-oriented economic adjustments, the necessity for inclusive growth, bottom-up planning and decentralization; challenges faced in the slow improvement and management of government institutions; a lagging collaboration with the international community especially in terms of human rights advancements. In emerging democracies and in stages of transition where many are the challenges governments face in advancing human rights, NHRIs can play a crucial role in bridging the divide between civil society and the state. The MNHRC even with its challenging mandate could still embrace this role and ease the government's transition burden, at least in the advancement and protection of human rights.

## The Mandate

The MNHRC was established under a presidential decree in September 2011, yet with no clear mandate until the MNHRC Law MNHRC Law No. 21/2014 was adopted by Parliament in March 2014, no real work had begun. Today the Commission is formed by seven all male commissioners. Following a recent scandal[1] in 2016, where four commissioners (two females) were dismissed, there is great expectation among civil society that new members will be selected to join the leadership of MNHRC,

[1] The two girls' case mediated by MNHRC and the resulting scandal in the media due to the 5 million kyat payout for slavery and torture.

yet the government has not yet requested the selection board to begin a nomination process.

The MNHRC is mandated to promote and protect the human rights enshrined in Myanmar's Constitution and is outlined in the Law No. 21/2014 in relation to the 2008 Constitution. Its main task is to monitor the government's compliance with international human rights obligations and to cooperate with regional and international mechanisms, such as the United Nations (UN) treaty bodies and the Universal Periodic Review (UPR).

A deeper understanding of the Commission's limitations would be of assistance to the main critics of MNHRC in formulating more effective recommendations that could be taken on board by the Commission itself.

## Critiques of the MNHRC

Public confidence in Myanmar among human rights defenders, rights-violations victims and the international community have plummeted spectacularly in the past six years. National media such as *The Irrawady*, *The Global New Light of Myanmar* as well as *The Myanmar Times* actively follow the actions and shortcomings of the Commission and diligently inform the population inflaming prejudice with their critiques. As there is very little academic work on the MNHRC (se de Lang in this volume and Lijleblad 2017), the following section will briefly outline the most common critiques fleshed out by national media and human rights defenders.

Already in 2015, when the outcome of the fact-finding mission[2] on the Impact and Effectiveness of the MNHRC conducted by Asia Forum and Burma Partnership was published, the key findings outlined a widening credibility deficit afflicting the Commission. A common theme as described by the investigators was the depiction of the MNHRC as a "for show"

[2]The fact-finding mission was conducted from 16 to 18 November 2015 by the Asian Forum for Human Rights and Development (FORUM-ASIA), as secretariat of the Asian NGO Network on NHRIs (ANNI), and Burma Partnership. The mission team comprised Professor Kyong-Whan Ahn, former Chairperson of the National Human Rights Commission of the Republic of Korea and Professor Emeritus, Seoul National University Law School; Mr. Nur Kholis, Chairperson of National Human Rights Commission of Indonesia (Komnas HAM); Ms. Betty Yolanda, Country Programme Manager of FORUM-ASIA; and Mr. Joses Kuan, Advocacy and Research Officer of Burma Partnership.

institution or a "post-office box".[3] The lack of trust is also reported in the 2017 ANNI report on the performance and establishment of national human rights institutions (NHRIs) in Asia: the chapter titled Suspicious Minds: The Myanmar National Human Rights Commission Trust Deficit specifically outlines some of the shortcomings of the Commission which compels national civil society not to trust the MNHRC (see Anni Report 2017).

In a joint report released in early December 2017, three known rights groups in the country, Progressive Voice, the Action Committee for Democracy Development and the Smile Education and Development Foundation, said that the MNHRC's greatest weakness is its failure to serve as a voice for the country's most vulnerable people.

The MNHRC is still seen by many as the well-planned window-dressing attempt, by U Thein's outgoing government, at deflecting calls in 2011 for an international commission of inquiry into alleged war crimes and crimes against humanity committed by the military regime in conflict-affected ethnic states (Reuters 2013). Governments and the international community subsequently rewarded the Myanmar government with hefty investment in the form of technical advice and money, following several new political and economic series of reforms, which triggered a new era where attention shifted from humanitarian assistance to development assistance and the lifting of sanctions (Reuters 2013).

Critics have highlighted numerous areas of weakness in Law No. 21/2014, among which are the nontransparent selection process, a questionable selection board, its witness protection and investigation powers, its complaints handling process as well as its independence. The lack of trust in the independence and possible functionality of the MNHRC is further compounded by its composition. In an article of *The Myanmar Times*, MNHRC Chairman U Win Mra responds to such criticisms: "People doubt whether we can do our job effectively. Yes, we were government officials in the past. Government officials must follow the policy of the government, whether it matches their personal beliefs or not. Now we have been appointed to work freely. I believe that we will be successful if we can use the experience we gained from our previous posts" (Myanmar Times 2011). These words by U Win Mra and his further attempts at defending the composition of the Commission in the following years have

[3] End of Mission Statement on the Impact and Effectiveness of the Myanmar National Human Rights Commission (MNHRC), 18 November 2015.

not been sufficient to change public opinion as well as that of many civil society organizations that still remain distant from the MNHRC.

Unfortunately, independence is an aspect that civil society, in this author's view, spends too much time debating and using as an excuse for nonengagement with the Commission. For example, Aung Khaing Min, Executive Director of Progressive Voice, is still caught up in the independence of the Commission and told DVB in December 2017 that the Commission should be composed of independent members as opposed to being appointed by the president (DVB News 2017).

Independence is not a prerequisite for effectiveness and efficiency.[4] Instead each NHRI needs to tackle the political reality, the law and the context of its own country. Furthermore, cultural nuances on negotiation modus operandi need to be considered. Experience with the MNHRC by this author has been revealed that in order to discuss and negotiate human rights issues with the Myanmar government, a country that has been for so many years in the spotlight for its weak human rights record, human rights advocates need to embrace an Asian style approach that is closer to policy dialogue than to confrontational naming and shaming advocacy. The reality is that because advice, counseling and assistance is better received from "friends", it follows that the Myanmar government would be more open to positive criticism and advice from a Commission composed of its peers.

The dissatisfaction toward the lack of effectiveness of the MNHRC since its establishment prompted 149 national civil society organizations to write a letter directly to the International Coordinating Committee of National Institutions for the Promotion and Protection of Human Rights (ICC) petitioning to reject the MNHRC's accreditation application altogether in 2016 (Myanmar Times 2016). Unsuccessful as the letter was, one must note that the ICC only accredited MNHRC with a "Status B" implying that the MNHRC does not fully meet the requirements mandated in the Paris Principles (ICC 2015). The ICC has sent a strong message of dissatisfaction that the Myanmar government needs to take onboard. To be able to sit at the same table with its peers in Southeast Asia, the new NLD government needs to take concrete steps to address all criticisms outlined above.

One main challenge that interferes with the work of the Commission is that due to existing constitutional provisions, it states that human rights

[4] See, for example, Michael J.V. White in this volume.

means the rights of citizens rather than the rights of all human beings, which impacts on its work in relation to all persons which the government does not recognize as being Myanmar citizens. The 2008 Constitution specifically states that only two categories of persons are citizens of Myanmar, namely: persons born of parents both of whom are nationals of the Republic of the Union of Myanmar; and persons who are already citizens according to law on the day the 2008 Constitution came into operation.[5]

## The Work of the MNHRC

NHRIs have a significant role to play in advancing the promotion of human rights and in holding governments accountable to their human rights commitments. Although NHRIs are established by the government, they are mandated to be independent bodies that scrutinize government's challenges in the promotion, protection and respect of human rights in their country.

The five departments that carry out the work of MNHRC are the International Relations Division, the Legal Division, the Human Rights Promotion & Education Division, the Human Rights Protection Division and the Planning and Finance Division. All the work of MNHRC is rolled out by the current (at the time of writing) 60 staff members of the Commission, posing important limitations to the amount of attention, time and follow-up needed to deal with a significant caseload, typical of countries in transition, subject still to ongoing conflicts.

Since its establishment under a full mandate in 2014, MNHRC has certainly progressed in its performance. From Table 6.1, we can see that actions taken by relevant government ministries in relation to reported cases by MNHRC on received complaints have increased gradually over the past three years. The data from 2016 is very encouraging compared to the data from 2014. It must, however, be noted that it is a common factor that the year an NHRI opens office and begins operations, there is a significant caseload of human rights issues that people seek attention on. With better information dissemination and development of legal expertise as well as experience and outreach by MNHRC, the number of reported,

[5] 2008 Constitution of Myanmar, Chapter 8: Citizen, Fundamental Rights and Duties of the Citizens http://extwprlegs1.fao.org/docs/pdf/mya132824.pdf.

**Table 6.1** Complaints submitted to the MNHRC by type of cases

| *No.* | *Subject* | *2014* | *2015* | *2016* | *Total* |
|---|---|---|---|---|---|
| 1 | Land confiscation cases | 944 | 626 | 274 | 1844 |
| 2 | Cases concerning legal matters | 166 | 141 | 80 | 387 |
| 3 | Cases concerning government officials | 147 | 92 | 36 | 275 |
| 4 | Police cases | 86 | 73 | 43 | 202 |
| 5 | Cases concerning township/village administrative officials | 96 | 53 | 24 | 173 |
| 6 | Cases concerning financial matters | 44 | 36 | 25 | 105 |
| 7 | Municipal | 42 | 44 | 15 | 101 |
| 8 | Women/labor/religious matters | 27 | 44 | 19 | 90 |
| 9 | Terrorism/prisons/trafficking | 32 | 13 | 15 | 60 |
| 10 | Others | 255 | 165 | 80 | 500 |
| | Total | 1839 | 1287 | 611 | 3737 |

Source: Data taken from 2016 MNHRC Annual Report, and May 2017 Presentations by MNHRC at LWF Consultation Meeting

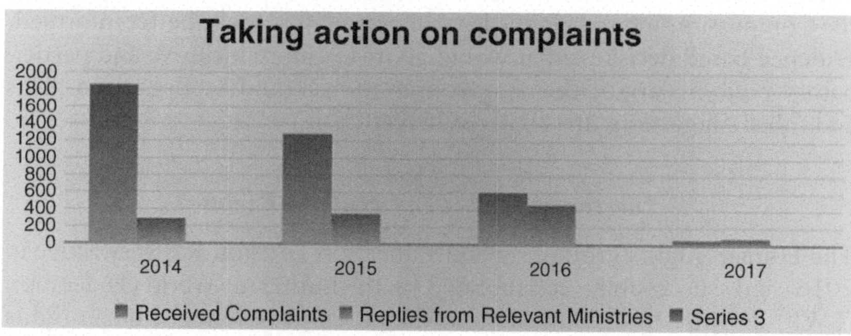


**Fig. 6.1** Inventory of Action taken on complaints. (Source: Data taken from 2014 MNHRC Annual Report, and May 2017 Presentations by MNHRC at LWF Consultation Meeting)

referred and responded to cases will continue to balance out over the next years (Fig. 6.1).

The Protection Division received 1021 letters of complaints in 2016 of which 400 were not recorded by the commission as human rights issues. The Complaint Handling Team held 94 meetings to examine 611 letters of complaints, and 311 cases were transmitted to the government departments concerned, as reported in the 2016 MNHRC Annual Report.

Unfortunately, data from 2017 has not yet been released at the time of writing in an annual report by the Commission; however, Table 6.1 shows the disaggregation, by topic, of the complaints received by the Commission from 2014 to 2016 (MNHRC 2016).

Many areas need improvement, many of which are outlined in the main criticisms on the work of the Commission analyzed above. Opportunities for improvement exist and are tangible in the context of MNHRC in the difficult transition process the country is undergoing.

### *Opportunities*

NHRIs can play an essential role in promoting and protecting human rights and consolidating democracy; this is also true in countries undergoing complex transition times like in Myanmar. Of the suggestions below, a particularly important one is to build closer, more constructive relationships and partnerships with civil society as envisaged by the Paris Principles. This is crucial to mobilize needed resources to alleviate the workload of the Commission and to help the legal department to make better informed, evidence-based decisions that would allow for more inclusive and participatory policymaking if thematic consultations could be organized. This and other suggestions are surveyed hereafter.

### *Increase Awareness on Human Rights*

The Human Rights Promotion and Education Division was very active in 2016 and successfully collaborated with Lutheran World Federation (LWF) in order to disseminate knowledge on government human rights commitments and the opportunities with the Universal periodic Review.[6] The Division is also in charge of awareness-raising, which can also include a review of the Myanmar legal framework against relevant treaty obligations.

### *Increase Access to the MNHRC*

In the most recent bilateral meeting between LWF and MNHRC, Chairman U Win Mra outlined the desire to increase the capacity of

[6] LWF facilitated trainings in 2016 at township level with a number of government departments, including the Township Medical Office, Township Education Office, members of staff from the Administration Department and the Police as well as the Township Land Committee, village tract Authorities and villagers in Chin, Ayewardy and Kayin State.

MNHRC via the establishment of branch offices; this will provide the MNHRC with the opportunity to set up regional offices to ensure effective outreach and communication with marginalized communities and minorities. The presence of MNHRC in more decentralized locations would close the gap that exists now between the people and the Commission.[7]

### *Ratification and Compliance with International Instruments*

It is important to note that MNHRC has already begun its work on advocating to the government for the adoption and ratification of the ICCPR. In December 2016, the commission has submitted a translated version of the covenant to the Parliament for its approval, opening the floor for discussion and Myanmar becoming signatory to the covenant (MNHRC 2016: 9).

The MNHRC could conduct a study on Myanmar's compliance with the UPR and Convention on the Elimination of Discrimination against Women (CEDAW) for which the government has recently undergone review, as well as a study on the ratification processes of International Covenant on Economic, Social and Cultural Rights (ICESCR) which was only signed in 2015. It could follow the example of Bangladesh, where the National Human Rights Commission conducted a study on state compliance with the ICCPR and it focused on recommendations on how to improve the government's implementation of the treaty (NHRC 2013). Here it is worthy to note that MNHRC has already recommended the full ratification of ICESCR to the government on 21 and 22 July 2016 during a government workshop on the covenant (MNHRC 2016: 8).

### *Fully Exercise Its Investigative Powers*

In relation to its legal powers, the MNHRC has the mandate to investigate human rights violations, for which it can summon witnesses, visit detention centers (with prior notification) and recommend further action to relevant government department and authorities. The MNHRC should push to have the ability to visit detentions centers without prior notification; this will allow the Commission to have a more realistic picture of the situation in detention centers.

[7]The MNHRC has already informed the President's Office on this plan and is waiting for adequate budget allocation to roll out the establishment of branch offices.

### *Respond in a Timely Manner to Complaints*

In relation to referred cases and responses from relevant government ministries, the MNHRC would gain more credibility and increase its effectiveness with timely responses from relevant government ministries in relation to referred cases. The government should take responsibility to follow the law that states a response must be provided to MNHRC within 60 days of the case being referred.

### *Cooperate with Other Mechanisms*

The MNHRC has the mandate for "consulting, engaging and cooperating with other national, regional and international human rights mechanisms". The Universal Periodic Review is a good monitoring mechanism accepted by government; therefore, the MNHRC should use this pathway in order to engage further with the government. Co-designing an action plan for implementing the accepted recommendations was a great initial step by the MNHRC in August 2017. Follow-up in building a monitoring framework for the implementation of the UPR Recommendations would allow the MNHRC to be further in contact with civil society and the government, providing a bridge for consultation and dialogue in the process of holding the government accountable for its international human rights commitments.[8]

### *Improve the Selection Process for Commissioners*

The selection procedure for the commissioners of MNHRC is coordinated by a selection board comprising a significant number of members of government, and yet there is no quorum requirement in the law. An important step forward in the transparency of appointments could include ensuring vacancies are published broadly, that there is an important promotion of broad consultation in the application, screening and selection process, and lastly, selection of commissioners should be based on predetermined and publicly available criteria.

[8] The National Human Rights Commission of Nepal cooperates with the international nongovernmental organization (NGO), UPR Info and LWF to conduct mid-term assessments of the implementation of UPR recommendations and consultations with civil society and other stakeholders.

### *Enhancing the Legal Department*

Strengthening the Legal Department of MNHRC is central to the success of the work of the Commission. Further legal expertise should be secured to ensure that investigatory functions are conducted according to fair procedures and the law. In addition, a subdivision within the Legal Department could focus on specialized case file management, the latter having the responsibility to ensure information flow and efficient monitoring of the caseload and follow-up.

### *Develop a Sound Communication Strategy*

Improving the public's understanding about MNHRC would help in countering the bad press the commission has been receiving in terms of criticisms to its work and effectiveness. A simple step that can be taken is to improve the internet presence of the Commission. A calendar of relevant events, access to an online library of relevant laws and a simple searchable database of human rights training materials and resources developed by the Commission.

To build on the latter suggestion, a good communication strategy that includes how to use press releases and media contacts as well as establishing a presence in social media will further strengthen the public's awareness about the MNHRC's work, helping to promote increased citizen engagement, better use of the complaints process and an improved awareness about the Commission's role in general.

### *Ensure Adequate Funding*

Out of the seven UPR Recommendations accepted by the government on the establishment of an independent national human rights commission, recommendation number 143.48 specifically states that the government of Myanmar should

> [p]rovide all necessary assistance in order that the national human rights institution is able to operate at full capacity and continue judicial reforms, including the increased capacity building of judicial institutions.[9]

[9] LWF Myanmar Analysis of UPR Recommendations: April 2016, page 10.

In order to fulfill the latter, sufficient funds should be provided to establish branch offices, to ensure that the Commission is accessible to rural areas, minorities and vulnerable groups in the country. In addition, funding should allow a robust communication infrastructure that includes complaint filing and information databases as suggested in points IX and X above.

The Commission submits yearly budgets to the President's Office and money is disbursed in the form of grants. MNHRC submitted a budget of 926,237,002 kyats for the period starting from September 2011 to September 2014. In this three-year period, 833,549,618 kyats was utilized in administrative matters and promotion and protection activities. The balance of 92,687,404 kyats had to be reimbursed back to the President's Office (MNHRC 2017).

A further impediment is the necessity to submit budgetary applications every three months for funds to be disbursed. To increase the autonomy of the MNHRC in making decisions on how to spend the money that is allocated to its budget it would be helpful if an amendment to the law would take place stipulating that it shall not be necessary for the Commission to take prior approval from the government to spend already allocated funds. The law, in section (24) (a) and (b), currently only states that the Commission has the right to act independently on matters "that falls within its powers" and has the right to act independently in respect of financial management and administrative matters in "conformity with the provisions of the law".[10]

Following Myanmar's second UPR of November 2015, the government indicated that it would consider developing a national human rights plan of action to support the implementation of the UPR recommendations the government had accepted.[11] In this situation, the MNHRC could work with civil society to identify priority areas for action and a program of work on a national action plan for the implementation of accepted UPR recommendations and its corresponding monitoring framework.

### *Cooperate with Civil Society*

Better cooperation with civil society is a key aspect that will improve the MNHRC's effectiveness. It must cooperate with nongovernment organi-

[10] 2016 Annual Report by the Myanmar National Human Rights Commission, page 36.

[11] LWF/MNHRC Workshop with Parliamentarians from Upper and Lower House, held in Nay Pyi Taw 9–10 August 2016.

zations as well as academic institutions or other experts in conducting thematic research activities, for example. Engaging and coordinating with civil society organizations in human rights monitoring is one of the four priority areas of the MNHRC's Strategic Plan for 2014–2016 that set out a roadmap for its early life—in addition to providing human rights information to the public, obtaining accreditation with A-Status at the SCA and providing information on the commission's complaint handling procedures. Since the Commission will undergo a strategy development process to frame its work for the next coming years, the inclusion of civil society in a coordinated and transparent process would be extremely beneficial to MNHRC. A participatory planning process would help to instill trust in the institution and provide concrete avenues for cooperation with different stakeholders as well as increase awareness about the MNHRC's work, available resources and organizational structure.

## MNHRC Work with Civil Society

Since November 2012, the Raoul Wallenberg Institute (RWI) has received important funds from Swedish International Development Agency (SIDA) for the overall objective to strengthen the MNHRC and its key partners.[12] RWI worked hard to increase the understanding of human rights and the role of NHRIS among both MNHRC commissioners and staff members. Furthermore, this cooperation has contributed to the development of increased capacity as well as enhanced internal tools to handle complaints and carry out inquiries. The Human Rights Protection Division prepared a comprehensive Complaint Handling Manual with the facilitation of RWI in 2014.

RWI worked closely with the government and MNHRC to develop the Myanmar National Human Rights Commission Law, yet the commission was heavily criticized by national civil society for lack of transparency and inclusiveness in the drafting process, at a time when civil society was reluctant to work with the Commission.

The cooperation between RWI and MNHRC showcased a high degree of trust between the two institutions, inspiring other civil society organizations like The Lutheran World Federation to start developing close collaborative relationships with MNHRC. The Lutheran World Federation is an international organization interested in building a well-

[12] SIDA Decentralized Evaluation of the Raoul Wallenberg Institute's project "Strengthening Human Rights in Myanmar" November 2014.

functioning MNHRC to contribute to the improvement of government accountability and the promotion and protection of human rights in Myanmar. Since 2009 the organization has been focusing on increasing the capacity of both communities and government to address together issues that limit human rights advancements in Myanmar. In the past two years, The Lutheran World Federation has developed a working relationship with MNHRC in order to work together to ensure awareness raising workshops and seminars on the UPR process in country would take place also at township level in areas far away from Yangon, Nay Pyi Taw and Bagan. In addition, the development of a joint monitoring mechanism for the implementation of UPR- and CEDAW- accepted recommendations was a primary focus in 2016 and 2017.

Exposure to other NHRIs and the participation of MNHRC Commissioner Dr. Myint Kyi in Asia Centre's International Conference on NHRI in Southeast Asia in Bangkok from 13 to 14 July 2017 were great opportunities to ensure that the only government staff, who is a current commissioner of MNHRC, would have the time to interact and learn about other models and challenges for NHRIs in Southeast Asia.

Lastly the most important focus of the work LWF is implementing is to close the gap between MNHRC and local government departments through supporting township level trainings for government staff, as well as to close the gap between MNHRC and civil society at the grass-roots through supporting township level trainings for village authorities and villagers as well as local organizations.

The other organization that successfully started to collaborate with the MNHRC in June 2016 was the International Court of Justice (ICJ), which, together with the Commission, co-organized a workshop with the aim of strengthening the capacity of parliamentarians and government officials with knowledge on international human rights norms and standards relating to minorities rights (MNHRC 2016).

Equality Myanmar (formerly HREIB) is a local nongovernmental organization which has facilitated a range of human rights education and advocacy programs in Myanmar. Famous for its work on Lesbian, Gay, Bi-sexual, Transgender and Intersex (LGBTI) but also for working on a national coalition report for the 2015 UPR of Myanmar, it was for many years reluctant to work with the Commission and focused its energy on criticizing the organization until recently.

In 2016, the organization was able to secure a three-year funding allocation through the EU EIDHR that will allow Equality Myanmar to focus more attention on stronger consultation processes with a wider range of civil society organizations across the country and will dedicate more time to work collaboratively[13] with the Commission. Examples of this change in their approach to human rights advocacy were finally seen in March 2018 when Equality Myanmar participated in the preparation of the UPR mid-term report with a number of other CSOs and presented it to the Myanmar Human Rights Commission officials, who in turn have offered their comments on the findings of the civil society mid-term UPR Report and have agreed to submit it to the government (Equality Myanmar 2018).

Burma Partnership was an international NGO based in Thailand that, over the last decade, has worked to mobilize and coordinate a solidarity movement with a common strategy for a democratic and free Burma. In 2011, the organization put together a toolkit, the MNHRC Monitor in order to train and give advocacy tools to national civil society in order to assess the work of the MNHRC.[14] For the organization MNHRC in order to be regarded as an effective NHRI had to demonstrate a commitment to the international standards set forth in the Paris Principles. This includes constructing a meaningful and recurring dialogue with civil society, abolishing the influence of the president and the Burma Army, and advocating for the protection of human rights defenders. For a decade the organization has been very confrontational on its human rights advocacy especially toward the MNHRC. As of 10 October 2016, Burma Partnership dissolved; however, it has been operating in a new direction, under the banner of Progressive Voice, which still focuses a lot of its work on monitoring and reporting on the performance of the Commission from afar. Collaboration between these two organizations has not yet been reported by either side.

Positive improvements like the new collaboration between Equality Myanmar and a network of CSOs that has begun in 2017 and 2018 lay the foundations for a new space of negotiations between the Commission, national civil society and the government—a turn which in 2016 was improbable. National civil society was reluctant to engage in any form of collaboration with MNHRC due to the heavy criticism the Commission

[13] Interview with Deputy Director of Equality Myanmar JMS on work planned for 2018 and 2019 of the human rights NGO.

[14] Burma Partnership MHNHRC Monitor. http://www.burmapartnership.org/tools-for-activists/.

was under and possibly the fear of being labeled as a forgiving human rights organization in collusion with the Commission and the government. Few were the organizations that up until then had worked with the Commission and as outlined above spearheaded a change in the realm of human rights advocacy in Myanmar introducing the policy dialogue method, namely, RWI, LWF and ICJ (MNHRC 2016: 28).

## Conclusion

As Myanmar continues along its path of transition, where there are both hopeful and worrying trends from a human rights perspective, the resistance to cultural globalization and the reactivation of a cultural protectionist stance in which minorities are seen as a barrier to the realization of a functioning Myanmar state, the MNHRC has great potential to play an effective role in assisting civil society in holding the government accountable to human rights commitments as well as providing useful guidance to government on necessary policy reform for improving the human rights situation in Myanmar.

But the pace of change for both Commission and government needs to match institutional absorptive capacity. Challenges include developing a culture of human rights and democratic governance; navigating plural legal systems; addressing issues related to federalism and governance, constitutional reform, appreciating diversity and addressing the aspirations of ethnic nationalities; ensuring equitable development; and reducing inequalities generated by market reform.

Despite the challenges, Myanmar's reforms and advancements since 2011 provide cause for balanced optimism, yet it remains to be seen what the new state councilor's plans are in relation to pushing forward on developing a culture of human rights and democratic governance in Myanmar. Having failed to become a beacon of hope, failing to fulfill expectations of its own people and that of the wider international community, Aung San Suu Kyi needs to step up. Community at large, scholars, lawyers, human rights defenders and more importantly rights violation victims, disheartened, await their political leaders in the NLD to take charge of positive improvements in the form of rights protection, better collaboration with international human rights mechanisms and political reform, where everybody is equal before the law and justice downplays military might and power.

## References

ANNI Report. 2017. Suspicious Minds: The Myanmar National Human Rights Commission's Trust Deficit, Available at https://www.forum-asia.org/uploads/wp/2017/12/ANNI-Report-2017-1.pdf.

DVB News. 2017. MNHRC Failing to Protect Human Rights says NGOs, 4 December, http://www.dvb.no/news/mnhrc-failing-to-protect-human-rights-say-ngos/78709.

Constitution of Myanmar. 2008. Chapter 8: Citizen, Fundamental Rights and Duties of the Citizens, http://extwprlegs1.fao.org/docs/pdf/mya132824.pdf.

Department for International Development (DFID). 2014. Operational Plan for Myanmar 2011–2016, Updated December 2014, Available at https://www.gov.uk/government/publications/dfid-burma-operational-plan-2014.

Equality Myanmar News. 2018. UPR Consultation Meeting with MNHRC, 23 March, Available at http://equalitymyanmar.org/upr-consultation-meeting-with-mnhrc/.

International Coordinating Committee of National Institutions for the Promotion and Protection of Human Rights. 2015. Report and Recommendations of the Session of the Sub-Committee on Accreditation (SCA) Geneva, 16–20 November, https://nhri.ohchr.org/EN/AboutUs/GANHRIAccreditation/Documents/SCA%20FINAL%20REPORT%20-%20NOVEMBER%202015-English.pdf.

Lee, Y. 2017. Special Rapporteur on the Situation of Human Rights in Myanmar, Statement at the 35th session of the Human Rights Council Agenda item 4, Geneva, 15 June 2017.

Lijleblad, J. 2017a. The 2014 enabling law of the Myanmar National Human Rights Commission and the United Nations Paris principles: A critical evaluation, Journal of East Asia & International Law, Vol. 9, no. 2, pp. 427–448.

———. 2017b. The efficacy of National Human Rights Institutions seen in context: Lessons from the Myanmar National Human Rights Commission, Yale Human Rights and Development Journal, Vol. 19, no. 1, article no. 3.

Myanmar National Human Rights Commission (MHNRC). 2016 Annual Report, Available at http://www.mnhrc.org.mm/en/publication/2016-annual-report-english/.

———. 2017. Report of activities for a (3) year period (5-9-2011 to 24-9-2014) Page 2, http://www.mnhrc.org.mm/app/uploads/2017/05/Report-for-3-years-Eng-version.pdf.

Myanmar Times. 2011. We won't be influenced by the government, Yadana Htun, 19 September 2011, Available at https://www.mmtimes.com/national-news/2090-we-won-t-be-influenced-by-the-govt.html.

———. 2016. Human Rights Commission comes under fire over record 03 February 2016, Available at https://www.mmtimes.com/opinion/18786-human-rights-commission-comes-under-fire-over-record.html.

National Human Rights Commission Of Bangladesh. 2013. The International Covenant on Civil and Political Rights: A Study on Bangladesh Compliance, March, Available at http://nhrc.portal.gov.bd/sites/default/files/files/nhrc.portal.gov.bd/page/348ec5eb_22f8_4754_bb62_6a0d15ba1513/Study%20Report%20ICCPR.pdf.

Reuters. 2013. EU lifts Myanmar sanctions despite human rights concerns, April 22, 2013, Available at https://www.reuters.com/article/us-myanmar-eu/eu-lifts-myanmar-sanctions-despite-human-rights-concerns-idUSBRE93L11G20130422.

The Guardian. 2016. Myanmar's Rohingya campaign 'may be crime against humanity', 19 December, Available at https://www.theguardian.com/world/2016/dec/19/myanmars-rohingya-campaign-may-be-against-humanity.

CHAPTER 7

# Komnas HAM: Discrepancies Between Its Mandate and the Indonesian Constitutional Framework

*Nukila Evanty*

## Introduction

This chapter argues that there is a discrepancy in the legislation that has caused the performance of the National Commission on Human Rights Indonesia (Komnas HAM) protection mandate to be suboptimal. A major issue is that the law does not clearly govern the institution of Komnas HAM. In particular, Law No. 39 of 1999 on Human Rights does not articulate a clear strategic function for Komnas HAM, resulting in many interpretations of the law's implementation. In addition, Komnas HAM also does not have strong authority under the law. Consequently, Komnas HAM can only provide recommendations that are not legally binding and can not be enforced.

This analysis contributes to emerging literature on NHRIs in Southeast Asia, surveyed in the introduction to this book (see also Faiz 2016; Crouch 2013; and Iskandar 2015). The chapter examines more specifically the understudied discrepancies between the Constitutional framework for

N. Evanty (✉)
School of Law, Atma Jaya Catholic University of Jakarta, Jakarta, Indonesia



J. Gomez, R. Ramcharan (eds.), *National Human Rights Institutions in Southeast Asia*,
https://doi.org/10.1007/978-981-15-1074-8_7

human rights and the specific mandates and powers of Komnas HAM (see generally, Government of Indonesia Constitution 1945 and Law No. 29 and 39; and Setiawan 2018).

This chapter draws on reports of the Asian NGO Network on National Human Rights Institutions (ANNI), which assess that Komnas HAM veered toward becoming an ineffective institution during the period 2012–2017 with its declining performance, although it has received an "A" rating from GANHRI (GANHRI 2017; see ANNI Reports 2012, 2014, 2015, 2016, 2017, 2018). An A rating indicates strong compliance with the Paris Principles (OHCHR 1993). The ANNI report 2017 explains the failure of Komnas HAM to formulate strategic plans. Furthermore, Komnas HAM's weakness has increased because it was not supported by government agencies and other state institutions. The chapter also analyzes the legal texts of the provisions in the problematic human rights laws that are an obstacle to the implementation of the mandate and authority of Komnas HAM in the protection of human rights, and examines the need for revision of the law that established the institution and recommendations.

Following a brief examination of challenges facing Komnas Ham, this chapter looks at needed revisions to the human rights laws, discrepancies between the Constitution and the legal mandates of Komnas Ham and the role of international standards in overcoming such discrepancies.

## Challenges to Komnas HAM

Komnas Ham, which operates in accordance with a number of laws related to human rights (see Table 7.1), faces a number of challenges (see annual reports of Komnas Ham). From Law No. 39 (1999) and Law No. 40 (2008), we can obtain a clear idea of the challenges it faces. Among the key challenges afflicting the institution, as noted by civil society, are:

- negative public perception, because of its slow response to the handling of complaints by the public;
- lack of responses of the commissioner on the substance of human rights violations reported by the public;
- neglected reports and problems among commissioners themselves;
- constraints in investigating and monitoring past human rights violations;

**Table 7.1** Human rights legislations affecting Komnas HAM

| *No.* | *Legislation* | *Issue* | *Explanation of mandate* |
|---|---|---|---|
| 1. | Law No. 39 of 1999 | On human rights | This regulation governs the role of the government and Komnas HAM in the protection and enforcement of human rights |
| 2. | Law No. 40 of 1999 | On press | This regulation governs the Press Council established to develop press freedom and improve the life of the national press |
| 3. | Law No. 26 of 2000 on Human Rights Court | On human rights court | This regulation provides for the functions and duties of Komnas HAM, the attorney and the human rights court |
| 4. | Law No. 23 of 2004 | On elimination of domestic violence | This regulation provides a mandate to the minister whose scope of duties and responsibilities are in the field of women's empowerment |
| 5. | Law No. 12 of 2006 | On citizenship | The regulation mandates the minister whose scope of duties and responsibilities are in the field of citizenship, officials appointed by the minister to deal with citizenship issues, as well as Indonesian representation abroad |
| 6. | Law No. 14 of 2008 | On the openness of public information | The Information Commission functions to enforce this law and its implementing regulations |
| 7. | Law No. 40 of 2008 | On the elimination of racial and ethnic discrimination | The National Commission on Human Rights (Komnas HAM) functions are to conduct research, extension, monitoring and mediation of human rights<br>Regulations govern the functions of the investigator, public prosecutor or judge |
| 8. | Law No. 21 of 2007 | On the eradication of human trafficking crime (PTPPO) | Regulations governing the functions of the investigator, public prosecutor, or judge |
| 9. | Government Regulation No. 56 of 2010 | On the procedures for monitoring racial and Ethnic Discrimination Efforts | This regulation mandates the National Commission on Human Rights (Komnas HAM), which functions to carry out research, counseling, monitoring and human rights mediation. Based on this regulation, Komnas HAM monitors all forms of efforts to eliminate racial and ethnic discrimination |
| 10. | Law No. 7 of 2016 | On the protection and empowerment of fishermen | This regulation provides responsibility to the central government, regional governments as well as ministers who administer government affairs in the field of marine and fisheries |

(*continued*)

**Table 7.1** (continued)

| *No.* | *Legislation* | *Issue* | *Explanation of mandate* |
|---|---|---|---|
| 11. | Law No. 31 of 2014 | On the protection of witnesses and victims | This regulation delegates the Witness and Victim Protection Agency (LPSK), the institution in charge and authorized to provide protection and other rights to witnesses and or victims |
| 12. | Law No. 35 of 2014 | On child protection | The regulation broadly assigns duties to the central government and regional governments, namely, governors, regents, and mayors as well as regional apparatus as elements of government organizers |
| 13. | Law No. 8 of 2016 | On persons with disabilities | The regulation mentions the responsibility of the National Disability Commission (KND), which is an independent nonstructural institution, then to the central government and the regional government and the minister who administers government affairs in the social field |
| 14. | Law No. 18 on 2017 | On the protection of Indonesian migrant workers | This regulation mentions several duty bearers on the issue of migrant workers; social security administering body, central government, local government, village government, representative of the government abroad, minister who conducts government affairs in the field of labor as well as non-ministerial government institutions/agencies |

- recommendations by Komnas Ham not obeyed; and
- long-standing cases under consideration remaining unresolved.[1]

Moreover, in the context of the Constitution, discrepancies exist between the human rights laws and related laws in connection with human rights protection, with the new commissioners, the weak power of

[1] Review of Komnas HAM 2012–2017. The NGOs Coalition comprises the Indonesian Legal Aid Foundation (YLBHI), the Commission for the Disappeared and Victims of Violence (Kontras), Lembaga Studi dan Advokasi Masyarakat (Elsam), the Indonesia Corruption Watch (ICW), the Walhi Environmental Forum (Walhi) and a number of other organizations.

Komnas HAM and its recommendations. Collectively, these point to a weak institution that is not yet able to effectively protect human rights (see Komnas Ham Reports).

A particularly telling indicator of the weakness of Komnas HAM is the fact that it only recommended three cases of gross human rights violations to the Court. These are: (1) the "Abepura" case, 7 December 2000 on the occurrence of gross human rights violations committed through a systematic and widespread form of torture, summary killings, persecution, unlawful arrest, detention and involuntary displace persons by suspected security personnel; (2) the " Tanjung Priok " incident which was a siege against Muslims in Tanjun Priok in 12 September 1984. Both gross human rights violations were established based on Presidential Decree (Keppres) No. 53/2001, which was renewed by Presidential Decree No. 96/2001; and (3) the incidents of gross violation of human rights in East Timor by elements of the security apparatus.

Hence, Komnas HAM established the Commission of Inquiry on Human Rights Violations (KPP-HAM) in East Timor on 18 September 1999. Komnas HAM accomplished investigations in the past, such as Talangsari case (1998), Semanggi I and II cases (1998–1999), Trisakti case (1998), Wamena case (2000) and Wasior case (2001), and recommended them to the Attorney General's Office (AGO), which is the relevant ad hoc human rights court for the cases. However, the formation of such human rights courts was hindered by the unwillingness of the Attorney General's Office to prosecute these cases (ICG Asia Report 2001).

## Legal Challenges Facing Komnas HAM

Komnas HAM in its report to the Universal Periodic Review (UPR) stated that it needs to be strengthened through a separation of the Human Rights Law from a proposed new law that would govern Komnas HAM.[2] The following sections describe the laws that mention the Mandate of Komnas HAM and concurrently outline its challenges.

[2] Submission to the United Nations Third Universal Periodic Review, 27th Session of the Working Group on the UPR Human Rights Council, September 2016, The Indonesian National Human Rights Commission (Komnas HAM).

### *Law No. 39 of 1999 on Human Rights*

The functions, works and authority of Komnas HAM are found in Article 76 (1) (Functions) and Article 89 (Works and Authority). Each one has specific challenges.

*Assessment and Research*

A key function is to conduct assessment and research for the purpose of providing advice on the possibility of accession and ratification of international agreements to provide recommendations on the enactment, amendment and revocation of laws relating to human rights, and to publish the results of the study and research. In the course of this function, Komnas HAM can conduct desk studies, field studies and comparative studies in other countries on human rights. It can conduct discussions related to the protection, enforcement and promotion of human rights. It can also collaborate with other organizations, institutions or parties, at national, regional, and international levels on the subject of human rights.

Key challenges in these areas are as follows: the government has a National Action Plan on Human Rights, referred to the NAPHR[3] (National Action Plan on Human Rights) which is regulated under Presidential Regulation No. 5 of 2015 on National Action Plans on Human Rights 2015–2019. The NAPHR contains targets, strategies and priority actions and is regulated by the central government, and local governments who are supposed to promote, protect and ensure the fulfillment of human rights in Indonesia. One of its task functions is the preparation and ratification of draft reports on the implementation of international human rights instruments. Komnas HAM has not been fully involved in the process of achieving the NAHPR, especially in the functions and authorities in the assessment and research. Komnas HAM should be active in conducting an assessment of the implementation of international human rights instruments that have been ratified by Indonesia.[4] The

[3] National Action Plan on Human Rights is regulated under Presidential Regulation No. 5 of 2015 on National Action Plans on Human Rights 2015–2019.

[4] PemerintahIndonesia telah meratifikasi 8 instrumen kunci hukum HAM internasional, yakni: International Covenant on Civil and Political Rights (ICCPR), International Covenant on Economic, Social and Cultural Rights (ICESCR), International Convention on the Elimination of All Forms of Racial Discrimination (ICERD), Convention on the Elimination of All Forms of Discrimination against Women (CEDAW), Convention Against Torture and Other Cruel, Inhuman or Degrading Treatment or Punishment (CAT), Convention on the Rights of the Child (CRC), International Convention on the Protection of the Rights of All

government of Indonesia has already ratified eight key international human rights law instruments. Besides that, Komnas HAM has not played a role in disseminating UPR recommendations and treaty body recommendations[5] to government and state agencies.

*Counseling*

Komnas HAM is mandated to disseminate human rights issues to increase public awareness and to cooperate with international and domestic organizations in the field of human rights. It is active in providing counseling on human rights including educational cooperation with law enforcement, universities, UN human rights agencies and others.

*Monitoring*

Komnas HAM is mandated to observe the implementation of human rights and the compilation of reports of observations, to investigate and examine incidents which by their nature or scope are reasonably suspected of constituting human rights violations, to summon the complainant, victim or the alleged violator for questioning and to call witnesses, to review facts at the scene and other places deemed necessary, to call for the parties concerned to provide written information or to submit the necessary documents in accordance with the original document with the approval of the Chief Justice, to examine relevant premises with the approval of the Chief Justice; and to give its opinion based on the approval of the Chief Justice of a particular case that is in the judicial process.

Komnas HAM's obstacle lies in summoning the complainant, victim, witness, or other parties. In the event that a person who has been summoned is absent or refuses to give his or her testimony, Komnas HAM needs to seek out the assistance of the Chief Justice for forced summons in accordance with the provisions of the law.

Migrant Workers and Members of their Families (CMW), Convention on the Rights of Person with Disabilities (CRPD).

[5] Available at http://www.ohchr.org/EN/HRBodies/Pages/TreatyBodies.aspx. The human rights treaty bodies are committees of independent experts that monitor implementation of the core international human rights treaties. Each state party to a treaty has an obligation to take steps to ensure that everyone in the state can enjoy the rights set out in the treaty. There are ten human rights treaty bodies composed of independent experts of recognized competence in human rights, who are nominated and elected for fixed renewable terms of four years by state parties.

*Mediation*

The Commission may mediate in order to achieve peace between parties in conflict. Case settlement may be achieved through consultation, negotiation, mediation, conciliation and expert judgment. It may provide advice to parties to resolve disputes through courts or submit a recommendation on a case of human rights violation to the government for follow-up to its resolution and to the House of Representatives for follow-up.

The mediation settlement is a written agreement signed by the parties and confirmed by the mediator, however Komnas HAM is incapable of enforcing it even though such mediation decision is legally binding and is considered valid evidence. Therefore, if a mediation decision is not executed by either party within the time period stipulated in the decision, the other party may submit a request to the local District Court to make such decision declared workable.

### *Law No. 40 of 2008 on the Elimination of Racial and Ethnic Discrimination*

Law No. 40 of 2008 on the Elimination of Racial and Ethnic Discrimination recognizes the function of Komnas HAM as an independent institution which conducts research, studies, counseling, monitoring and human rights mediation. It must monitor all efforts to eliminate racial and ethnic discrimination.

The monitoring of Komnas HAM includes monitoring and assessing policies at all levels of government that may give rise to racial and ethnic discrimination. It has similar functions to Law No. 39 of 1999 on Human Rights, namely to conduct fact finding, to make recommendation to the central government and regional governments on the results of monitoring and assessment of laws containing racial and ethnic discrimination, to monitor and assess central government, local governments and communities in the implementation of the elimination of racial and ethnic discrimination; and to give recommendation to the House of Representatives of the Republic of Indonesia to supervise the government that does not obey the findings of Komnas HAM.

The challenges are obvious here. Difficulties encountered include the actual conduct, monitoring and assessment of government policies and local government given resource constraints, of gathering credible facts from suspected persons, obtaining government cooperation and getting Parliament to act as the latter does not heed the findings of Komnas HAM.

Based on a review of several human rights laws already mentioned, only four of the laws stipulate the function and role of Komnas HAM clearly, which are Law no. 39 of 1999 on Human Rights, Law No. 26 of 2000 on Human Rights Courts, Law No. 40 of 2008 on the Elimination of Racial and Ethnic Discrimination, and Government Regulation no. 56 of 2010 on the procedures for monitoring racial and ethnic discrimination efforts.

The exclusion of Komnas HAM as the implementer of the law on human rights indicates that the state has not placed Komnas HAM as a partner in the protection of human rights and the low level of political support for Komnas HAM because the government prefers other commissions, institutions or ministries as implementers of a law on human rights.

## Revising the Human Rights Law(s)

There are two reasons necessitating revisions to the Human Rights Law. First, the 1945 Constitution in Article 1(3) clearly stipulates that Indonesia is governed by the rule of law. In addition to that, the 1945 Constitution states that human rights should be upheld in accordance with the principles of a democratic and law-based state. Hence, the human rights law should contain constitutional issues. However, the Human Rights Law No. 39 of 1999 was formulated before the second amendment of 2000 of the 1945 Constitution. The new amendment introduced an expanded list of human rights under Chapter XA Articles 28A to 28J[6] which have not been listed in the previous version of the 1945 Constitution.

The 1945 Constitution, Article 28I, paragraph (4) mentions: "The protection, promotion, enforcement and fulfillment of human rights is the responsibility of the State, particularly the government." Paragraph (5) states: "To uphold and protect human rights in accordance with the principles of a democratic constitutional State, the implementation of human rights is guaranteed, regulated, and set forth in the laws and regulations."

[6] Articles 28A–28J 1945 Constitution regulates the right to life, the right to form a family and to continue the offspring, the child is entitled to protection from violence and discrimination, the right to education, the protection of the law, the right to receive fair remuneration in the employment relationship, the freedom of every believer in trust, the right to adequate health services, the right not to be tortured, the right to religion, the right not to be enslaved and others.

Thus the 1945 Constitution explicitly mandates the state, in particular the government to be responsible for the protection, promotion, enforcement, and fulfillment of human rights on the principles of democratic state law, whose implementation is guaranteed, regulated in legislation. This is in line with Article 2 of Law No. 39 of 1999 on Human Rights, which states:

> The State of the Republic of Indonesia recognizes and upholds human rights and basic human freedoms as rights which are inherent in nature and inseparable from human beings, which must be protected, respected and enforced for the enhancement of human dignity, prosperity, happiness, intelligence and justice.

Then Article 71 of Law No. 39 of 1999 mentions:

> The Government shall be responsible for respecting, protecting, upholding and promoting the human rights provided for in this Law, other laws and regulations and international human rights law adopted by the Republic of Indonesia.

Furthermore, Article 72 of Law No. 39 of 1999 states:

> The obligations and responsibilities of the Government as referred to in Article 71 shall include effective implementation steps in the legal, political, economic, social, cultural, defense and security of the country and other fields.

The second reason is that the Human Rights Law(s) is considered not to meet the standards as stipulated in the Paris Principles. The core instrument relevant to NHRIs at the international level is the United Nations Principles relating to the Paris Principles.[7] The Paris Principles established the minimum international standards (competence, structure, working procedures) required for the independence and effective functioning of NHRIs. These principles provide guidance on the role that NHRIs are expected to perform and to be independent from government and civil society. They address aspects of promotion and protection of the mandate and even provide some direction about the quasi-jurisdictional competence

[7] Principles relating to the status of national institutions (the Paris Principles), GA Resolution 48/134 20 December 1993.

of NHRIs that owns such powers; as a general feature of some NHRIs in Asia. Principle 3 of Paris Principles mentions:

> A national institution shall, inter alia, have the following responsibilities:
> (a) submitting opinions, recommendations, proposals and reports on any matters concerning the promotion and protection of human rights, including with respect to: (i) Legislative or administrative provisions: the national institution shall examine the legislation and administrative provisions in force, as well as bills and proposals, and shall make such recommendations as it deems appropriate in order to ensure that these provisions conform to the fundamental principles of human rights.

Article 76 of Law No. 39 of 1999 stipulates that "to achieve its objectives, Komnas HAM carries out the functions of study, research, counseling, monitoring and mediation on human rights."

However, there is no regulation on the authority of Komnas HAM to summon the parties and there is no sanction for witnesses who are unwilling to be summoned in the articles of the Human Rights Law. Although Komnas HAM has the function of upholding human rights, it is legally limited to enforcing recommendations and has no ability to bring cases to the administrative law bodies or legal enforcement institutions hence rules governing the explicit position of Komnas HAM are required in order to provide certainty when Komnas HAM carries out its mandate.

## Discrepancies Between the Constitution and the Legal Mandate of Komnas HAM

In light of the preceding analysis, this section examines key aspects of the mandate of Komnas HAM in order to demonstrate how they must be improved in line with the current Constitution of Indonesia.

Komnas HAM was established based on Law No. 39 of 1999 on Human Rights. Key problems lie with the mandate of Komnas HAM that renders it incompatible with the Constitution, and the weak capacity to investigate gross violations of human rights.

Article 89 of the Law No 39 of 1999 on Human Rights stipulates, inter alia, that in carrying out Komnas HAM's functions in mediation, the duties and authorities of Komnas HAM may be exercised through (a) arbitration; (b) settlement of cases by means of consultation, negotiation, mediation, conciliation and expert judgment; (c) advising the parties to settle disputes through courts; (d) submitting a recommendation on a case of human rights violation to the government for follow-up to its resolution; (e) submitting a recommendation on a human rights violation to the House of Representatives of the Republic of Indonesia for follow-up.

Therefore, as stipulated in Article 89, Komnas HAM may issue recommendations after a mediation process. Outside the mediation process the Human Rights Law does not regulate further on whether Komnas HAM may issue recommendations or not. In practice, however, recommendations may be issued after Komnas HAM has conducted monitoring tasks. This poses a problem because the parties can reject the recommendation on the grounds that it is not strictly regulated in the Human Rights Law.

Komnas HAM is not authorized to investigate the findings of human rights violations in the field. The authority of Komnas HAM merely conducts research, monitoring and investigation as well as issuing recommendations. The Human Rights Law does not give any consequences if the party concerned does not carry out the recommendation. Article 95 of the Human Rights Law states that *"[i]f a person who is summoned does not come to face or refuse to give his statement, Komnas HAM may request the assistance of the Chief Justice for the enforcement of forced vocations in accordance with the provisions of the law."*

The Human Rights Law does not give Komnas HAM *explicit* authority to call the alleged perpetrators of human rights violations or question other parties, nor the power to enforce.

The importance of the revision of the Human Rights Law is that Komnas HAM is only regulated in Law No. 26 of 2000 on Human Rights Courts and Law No. 40 of 2008 on the Elimination of Racial and Ethnic Discrimination. Law No. 26 of 2000 on Human Rights Courts, in general, regulates two matters, first, the regulation of criminal acts categorized as serious human rights violations, which covers the crime of genocide and crimes against humanity generally derived from the Rome Statute, while the procedural laws govern arrest, detention, investigation, prosecution, examination in the hearing and the terms of appointment of judges to the provisions of execution. Law No. 26 in Article 18 (1) mentions, *"The National Human Rights Commission (Komnas HAM) in conducting investigations may establish an* ad hoc *team comprising the National Commission on Human Rights and the community element.* With Law No. 26 of 2000, Komnas HAM is the only institution with authority to investigate gross human rights violations.

However, the attempts to prosecute gross violations of human rights are hampered by Article 43 of the Human Rights Court Law (2), which mentions:

> The ad hoc Human Rights Court as referred to in paragraph (1) shall be established upon the proposal of the House of Representatives of the Republic of Indonesia based on certain events by Presidential Decree.

Furthermore, Article 43 (2) of the Human Rights Court Law explicitly states, "In the case of the House of Representatives (DPR) proposing the establishment of an ad hoc human rights court, therefore the House should be based on allegations of serious human rights violations restricted to locus delicti or the scene of the crime that occurred prior to the enactment of Law." This means that for any serious human rights violations that occurred "before" Law No. 26/2000 was established, the DPR should recommend or propose the establishment of an ad hoc human rights court adjudicating the alleged cases of gross human rights violations based on the findings of Komnas HAM and the Attorney General.

In addition to that, Komnas HAM recommendations are hampered by the Attorney General authorities when it is not followed up with investigation. The construction of Law No. 26 of 2000 mentions Komnas HAM as "pro justitia" (a Latin phrase "on behalf of justice") investigator and the Attorney General (AGO) is an investigator of cases of gross human rights violations. The separation between implementing agencies of investigation and prosecution functions, such as pursuing serious violation of human rights under Law No. 26 of 2000, results in a lack of effective protective relationship between the two institutions, as can be seen in the Table 7.1 (see Soeprapto 2011).

## *Law No. 26/2000 on Human Rights Courts*

A discussion of Law No. 26 further highlights the difficulties faced by Komnas HAM. These can be seen by examining the mandate of Komnas HAM and the role of the attorney counsel. Challenges are distilled from this contrast.

### *Mandate of Komnas HAM*

Investigation of gross human rights violations is conducted by the National Commission on Human Rights. Komnas HAM may establish an ad hoc team comprising members of the Commission itself and community representatives. In carrying out such investigations, the Komnas HAM researcher is authorized:

(a) to conduct an investigation and examination of events arising in a society which by its nature or scope is reasonably suspected of gross violations of human rights;
(b) to receive reports or complaints from a person or group of people about the occurrence of gross violations of human rights, and to seek information and evidence;
(c) to call the complainant, victim, or complainant to be solicited and heard;
(d) to summon witnesses to be asked and heard his or her testimony;
(e) to review and collect information on the scene and other places deemed necessary;
(f) to call the parties concerned to provide written information or submit the necessary documents in accordance with the original one.

On the orders of the investigator, following actions may take place:

(a) mail examination;
(b) search and seizure;
(c) local examination of the house, yard, buildings and other places occupied or owned by certain parties;
(d) bring in experts in connection with the investigation.

In case the Komnas HAM researcher starts investigating an event that is suspected to be a gross human rights violation, the researcher informs the person responsible—the investigator.

In case Komnas HAM finds that there is sufficient initial evidence of serious human rights violations, the conclusions of the investigation shall be submitted to the investigator. No later than seven working days after the conclusion of the investigation is submitted, Komnas HAM submits the full investigation to the investigator.

In the event that the investigator believes that the results of the investigation are still incomplete, the investigator shall promptly return the results of the investigation to the Komnas HAM researcher with instructions to be completed. Within 30 days from the date of receipt of the investigation results the Komnas HAM researcher shall supplement the deficiency.

Komnas HAM may at any time submit a written request to the prosecutor general regarding the progress of the investigation and prosecution of cases of gross violations of human rights.

*Mandate of Attorney General*

The Attorney General as the investigator is authorized to make arrests for the purpose of investigating a person alleged to have committed gross human rights violations on the basis of sufficient initial evidence. The execution of the duty of arrest is carried out by the investigator by showing the assignment letter and giving the suspect an arrest warrant mentioning the identity of the suspect, the reason of the arrest, the place of the examination and the brief description of the case of gross violation of human rights which is suspected.

The Attorney General as investigator and prosecutor has the authority to arrange the extension for investigation and prosecution or detain. The judge of the human rights court with his/her determination is authorized to hold detention for the purpose of examination in court. The investigation of cases of gross human rights violations is conducted by the Attorney General. The investigation does not include the authority to receive reports or complaints. In the performance of this task, the Attorney General may appoint an ad hoc investigator composed of government and/or community representatives. The prosecution of cases of gross human rights violations is conducted by the Attorney General. In the performance of such duties, the Attorney General may appoint an ad hoc public prosecutor comprising government and/or community representatives.

*Challenges*

The authority of Komnas HAM is limited by the authority and powers of the Attorney General. Komnas HAM can only conduct mail examination; search and seizure; local examination of houses, yards, buildings and other places occupied or owned by certain parties; bring in experts in connection with the investigation on the order of the investigator (Attorney General).

When Komnas HAM begins to investigate an incident that was allegedly a gross violation of human rights, Komnas HAM informs the investigator (Attorney General). The Attorney General has a clear duty in detaining, continuing detention and prosecuting the case.

Komnas HAM relies heavily on investigators (Prosecutor's Office) for the confirmation of preliminary evidence showing that there have been considerable incidents of gross violations of human rights.

Three cases of serious or gross human rights violations have been resolved by the Indonesian human rights courts: the East Timor 1999 case and Tanjung Priok 1984 cases were handled by the Jakarta Ad Hoc Human Rights Court, and the Abepura 2000 gross human rights violation case was handled by the Makassar Human Rights Court (Komnas HAM reports). The law also has a fundamental weakness, since the crime of genocide and crimes against humanity is a category of international crimes handled directly by the International Criminal Court and it does not fall within the jurisdiction of human rights courts. Human rights courts are different conceptually from the International Criminal Court. The weakness of Law No. 26 of 2000 is the conceptually deliberately misplaced, incorrect, and even intentional law made to legalize past human rights violations through the court (Suparman 2010) Next, Law No. 40 of 2008 mentions in Article 8 (1):

> "Supervision of all forms of efforts to eliminate racial and ethnic discrimination by Komnas HAM". (2) "Supervision as referred to in paragraph (1) shall include:
>
> (a) monitoring and assessing the policies of the government and local government that are deemed to have the potential to cause racial and ethnic discrimination,
> (b) fact finding and assessment to individuals, community groups or public institutions or private sector alleged to engage in racial and ethnic discrimination,
> (c) recommendation to the government and local government on the results of monitoring and assessment of acts that contain racial and ethnic discrimination,
> (d) monitoring and assessment of government, local government and community in the implementation of elimination of discrimination race and ethnicity, and
> (e) recommendation to the House of Representatives of the Republic of Indonesia to supervise the government that ignores the findings of Komnas HAM."

With the existence of Law No. 40 of 2008, the mandate of Komnas HAM was broadened. The purpose of the provisions of the supervisory function of Law No. 40 of 2008 is that Komnas HAM evaluates the central and regional government policies that are conducted periodically or incidentally by monitoring, fact-finding, assessing whether or not racial and ethnic discrimination is followed up with recommendations. Law No. 40 of 2008 is a regulation governing the substance of the Convention on the Elimination of Racial Discrimination which has been ratified by the state. Hence, any state that has ratified an international human rights covenant such as the International Covenant on Civil and Political Rights (ICCPR) should provide the role of Komnas HAM for oversight and enforcement through legislation. According to the Paris Principles, the mandate of the National Human Rights Commission should be as broad as possible. A broad mandate means that the institution possesses the power to investigate human rights. However, in the context outlined above, these conditions make Komnas HAM unable to solve human rights issues submitted by the community. Komnas HAM should be given a stronger mandate and the power to act to resolve human rights violations since the majority of human rights violators are committed by the government and armed apparatus. Therefore, the only institution capable of conducting examinations related to human rights violations committed by government institutions is Komnas HAM.

## Enforcing International Standards: An Opportunity to Overcome Discrepancies

An opportunity for Komnas HAM in overcoming such weaknesses lies in the increasing adherence of Indonesia to international human rights standards. They are powerful tools with which to bring about the legal and procedural changes to bring KOMNAS Ham in line with the Constitutional framework for human rights. Close coordination with the UN Office of the High Commissioner for Human Rights and the UPR process is warranted. In this vein the former high commissioner for human rights encouraged Indonesia to strengthen its national human rights mechanism as well as to follow up and report on its international and regional treaty obligations (OHCHR 2017).

Komnas HAM uses various national and international human rights instruments that are binding and nonbinding as its reference in performing functions, duties and authorities. Indonesia has accessed and ratified eight of nine international human rights treaties. These several provisions of international human rights laws that should be the legal references of Komnas HAM are:

1. Universal Declaration of Human Rights (UDHR), 1948.
2. International Covenant on Civil and Political Rights (ICCPR), 1966, ratified by Law No. 12 of 2005.
3. International Covenant on Economic, Social and Cultural Rights (ICESCR), 1966, ratified by Law No. 11 of 2005.
4. The International Convention on the Elimination of Racial Discrimination (ICERD), 1965, was ratified by Law No. 29 of 1999.
5. The International Convention on the Elimination of Discrimination Against Women (CEDAW), 1979, was ratified by Law no. 7 of 1984;
6. The International Convention Against Torture and Cruel, Inhuman or Degrading Treatment or Punishment (CAT), 1984, was ratified by Law No. 5 of 1998.
7. Convention on the Rights of the Child (CRC), 1989, ratified by Law No. 10 of 2012.
8. The International Convention on the Rights of Persons with Disabilities (ICRPD), ratified by Law No. 19 of 2011.
9. The International Convention for the Protection of Migrant Workers and Their Families (ICMW), 1990, was ratified by Law No. 6 of 2012.

During the third cycle of the UPR, Komnas HAM recommended that Indonesia should ratify the Optional protocol of the Convention Against Torture, the Rome Statute of the International Criminal Court and the International Convention on the Protection of All Persons from Enforced Disappearance and the OP-CRPD (UN General Assembly 2017).

Article 7 of Law No. 39 of 1999 on Human Rights provides an opportunity for provisions of international law that have been ratified for promulgation into national law. This mechanism is called the treaty-based mechanism, a grievance mechanism established under international human rights treaties or conventions. Such agreements are only valid and binding for a country that has signed and ratified them. As is well known, for example, Indonesia submits reports to the Human Rights Committee (HRC) established under the 1976 International Covenant on Civil and Political Rights (ICCPR) ratified by Indonesia through Law No. 12 of 2005 on the Ratification of the International Covenant on Civil and Political Rights (International Covenant on Civil and Political Rights).

Over the period 2010–2015, it has reported to: Committee on the Elimination of All Forms of Discrimination against Women (CEDAW), New York, 11 July 2012; United Nations Civil and Political Rights Committee (CCPR), Geneva, 10–11 July 2013; United Nations Committee on Economic, Social and Cultural Rights (CESCR), Geneva, 30 April to 1 May 2014; and the United Nations Child Rights Committee (CRC), Geneva, 5 June 2014 (Ministry of Foreign Affairs 2019).

Greater compliance with international standards will undoubtedly be of benefit given that, as provided in Article 7 of Law 39 (1999) Concerning Human Rights:

1. Everyone has the right to use all effective national legal means and international forums against all violations of human rights guaranteed under Indonesian law, and under international law concerning human rights which has been ratified by Indonesia.
2. Provisions set forth in international law concerning human rights ratified by the Republic of Indonesia are recognized under this Act as legally binding in Indonesia.

## Conclusions

This chapter has shown that Law No. 39 of 1999 on Human Rights has a fundamental weakness, namely, the limitation of the mandate, role and function of Komnas HAM itself. Hence, the law stipulates powers possessed by Komnas HAM but the authority is very weak because the law does not provide recommendations that have legally binding powers for Komnas HAM. Moreover, some of the authority possessed by Komnas HAM is perceived as insufficient and ineffective in its efforts to protect human rights.

Therefore, to enhance and strengthen the effectiveness of Komnas HAM apart from strengthening its existing authority, the following legal arrangements must be made. Firstly, to strengthen the mandate to subpoena someone to appear in legal proceeding and Komnas HAM's power to request the production of documents by Komnas HAM should be authorized to request assistance from law enforcement agencies to present the concerned person by force. Secondly, Komnas HAM should be able to conduct an investigation into cases of human rights violations with full powers, unfettered by powers of the Attorney General's Office. Thirdly, reforms must give more authority to Komnas HAM as a recommender to the president for the establishment of an ad hoc human rights court for cases of gross human rights violations and replacing the role of the House of Representatives (DPR) as a political institution whose involvement in the legal process of handling cases of human rights violations is not appropriate. Fourthly, there is a need for regulation in the law allowing binding obligations upon the parties receiving recommendations from Komnas HAM to implement the recommendations. If the recipient of the recommendation rejects some or all of the recommendations, it shall explain its rejection in writing to Komnas HAM in a certain period. If Komnas HAM can not accept the reason of the recipients of the recommendations, Komnas HAM may file a court decision. Fifthly, there is a need for a provision on how Komnas HAM is building networks with civil society (NGOs) or other state institutions in coordinating and implementing its recommendations.

Together, these will bring the mandate of Komnas HAM more in line with the overall constitutional framework on human rights in Indonesia. These changes are necessary in light of the fact that Komnas HAM faces considerable challenges in its ability to adequately protect human rights of Indonesian citizens. Among the human rights challenges that affect its work, as noted by stakeholders in the 2017 UPR (third cycle) review of Indonesia, are:

- members of law enforcement agencies or investigative bodies regularly subjected Indonesian lawyers to improper interference or attempts to put pressure on them;
- lawyers were victims of threats, intimidation and physical attacks, including by members of law enforcement agencies or investigative bodies;
- impunity was still firmly entrenched and perpetrators of human rights violations were not brought to legal proceedings;
- lack of an independent, effective, and impartial oversight mechanism to investigate human rights violations committed by the security forces and to take forward its findings in prosecution (UN General Assembly 2017, paras 32–35).

Improving Komnas Ham's powers and performance is a pressing task in light of ongoing critical human rights assessment by civil society groups, notably Amnesty International. The latter has noted in the lead up to elections in Indonesia in 2019, that despite some progress since 1998:

> Indonesia's human rights record in many areas has been floundering, including ongoing human rights violations committed by the security forces; undue restrictions in law and practice on the rights to freedom of expression and freedom of religion; entrenched gender-based discrimination and other violations of women's human rights; failure to ensure justice, truth and reparation for past abuses; ongoing human rights violations in Papua; and the continued use of the death penalty. (Amnesty International 2019; 5)

## References


Amnesty International. 2019. Rights Now. 9-POINT HUMAN RIGHTS AGENDA FOR INDONESIA'S ELECTION CANDIDATES. Available at https://www.amnesty.org/download/Documents/ASA2101532019ENGLISH.PDF.

Asian NGO Network on National Human Rights Institutions (ANNI). 2012. ANNI Report on the Performance and Establishment of National Human Rights Institutions in Asia. Forum Asia.

———. 2014. ANNI Report on the Performance and Establishment of National Human Rights Institutions in Asia. Forum Asia.

———. 2015. ANNI Report on the Performance and Establishment of National Human Rights Institutions in Asia. Forum Asia.

———. 2016. ANNI Report on the Performance and Establishment of National Human Rights Institutions in Asia. Forum Asia.

———. 2017. ANNI Report on the Performance and Establishment of National Human Rights Institutions in Asia. Forum Asia.

———. 2018. ANNI Report on the Performance and Establishment of National Human Rights Institutions in Asia. Forum Asia.

Crouch, M.A. 2013. Asian Legal Transplants and Rule of Law Reform: National Human Rights Commission in Myanmar and Indonesia. *5 Hague Journal on the Rule of Law*, pp. 146–177.

Faiz, Pan Mohamad. 2016. The Protection of Civil and Political Rights by the Constitutional Court of Indonesia. *Indonesia Law Review*, vol. 6, no. 2, pp. 159–179, 2016. Available at SSRN: https://ssrn.com/abstract=2838900.

Global Alliance of National Human Rights Institutions (GANHRI). 2017. *Report and Recommendation of the Session of the Sub-Committee on Accreditation (SCA)*. Geneva. 13–17 March 2017. Available at https://nhri.ohchr.org/EN/AboutUs/GANHRIAccreditation/Documents/SCA%20Final%20Report%20-%20March%202017-%20English.pdf.

Government of Indonesian Constitution. 1945. Secretariat General MPR RI, 2011.
ICG Asia Report. 2001. Indonesia: Impunity versus Accountability for Gross Human Rights Violations, ICG Asia Report N° 12 Jakarta/Brussels.
Iskandar, P. 2015. *Reclaiming Human Rights Universality in 'Nonconstitutional' Constitution: Toward a New Reading of the 1945 Constitution*. April 4. Available at SSRN: https://ssrn.com/abstract=2589985 or https://doi.org/10.2139/ssrn.2589985.
Komnas HAM. Various reports. Available at https://www.komnasham.go.id/index.php/laporan-tahunan/.
Ministry of Foreign Affairs of Indonesia. 2019. Indonesia and Human Rights. 5 August. Available at https://kemlu.go.id/portal/en/read/97/halaman_list_lainnya/indonesia-and-human-rights.
Office of the High Commissioner for Human Rights (OHCHR). 1993. Principles Relating to the Status of National Institutions (Paris Principles). 1993. Adopted by General Assembly Resolution 48/134 of 20 December 1993, OHCHR. Available at http://www.ohchr.org/EN/ProfessionalInterest/Pages/StatusOfNationalInstitutions.aspx ), available also at https://www.un.org/ruleoflaw/files/PRINCI~5.PDF.
———. 2017. Letter from UN High Commissioner for Human Rights to Indonesian Foreign Minister. 23 October 2017. Available at https://lib.ohchr.org/HRBodies/UPR/Documents/Session27/ID/IndonesiaHCLetter.pdf.
Setiawan, K. 2018. Between Law, Politics and Memory: The Indonesian National Commission on Human Rights (Komnas Ham) and Justice for Past Human Rights Crimes. August 28. *Australian Journal of Asian Law*. vol. 19, no. 1, article 8, 2018. Available at SSRN: https://ssrn.com/abstract=3239774.
Soeprapto, E. 2011. Review Law No. 26 of 2000 on the Human Rights Court. Paper presented at Advanced Human Rights Training for Lecturer of Law and Human Rights, *Center for Human Rights Studies of Universities Islam Indonesia (PUSHAM UII) in collaboration with Norwegian Center for Human Rights (NCR), University of Oslo*, Yogyakarta June 8–10, 2011, pp. 23–26.
Suparman M. 2010. Politics of Human Rights Law in Indonesia in the Reform Era (Study of the Enforcement of human rights laws in the Settlement of Past Human Rights Violations), Yogyakarta: *Summary of Dissertation of Doctoral Program of Legal Science of Post Graduate Program of Faculty of Law UII*, 2010, pp. 43–55.
UN General Assembly. 2017. Summary of stakeholders' submissions on Indonesia, Report of the Office of the United Nations High Commissioner for Human Rights. 20 February. A/HRC/WG.6/27/IDN/3.

CHAPTER 8

# Strengthening Komnas HAM and Building Synergies with Other National State Institutions on Human Rights

*Inosentius Samsul*

## Introduction

This chapter builds on emerging literature on NHRIs noted in the Introduction and in Chap. 6. It argues that, despite the creation of Komnas HAM as an independent institution with more powers compared with other national rights bodies, Komnas HAM has not been able to produce results in terms of protection of human rights in Indonesia. In addition, Komnas HAM competes with other national institutions for the protection of rights, but such institutions are self-running, not consolidated and therefore unable to improve the protection and enforcement of human rights in Indonesia. A much-understudied aspect of the national human rights architecture in Indonesia is the lack of synergy between national commissions, government institutions, and the community in strengthening the protection of people's rights. Building synergy is a necessity. This chapter seeks to address this gap in the literature. A 2018 report on research on the effectiveness of NHRIs by the Danish Institute for Human

I. Samsul (✉)
Faculty of Law, University of Indonesia, Depok, Indonesia



J. Gomez, R. Ramcharan (eds.), *National Human Rights Institutions in Southeast Asia*,
https://doi.org/10.1007/978-981-15-1074-8_8

Rights noted that between 1996 and 2017, a total of three works were produced on Indonesia's Komnas HAM (Jensen 2018). It also notes some attention to the interaction between national commissions. This and other works are therefore timely additions to this literature.

Research questions guiding this chapter include: Why is Komnas HAM not able to perform its expected mandate? What synergies exist between Komnas Perempuan and KPAI (Komisi Perlindungan Anak Indonesia) based on their mandate, position, function, and coordination? How is the relationship and division of tasks and functions between the commissions of human rights protection and other government agencies such as the witness and victim protection agency, the Ministry of Law and Human Rights (MLHR), and the Ministry of Foreign Affairs (MFA)? What measures are needed to support Komnas HAM to carry out its duties and authorities as the leading national human rights institution?

Based on Article 28 I, Paragraph 4, of the 1945 Constitution, protection, promotion, enforcement, and fulfillment of human rights are the responsibility of the state; thus the 1945 Constitution provides the normative foundation for the establishment of Komnas HAM as an independent institution. Then, the government ratified Law No. 39 of 1999 on Human Rights as the legal basis for the establishment of Komnas HAM. Therefore, Komnas HAM is a state auxiliary agency, or in the parlance of the Paris Principles and in this chapter, the term NHRI (or national human rights institution) applies (GA Resolution 48/134, 1993). From Law No. 39 of 1999 on Human Rights, it can be observed that the position of Komnas HAM is an independent institution which helps the government develop conditions conducive to protect human rights in Indonesia. Komnas Ham falls under the purview of the president and the House of Representatives.

NHRIs include the National Commission on Violence Against Women (Komnas Perempuan) and National Commission on Child Protection (KPAI). This qualitative study draws on primary sources and legal texts, as well as secondary work by experts in the field.

The chapter, which undertakes an original, textual analysis of relevant laws, proceeds by highlighting the political context on the establishment of the rights institutions, on synergies between Komnas HAM and other human rights institutions, NGOS and civil society, and examines challenges to fulfilling the mandate of Komnas HAM and recommendations for its improvement.

## The Political Context

As noted in the introduction to this work, NHRIs were established in the political contexts by which governments needed to improve their human rights image. Indonesia was no exception.

Politically, the history of Indonesian government was divided into three eras, namely, the era of the old order under President Soekarno, the new order era under President Soeharto, and the reform era under the governments of several presidents, namely, President B. J. Habibie, President Abdurahman Wahid, President Megawati Soekarno Puteri, President Susilo Bambang Yudhoyono, and President Djoko Widodo. The three successive rounds of governments were intimately connected to the evolution and growth of political development of Indonesia's nation building—that recognized its independence—to the stage of industrialization (Organski, in S. Amran Tasai 2010: 40). The most important for the history and policy of human rights protection in Indonesia was Indonesia's independence, which was declared only 3 years prior to the Universal Declaration of Human Rights (UDHR) in 1948. Therefore, human rights have been debated since the preparation of Indonesian independence (Satya 2008: 6). Subsequently, many international human rights instruments were incorporated into the 1945 Constitution. The second amendment of the Constitution in 2000 adopted more articles on human rights. The ratification of eight United Nations human rights covenants led to the adoption of legislation codifying international standards and values. One of the main features of modern constitutional law content is the existence of the protection of human rights, so that Komnas HAM as an institution was specifically created by the state for the purpose of promoting, respecting and protecting human rights. Human rights has been positioned in the design of the 1945 Constitution, the highest legal source in the Republic of Indonesia based on Pancasila or Five Principles (Rommy Patra 2012: 210). The 1945 Constitution contains a plethora of articles on human rights. So, we must say that human rights protection material becomes the core business of Indonesia in the new Constitution (Asshiddiqie 2017: 1).

With so many articles in the 1945 Constitution, the Indonesian government established several human rights protection institutions. Therefore, there are many institutions that have mandates to carry out their duty of human rights promotion and protection. Indonesia is the only country in Southeast Asia that has three NHRIs: National Commission on Human Rights (Komnas HAM), National Commission on Violence against Women (Komnas Perempuan), and National Commission on Child Protection (KPAI); however, Komnas Perempuan and KPAI have different positions from that of Komnas HAM, although the name is the National Commission. Komnas HAM has "more power" in terms of its position as an independent institution as the NHRI.

Therefore, civil society's hope about Komnas HAM remains high. This is evident from the many complaints submitted to Komnas HAM to be resolved. For example, in July 2017 there were 399 complaints, and in August 2017 there were 602. The complaint is grouped into 12 sections, as shown in Tables 8.1 and 8.2:

However, the presence of Komnas HAM has been unable to improve the protection and enforcement of human rights in Indonesia. Further, the image of Komnas HAM is worse than in the previous period. Komnas HAM received criticism and was perceived to be a tool of the government to improve its image. However, it also showed satisfactory results and received sympathy from the society (Rommy 2012: 210).

It is unfortunate that Komnas HAM, in the period 2012–2018, was fraught with problems of integrity and institutional accountability, namely, the practice of fictitious rent-house practices by a vice chairman of Komnas HAM and budget deviation of Komnas HAM to obtain the title of

**Table 8.1** Complaint files to Komnas HAM from 1 to 31 July 2017

| *No.* | *Classification of Violation of Rights* | *No. of files* |
|---|---|---|
| 1. | Right to life | 4 |
| 2. | The right to marry and have children | 0 |
| 3. | Right to self-development | 3 |
| 4. | Right to justice | 103 |
| 5. | Right to personal freedom | 6 |
| 6. | Right to security | 30 |
| 7. | Right to prosperity | 167 |
| 8. | The right to participate in government | 3 |
| 9. | Women's rights | 0 |
| 10. | Rights of the child | 0 |
| 11. | Rights are not treated discriminatory | 0 |
| 12. | Non-human rights | 83 |
| Total number of files | | 399 |

Source: https://www.komnasham.go.id/index.php/data-pengaduan

**Table 8.2** Complaint files to Komnas HAM from 1 to 30 August 2017

| *No.* | *Classification of Violation of Rights* | *No. of Files* |
|---|---|---|
| 1. | Right to life | 13 |
| 2. | Right to marry and have children | 0 |
| 3. | Right to self-development | 6 |
| 4. | Right to justice | 218 |
| 5. | Right to personal freedom | 16 |
| 6. | Right to security | 52 |
| 7. | Right to prosperity | 232 |
| 8. | The right to participate in government | 9 |
| 9. | Women's rights | 2 |
| 10. | Rights of the child | 4 |
| 11. | Rights are not treated discriminatory | 1 |
| 12. | Non-human rights | 49 |
| Total number of files | | 602 |

Source: https://www.komnasham.go.id/index.php/data-pengaduan

Disclaimer from the State Audit Board of the Republic of Indonesia in 2015 (KPK, Commission of Eradication of Corruption's press release 31 June 2016). In addition, based on Civil Society Organization research and searches of Komnas HAM commissioner candidates 2017–2022, 9 people from 60 Komnas HAM commissioner candidates have links with radical organizations (data from the Coalition for Save Komnas HAM, July 2017).

Moreover, Totok Yulianto from Indonesian Legal Aid Center, in his press briefing at Cikini, Central Jakarta, expressed that from the aspect of independence, 13 people were affiliated with political parties and 13 people with corporations. In terms of integrity, 5 people are suspected of corruption and gratification, 11 people in trouble in the right of honesty, 8 people related to sexual violence, and 14 people in trouble regarding diversity issues (News.detik.com 03 July 2017, 14:13).

## Synergies and Limitations Between Komnas HAM, Komnas Perempuan, KPAI, and Government Institutions

There are important synergies between Komnas HAM, KPAI, and other government institutions across their mandates. These lie principally in the following areas:

1. Counseling
2. Assessment and Research
3. Monitoring
4. Mediation
5. Initiator of changing and drafting of legal policy

Komnas HAM was established on 7 June 1993 based on the Presidential Decree No. 50 of 1993 on the Indonesian Human Rights National Commission (Presidential Decree No. 50/1993). The legal status of Komnas HAM was subsequently strengthened through the Act No. 39 of 1999 on Human Rights. According to Article 1 point 7 of the Act No. 39/1999, Komnas HAM is an "independent institution" of an equal level to other state institutions and which holds the functions of carrying out research and study, education, monitoring, and mediation of human rights.

When compared to Komnas Perempuan and KPAI in terms of mandate, Komnas HAM has a broad mandate. Although the formation of KPAI is regulated in law, Komnas HAM has a stronger mandate than Komnas Perempuan and KPAI. In terms of duties and functions, the three institutions have the same function, namely, counseling; mediation; assessment and research; and monitoring with the same objects on violation of human rights, so their mandates seem to overlap. Therefore, it needs to be consolidated.

From the authority of Komnas HAM, Komnas Perempuan, and KPAI, there are several tasks that require synergy between the institutions to strengthen the protection of human rights. Some of the functions are counseling; mediation; assessment and research; monitoring; and initiator of the changing and drafting of legal policy (Table 8.3).[1]

[1] For more detailed discussions about the integration of the three commissions in Indonesia and other contexts, see, for example, Mayrhofer, M., Francisco Aquilar, Mehdi Azeriah, Renata Bregaglio, Jeremy Gunn, Patrick Harris, Amal Idrissi, Alvaro Lagresa, Adrián Lengua, Y.S.R. Murthy, Bright Nkrumah, Kristine Yigen. 2016. European Commission. International Human Rights Protection: The Role of National Human Rights Institutions—a Case Study; Khalid, Hari Purwadi, Hartiwiningsih. 2018. Integration of Human Rights Institutions for Strengthening the Independence and Effectiveness of Human Rights Protections in Indonesia. *UI Proceedings on Social Science and Humanities Vol. 2 2018*; and Khalid, Hari Purwadi, Hartiwiningsih. 2018. Strengthening of Institutions and Protections Enforcement of Rights of Women and Children in Constitution, *International Journal of Business, Economics and Law*, Vol. 15, Issue 5 (April).

**Table 8.3** Comparison of Komnas HAM, Komnas Perempuan, and KPA

| *Subject* | *Komnas HAM* | *Komnas Perempuan* | *KPAI* |
|---|---|---|---|
| Establishment | Established on 7 June 1993 based on the Presidential Decree No. 50 of 1993 on the Indonesian Human Rights National Commission. Then, the legal establishment was strengthened through the Act No. 39 of 1999 on Human Rights | Established on 9 October 1998 based on the Presidential Decree No. 181 of 1998 on the National Commission on Violence Against Women and renewed by Presidential Regulation No. 65 of 2005 on the National Commission on Violence Against Women | Established on 20 October 2002 based on the Act No. 23 of 2002 on Child Protection in conjunction with Act No. 35 of 2014 on Amendment of Act No. 23 of 2002 on Child Protection |
| Membership | Maximum 35 commissioners; currently 7 commissioners were elected | 15 commissioners, currently 13 commissioners were elected | National Forum on Child Protection as the highest authority and the decision-maker |
| | Proposed by National Commission on Human Rights, elected by the House of Representative | Chairman and 2 vice chairs selected from and by members; | |
| | Inaugurated by the president; | 5 subcommissions, 3 task forces, and 2 teams; | |
| | chairman and 2 vice chairs selected from and by members; | 5 years term of office and may be re-elected for just one more term | |
| Objectives | To develop conditions which are conducive to the implementation of human rights; | To develop a conducive condition to eliminate all forms of violence against women and to enforce women's rights in Indonesia; | To influence policymakers. |
| | To improve the protection and enforcement of human rights. | To improve prevention and monitor regarding all forms of violence against women and | To promote the participation of children |
| | | Protection of women's rights | To raise awareness of child rights; To ensure that children have effective means of redress when their rights are violated |

(*continued*)

**Table 8.3** (continued)

| *Subject* | *Komnas HAM* | *Komnas Perempuan* | *KPAI* |
|---|---|---|---|
| Functions | Counseling;<br>Mediation;<br>Assessment and research; and | Resource center;<br>Negotiator and mediator;<br>Initiator of the changing and the drafting of legal policy;<br>Monitoring;<br>Facilitator; | Counseling<br>Mediation<br>Assessment and Research<br><br>Monitoring; |
| National Instruments | The Constitution of the Republic of Indonesia 1945;<br>MPR Decree No. XVII/MPR/1998 on Human Rights; | The Constitution of the Republic of Indonesia 1945;<br>Act No. 39 of 1999 on Human Rights; | The Constitution of the Republic of Indonesia 1945;<br>Act No. 23 of 2002 on Child Protection and renew by Act No. 35 of 2014 on Amendment of Act No. 23 of 2002 on Child Protection; Presidential Decree No. 77 of 2003 on Child National Commission |
| | Act No. 39 of 1999 on Human Rights | Presidential Decree No. 181 of 1998 on the National Commission on Violence Against Women and renew by Presidential Regulation No. 65 of 2005 on the National Commission on Violence Against Women | Act No. 4 of 1979 on Children Welfare |
| | Act No. 26 of 2002 on Human Rights Court | | Presidential Decree No. 36 of 1990 Ratification on the Convention on the Rights of the Child |
| | Act No. 40 of 2008 on The Elimination of Discrimination, Race, and Ethnic; | | |

(*continued*)

**Table 8.3** (continued)

| *Subject* | *Komnas HAM* | *Komnas Perempuan* | *KPAI* |
|---|---|---|---|
| Outstanding Cases on Human Rights | Freeport Indonesia; | Domestic violence; | JIS (Jakarta International School) |
| | Trisakti; Marsinah; Tanjung Priok;<br>Munir<br>Sampit | The attack on women of Chinese descent on May 1998 | |

Source: Compiled from various laws and regulations

**Table 8.4** Mandate to examine gross violations of human rights: Komnas HAM, Attorney General, the Court

| *Pre-investigation* | *Investigation* | *Prosecution* | *Court* |
|---|---|---|---|
| Komnas HAM | Attorney General | Attorney General | Human Rights Court |
| Komnas HAM establishes an Ad Hoc Team consisting of members of Komnas HAM and the elements of the society; | It does not include the authority to receive reports; | Prosecution performed by the Attorney General; may appoint an ad hoc claimant; the prosecution must be done no later than 70 days from the time the investigation is received; Komnas HAM may request written information from the Prosecutor regarding the progress of the investigation | Conducted by a panel of five Human Rights Court judges, consisting of 2 persons from the relevant human rights court and 3 ad hoc judges; Judicial hearings up to 180 days from the date of judgment; In case of appeal, it must be terminated within 90 days; |
| If its sufficient for initial evidence, then it can submit the conclusions to the Investigator | The Attorney General may appoint an ad hoc investigator; | It must be completed within 90 days of receiving the results of the investigation. 90 days and 60 days extended | In case of appeal, it must be terminated within 90 days |

The mandate of Komnas HAM was also increased with Act No. 26 of 2000 of Human Rights Court (Act No. 26/2000). This Act has appointed Komnas HAM as the institution that has the mandate to carry out inquiries of gross human rights violations, which according to the Act No. 26/2000 comprises genocide and crimes against humanity.

However, as observed in Table 8.4 the authority of Komnas HAM in handling cases of gross human rights violations is also very constrained. Implementation of duties in the field of gross human rights violations as mandated by Act No. 20 of 2000 is dependent on the willingness of other institutions, the House of Representatives of the Republic of Indonesia (Parliament) and the Attorney General. Komnas HAM's relationship with the Parliament is that the latter has the authority to formulate ad hoc human rights court while the working relationship with the Attorney

General is that the investigation and prosecution are the core authorities of the Attorney General. In some cases, the investigations conducted by Komnas HAM were not followed up by the Attorney General. Naturally, the Attorney General is a government body, and most of the human rights violations are conducted by state apparatus.

Building synergy between Komnas HAM, the Attorney General and the Human Rights Court is very important because the authority of Komnas HAM is only at the stage of pre-investigation. The work of Komnas HAM is highly regulated by the Attorney General's office and affects its ability to continue investigations and prosecutions. The work of Komnas HAM is not meaningful if the Attorney General does not proceed at the stage of prosecution, up to trial by the Human Rights Court. Synergy is also required between independent institutions, such as Komnas HAM, Komnas Perempuan and KPAI, and the government institutions on human rights because human rights protection is also carried out by government agencies, namely the Ministry of Justice and Human Rights (Kemenhukham) and the Ministry of Foreign Affairs (Kemenlu). The authority of the Ministry of Justice and Human Rights is very broad in the field of human rights protection. A high level work unit falls directly under the Minister. Similarly, the Ministry of Foreign Affairs has a mandate in handling human rights protection, although its work unit is two levels below the Minister. This shows the number of government institutions that deal with human rights in Indonesia but has not been consolidated well. This has led to inefficiency in the protection of human rights.

Table 8.5 illustrates the duties and functions of the Ministry of Justice and Human Rights and the Ministry of Foreign Affairs in the human rights protection. The most strategic synergy with government institutions is in the formulation of regulations and policies on the protection of human rights. Komnas HAM, Komnas Perempuan and KPAI should be actively involved in the formulation of policies and regulations imposed by government institutions. This involvement is important in order to avoid the impression that the independent human rights institution and the government institutions on the protection of human rights have any contradictory agenda in human rights protection. Komnas HAM and the government human rights institutions must have a common vision and platform for human rights protection.

Similarly, in the field of women's empowerment and child protection, Indonesia has a Ministry for Women Empowerment and Child Protection (PP-PA). The Indonesian government must give attention to the

**Table 8.5** Comparison between Ministry of Law and Human Rights (MLHR) and Ministry of Foreign Affairs (MFA)

| *Subject* | *Directorate General on Human Rights Ministry of Law and Human Rights* | *Directorate on Human Rights and Humanity, Directorate General on Multilateral Cooperation, Ministry of Foreign Affairs* |
|---|---|---|
| Establishment | Based on Government Regulation No. 2 of 1945 on Establishment of Department in the Republic of Indonesia | Based on Minister of Foreign Affairs Regulation No. 2 of 2016 on Organization and Working Procedures of the Ministry of Foreign Affairs |
| Objectives | Formulating and implementing policy and technique standardization on human rights | Formulating and implementing policy on foreign and political affairs on multilateral cooperation of civil and political rights, economic rights, social and cultural rights, development rights, minority rights, and humanity |
| Functions | Formulating policy;<br>Policy implementation; | Preparing the formulation of foreign affair policy on multilateral cooperation of civil and political rights, economic rights, social and cultural rights, development rights, minority rights, and humanity; |
| | Formulating, standard, norms, guidelines, criteria, and regulations on progression and protection of human rights;<br>Consulting on technical and evaluation; | Policy implementation of foreign affairs policy on multilateral cooperation of civil and political rights, economic rights, social and cultural rights, development rights, minority rights, and humanity;<br>Preparing the drafting of standards, norms, guidelines, and criteria of foreign affair policy on multilateral cooperation of civil and political rights, economic rights, social and cultural rights, development rights, minority rights, and humanity; |
| | Implementing administration on Directory General of Human Rights; | Monitoring and evaluating foreign affair policy on multilateral cooperation of civil and political rights, economic rights, social and cultural rights, development rights, minority rights, and humanity |
| | Foreign and home Affairs Cooperation;<br>Organizing the implementation of National Human Rights Action Plan; | |

(*continued*)

Table 8.5 (continued)

| *Subject* | *Directorate General on Human Rights Ministry of Law and Human Rights* | *Directorate on Human Rights and Humanity, Directorate General on Multilateral Cooperation, Ministry of Foreign Affairs* |
|---|---|---|
| | Securing Technical on Implementing the task on progression and protection of human rights | |

protection of children in various aspects (Ministry of Women Empowerment and Child Protection 2016a: 2). The number of children aged 0–17 years is estimated around 87 million people or about one third of the total population of Indonesia. The rights of the children are included in various laws, including the 1945 Constitution. Article 28 B (2) states that "every child has the right to survival, growth and development, and is entitled to protection from violence and discrimination." However, the implementation of the mandate of the law is not as expected. It is marked by the frequent occurrence of violations of children's rights reflected in the existence of children who experience violence, exploitation, and discrimination.

However, according to Komnas Perempuan, during the commemoration of Women's Day on 18 March 2017, the protection of children and women still faced several problems, namely:

1. It is possible and legal to marry before 16 even though Indonesia's Marriage Law (1974) sets the minimum age for marriage at 19 for males and 16 for females. This is done through an official dispensation from the Religious Court or a government officer—a practice that contradicts the UN Convention on the Rights of the Child which defines child marriage as those under the age of 18. The policy of providing marriage dispensation even for very young children is followed by local religious courts.
2. The constitutional court's decision to reject the petition for review to raise the marriage age limit of children also confirmed the practice of child marriage and violence against girls.
3. Femicide, or murder of women because she is female, is a serious issue that concerns the world but still gets minimal attention in Indonesia.

4. Close relationship between drug crime, human trafficking, and migration and death penalty in Indonesia.
5. Tensions between development policies and political priorities of infrastructure on the one hand with human rights issues.
6. Criminalization of women victims of domestic violence by their husbands or ex-husbands should also be of concern to the state.
7. Victims still tend to rely on services provided by NGOs or civil society.

The above issues indicate a strong need to build synergy between rights protection institutions, particularly the rights of women and children. Building synergy between Komnas HAM, Komnas Perempuan and Komnas Pembantu Anak with Ministry of Women Empowerment and Child Protection is necessary, especially in the formulation of policies and regulations. The Child Rights Protection Commission should be able to establish communication with ministries in the creation and implementation of various policies in the area of child protection.

The final point is the synergy between Komnas HAM, Komnas Perempuan, and Komnas Perlindungan anak with NGOs and civil society. Building synergy with NGOs and civil society opens access for public participation and support in the handling of human rights protection activities. Communities need to be involved in advocacy activities, formulation of regulations and public policy, even in the implementation of negotiations and mediation.

## Challenges in Implementing Komnas HAM's Mandate

The many challenges faced by Komnas HAM should not obscure some good work it has performed. It must be recognized that Komnas HAM has succeeded in conducting several research and mediation activities and giving attention to the handling of cases of human rights in the past.[2]

First, the results of research have been used to provide input for the drafting of laws that pay attention to human rights. Some research activities

[2] See for example, Statement By Komnas Ham (National Commission For Human Rights) on the results of its investigations into grave violation of human rights during the events of 1965–1966, 16 August 2012, available at http://tapol.org/sites/default/files/sites/default/files/pdfs/Komnas%20HAM%201965%20TAPOL%20translation.pdf; and "Human Rights Commission reveals the truth about 1965/66 crimes against humanity," Tapol, 23 August 2012, available at. http://www.tapol.org/press-statements/human-rights-commission-reveals-truth-about-196566-crimes-against-humanity.

were undertaken and used in discussions on drafting Act No. 8 of 2016 on Persons with Disabilities.[3]

Second, Komnas HAM mediated the cases of violations of the rights of the people. It carried out its mediation function by facilitating mediation meeting between Parangkusumo residents, Kabupaten Bantul, affected by the policy of regional regulation; Komnas HAM settled disputes over the construction of houses of worship; land disputes involving large groups of citizens such as land disputes around Tesso Nilo National Park in Riau, Kerinci Seblat National Park in Jambi, and Bukit Raya National Park in West Kalimantan; and Komnas HAM has submitted recommendations to government agencies.

Third, Komnas HAM opened the case on "1965". The reform era government is committed to the settlement of past human rights violations (Suparman 2010: 7). In order to address past human rights violations, namely the 1965 incident, Komnas HAM was involved in coordinating with the Politics, Law and Human Rights Coordinating Ministry. The government has responded by conducting a symposium on human rights violations in 1965. Hence, to organize the symposium was a small step in disclosing cases of human rights violations and Komnas HAM will take other steps.

Nevertheless, serious challenges remain. Komnas HAM faced several obstacles in 2016. First is the inclusion of Komnas HAM in the 1945 Constitution so that in case there is a dispute over the authority between state institutions in the constitutional court (MK), Komnas HAM will not be ignored. Second, from the perspective of Act No. 9 of 1999 on Human Rights, Komnas HAM acknowledges that the weakness of the law for Komnas HAM is that it cannot summon witnesses (subpoena). Third, the weakness of the commitment of Komnas HAM as mandated by Act No. 39 of 1999 caused the recommendations of Komnas HAM to be abandoned by several government agencies/other law enforcement agencies. Fourth, Komnas HAM does not have its own authority to force the judiciary to hear Komnas HAM's information in prosecuting cases of human rights violations. Fifth, regarding budgetary support, Komnas HAM informed the House of Representatives Commission III that its budget support in 2016 was insufficient to support Komnas HAM's tasks,

[3] See Comments of the National Human Rights Commission (Komisi Nasional Hak Asasi Manusia) of the Republic of Indonesia on Indonesia's Compliance with the International Covenant on Economic, Social and Cultural Rights, April 2014, The Indonesian National Human Rights Commission.

particularly in relation to the investigation and execution of tasks to the regions (*The House of Representative Report*, April 2017). As a follow-up to the hearing, a conclusion and joint commitment have been reached between Komnas HAM and DPR RI:

1. The structural and institutional reform of Komnas HAM, one of which can be done by bringing greater discipline in relation to internal conflicts within Komnas HAM. A great number of Komnas HAM commissioners would hinder the performance of Komnas HAM due to commissioners holding different interests in settling each case of human rights violations.
2. Commission III of the House of Representatives urged Komnas HAM to immediately undertake structural and institutional improvements and improve professionalism in carrying out its duties and functions in accordance with legislation and strengthening Komnas HAM through the revision of Act No. 39 of 1999 on Human Rights and open opportunities for the drafting of the Bill on Komnas HAM in the National Legislation Program.
3. Commission III of the House of Representatives urged Komnas HAM to submit the results of the study and research on legislation that has the potential to trigger human rights violations.
4. Commission III of the House of Representatives urged Komnas HAM to submit the results of the study and research on legislation and the Draft Law which have the potential to bring the occurrence of human rights violations to the attention of the House of Representatives.
5. Commission III of the House of Representatives supports Komnas HAM by increasing its authority in carrying out the investigation function through the amendment of Act No. 39 of 1999 on Human Rights.
6. Human rights violations have occurred with respect to the government's policy on the moratorium on the granting of remissions, parole, conditional leave, and free-time leave for inmates of corruption and terrorism;
7. There have been allegations of human rights violations in the Mesuji case in Mesuji District (Lampung), Mesuji case in OKI, Palembang (South Sumatra), Bima case, Papua case, Aceh case, Sijunjung (West Sumatera) case (Sampang), which will be resolved thoroughly (*The House of Representative Report*, April 2017).

Finally, the important point of the joint commitment was that the House of Representatives strongly supports the efforts to strengthen the protection of human rights in Indonesia and puts Komnas HAM as the leading National Human Rights Institution.

## Conclusion

Indonesia is paying close attention to the protection of human rights by adopting the principles of human rights protection in 1945 amendment and establishing many institutions performing the duty of human rights protection. However, these institutions operate independently, not in a consolidated manner and their respective authority and tasks seem to overlap. As a result, the contribution of these institutions in the protection of human rights is in decline.

It is therefore necessary to consolidate human rights protection institutions in Indonesia by placing Komnas HAM as the coordinator and the leading institution and to revise the Law on Human Rights. It is necessary to strengthen Komnas HAM so that it becomes the leading institution. This requires strengthening of human resources, budget, and overall strategic development.

First, Komnas HAM needs to be given the legal standing to file a judicial review to the Supreme Court and the Constitutional Court. Komnas HAM is expected to test the laws and regulations that are considered to violate human rights. This authority is important so that Komnas HAM can provide assurance that the laws produced by Parliament and government contain human rights aspects or values.

Secondly, Komnas HAM should be equipped with the authority to conduct investigations and prosecutions in every case of human rights violations. At the same time the police should be released from the task of investigating alleged cases of human rights violations because the security apparatus, especially the police, are prone to being perpetrators of human rights violations. When the authority of investigating and prosecuting lies with the police and prosecutorial institutions with conflict of interest present, the results of investigation from Komnas HAM do not proceed to investigation and prosecution.

Third, building synergy between Komnas HAM and Komanas Perempuan, Komnas Anak, and government institutions as well as NGOs and civil society is urgently needed in the future to strengthen the protection of human rights. In order to strengthen Komnas HAM's role in fostering this synergy, it is necessary to stipulate the duty of Komnas HAM to coordinate the implementation of the human rights protection of the Ministry of Justice and Human Rights, the Ministry of Foreign Affairs, and even with the Witness and Victim Protection Agency and the Ombudsman Institution.

Fourth, Komnas HAM needs to be strengthened in terms of competence and integrity, and the number of commissioners should be reduced, while there should be more professional support staff, lawyers, researchers, and experts. The personal integrity of the commissioner is very important. For example, Komnas HAM was established during the authoritarian rule of President Soeharto, who was pessimistic regarding the formation of Komnas HAM and saw it merely as a facade. Thanks to the integrity of Komnas HAM members, Komnas HAM was highly appreciated by the civil society.

Fifth, Komnas HAM needs more budget for research, monitoring, and mediation functions. Komnas HAM is mandated by four laws, but it is not given adequate budget.

Sixth, Komnas HAM needs to establish representative offices, based on the needs in provincial communities. The main function is to provide more access for local people in some provinces and regencies to voice their rights to the government. Representative offices will "pick up the ball" against the voices of communities in remote areas, such as offshore, islands, coastal, inland, and mountains. Komnas HAM has six representative offices located in Aceh, West Sumatra, West Kalimantan, Central Sulawesi, Maluku, and Papua. A new proposal was coming from West Papua and Lampung Provinces. The West Papuan Representative Office is a sign of the seriousness of the human rights organization in Indonesia's eastern regions. Finally, establishing Representative Offices is important because (1) Indonesia has a vast population that is vulnerable to human rights violations; (2) it allows for the expansion of human rights awareness agencies; and (3) it strengthens human rights protection. In fact, there are several obstacles in the establishment of representatives in the provinces: budgetary reasons, because it will increase the budget for facilities and infrastructure; and the rejection by a group of people from the province concerned, such as from Lampung Province, for the reason that establishing representative office implies that the area is not safe and full of human rights violations.

## References


Asshiddiqie, J. 2017. Efforts to strengthen KOMNAS HAM through the drafting of the draft of human rights law.

KOMNASHAM, *Paper Presentation in the framework of public discussion on the Future of Komnas HAM and Proposed Bill of Komnas HAM*, in Jakarta, 4 April, 2012.

Jensen, S. 2018 Lessons From Research On National Human Rights Institutions A Desk Review On Findings Related To NHRI Effectiveness. Copenhagen: *Danish Institute for Human Rights.*

Khalid, Hari, and Purwadi, Hartiwiningsih. 2018a. Integration of Human Rights Institutions for Strengthening the Independence and Effectiveness of Human Rights Protections in Indonesia. *UI Proceedings on Social Science and Humanities Vol. 2 2018.*

———. 2018b. Strengthening Of Institutions And Protections Enforcement Of Rights Of Women And Children In Constitution, *International Journal of Business, Economics and Law, Vol. 15, Issue 5 (April).*

Mayrhofer, M., Francisco Aquilar, Mehdi Azeriah, Renata Bregaglio, Jeremy Gunn, Patrick Harris, Amal Idrissi, Alvaro Lagresa, Adrián Lengua, Y.S.R. Murthy, Bright Nkrumah, Kristine Yigen. 2016. European Commission. International Human Rights Protection: The Role of National Human Rights Institutions—A Case Study.

Ministry of Women Empowerment and Child Protection. 2016a. Explanation of the Minister of Women's Empowerment and the Protection of the Children of the Republic of Indonesia on the Progress of the Issues of Children in Indonesia and its Settlement Measures at Working Meetings with Commission VIII with the Minister of Social Affairs, the PP-PA Minister, the Head of the Republic of Indonesia, and the Indonesian Child Protection Commission, Jakarta, 30 May 2016.

———. 2016b. Explanation of Minister of Women Empowerment and Child Protection of the Republic of Indonesia at *Working Meeting with Commission VIII DPR RI (Parliament) In the Framework of Budgetary Talk Introduction 2017.* Jakarta 1 September 2016.

Organski, A.F. 2010. *The Stages of Political Development, in Amran Tasai* Akademika Presindo (Ed) Jakarta, Indonesia, 2010.

Rommy, P. (2012) *Institutional Strengthening of Komnas HAM in the State System of Indonesia.* Available at http://ejournal.undip.ac.id/index.php/mmh/article/viewFile/5749/9838.

Satya A. 2008. *Human Rights in Political Transition in Indonesia,* Center for Constitutional Law, Faculty of Law, University of Indonesia, 2008.

Suparman, M. 2010. Politics of Human Rights Law in Indonesia in the Reform Era (Study of the Enforcement of Human Rights Laws in the Settlement of Past Human Rights Violations), Yogyakarta: *Summary of Dissertation of Doctoral Program of Legal Science of Post Graduate Program of Faculty of Law UII,* 2010.

CHAPTER 9

# The Protection Capacities of NHRIs in the Philippines, Thailand and Timor-Leste

*James Gomez and Robin Ramcharan*

## Introduction

This chapter surveys the key challenges and opportunities in relation to other NHRIs, notably the Philippines, Thailand and Timor-Leste. A review of the literature on NHRIs in the region having been provided in the introduction to this work, suffice it to note Vitit Muntarbhorn's review of human rights commissions at the national level in Southeast Asia, which complements Burdekin's prior work and other works noted in this book (Muntarbhorn 2013; Burdekin 2007).

In a more recent work, Muntarbhorn (2014) recalled the overall capacities of NHRIs in Southeast Asia, including the three reviewed here: the power to protect human rights through monitoring of the human rights situations in their respective countries, receiving complaints from individuals, investigating and fact-finding, recommending change and pressuring their governments. A problem area he noted was the appointment of Commissioners, which in some cases remained too close to the executive branch. In addition, whereas promotion was easy,

J. Gomez (✉) • R. Ramcharan
Asia Centre, Bangkok, Thailand
e-mail: james@asiacentre.co.th; robin@asiacentre.co.th



J. Gomez, R. Ramcharan (eds.), *National Human Rights Institutions in Southeast Asia*,
https://doi.org/10.1007/978-981-15-1074-8_9

hard protection—the application and monitoring of human rights protection—was more of a challenge.

Lorenzo (2011) and Wolman (2011) further advanced that NHRIs exhibit distinct types of interactions especially with the courts—namely collaboration rather than hard protection, and that they prove inadequate in affording remedies against human rights violations due to their limited independence within their respective jurisdictions.

While Timor-Leste's Ombudsman, or Provedor, has generally been praised for its adherence to the Paris Principles and its procedures, the Philippines and Thailand Commissions have not been able to perform properly as a result of political meddling and interference by the State or lack of capacity. Both latter Commissions have come under attack by their own Governments, a military dictatorship in Thailand and a recalcitrant President in the Philippines. Timor-Leste, despite its good ratings, also faces difficulties. For all three, the analysis below points to a gap between their mandates and the capacity to deliver justice through remedies and redress.

This chapter examines briefly their protection mandates and capacity to protect human rights. It is based on an examination of primary documents over the past five years, notably annual reports of the Commissions, the Asian NGO Network on National Human Rights Institutions (ANNI) reports and documentation from various UN bodies, such as the Universal Periodic Review.

This chapter is not intended to provide a comprehensive overview of the NHRIs being treated but rather to highlight the key challenges that they face. It briefly reviews some of these based on original analysis already undertaken by the authors in the past few years.

## Philippines

### *Protection Mandate*

The Commission on Human Rights is the oldest NHRI in Southeast Asia, created and enshrined in the 1987 Constitution under the Aquino administration following the People Power revolution that ousted the Marcos dictatorship. It was first established in 1986 as a Presidential Committee and was then institutionalized as an independent constitutional body. Executive Order No. 163 of 1987 serves as the Commission's Charter to today. Its role was progressively expanded over the years beyond the

Constitution through designated powers and functions in special laws, notably: The Magna Carta for Women, the Anti-Torture Law, the Anti-Enforced Disappearance Law and as Children's Ombudsman, among others. It cooperates with different stakeholders and has assisted the Human Rights Offices of the Security Sector, as well as the Presidential Human Rights Committee (Commission on Human Rights of the Philippines 2017a).

Several Bills were introduced in the past five years in the Philippines Congress aimed at strengthening the Commission of Human Rights of the Philippines (CHRP) notably through the provision of prosecutorial powers and the appointment of Human Rights Attaches to Philippine embassies and consulates to protect and promote human rights of Filipinos living abroad. Bills were not approved before the end of the 14th Congress at the end of June 2010 (ANNI Report 2011: 216; Philippines House of Representatives). Among other things, the Bills provided that the CHRP may investigate on its own or on complaint by any party in relation to all forms of human rights violations involving civil and political rights (ANNI 2011: 223). In carrying out its functions, it would grant immunity to a witness or to any person in possession of evidence deemed to be important. It would also be entitled to adopt its own operational guidelines and rules of procedure and may cite for contempt those who do not comply with orders pursuant to the guidelines and procedures (ANNI 2011: 224). The various Bills were referred to stakeholders and given for consideration in relevant committees in Congress in 2012. As of early 2016, Bill HB 02152, "An Act to Strengthen the Commission on Human Rights, and for Other Purposes," which was filed in July 2013, was referred to the Committee on Human Rights of the House for deliberation and has remained "Pending with the Committee on HUMAN RIGHTS since 2013-08-07" (Philippines House of Representatives 2018). The Commission expressed concern at expletives uttered by President Duterte against the UN Special Rapporteur on Extra-Judicial, Summary, or Arbitrary Executions, Agnes Callamard, and other human rights defenders, for reminding the Government to uphold its human rights duties in its problematic war on drugs (Commission on Human Rights 2017b).

The Commission has been under siege since the election of President Duterte in 2016. The Commission's leader, Chito Gascon, and human rights defenders generally, have come under attack directly by the President. Though the Commission's budget was doubled the CHRP regretted that "the House of Representatives opted to undermine our role as a check-and-balance mechanism of the government by allocating PHP

1,000 for our budget. "The Philippines Congress," it continues, had "now chosen to deny the Commission its ability to meaningfully pursue its human rights protection, promotion, and policy-advisory functions through insufficient appropriations" (Commission on Human Rights of the Philippines 2017a).

### *Protection Capacity*

The CHRP has recorded its fair share of complaints. The ANNI 2011 report noted of the 2792 complaints recorded, none of the cases had reached the Commission for resolution and a majority remained in the investigation stage. Indeed, the Commission on Human Rights of the Philippines had reported in 2010 that "[u]nresolved cases of violations of civil and political rights, particularly enforced disappearances, extra judicial killings, and arbitrary deprivation of life and liberty contribute to a growing perception of state impunity" (Commission on Human Rights of the Philippines 2010: vi). The non-resolution of human rights violation was mostly attributed to a "lack of witnesses and insufficiency of evidence" (Commission on Human Rights of the Philippines 2010: vi). Moreover, domestic laws to penalize enforced disappearances and extra judicial killings had yet to be enacted by Congress. A critical concern of the Commission was how to address "justiciability" of violations of economic, social and cultural rights, in such issues as homelessness, hunger, social security, and other human rights degradation attributable to the poverty and hunger suffered by the poor and vulnerable sectors in many parts of the country (Commission on Human Rights of the Philippines 2010: vi).

In seeking to remedy this situation through action in the 15th Philippine Congress, Representative Salvador H. Escudero III provided a poignant indictment of the "toothless" nature of the Commission in an explanatory note to House Bill 2974 (Philippines House of Representatives Bill 2974 2010). He noted that: it is neither a judicial nor a quasi-judicial body. It can only extend preventive measures, such as initiating applications in court for judicial writs and order, conduct investigation and receive evidence of violations of human rights, among others (Philippines House of Representatives Bill 2974 2010). The Bill sought to equip the CHRP with prosecutorial powers over delineated forms of human rights violations. At the time of writing, the Bill was under review by stakeholders since May 2012. Senate Bill 2818, purported to do just that. During the Universal

Periodic Review of the Philippines in May 2017, the Office of the UN High Commissioner for Human Rights reported that information noted that

> 10. The Committee on Economic, Social and Cultural Rights urged the Philippines to expedite the adoption of the Commission on Human Rights Charter (Senate bill No. 2818). 13. The Committee against Torture recommended providing the Commission with full functional, structural and financial support. 14. In 2012, the Human Rights Committee recommended ensuring that the Commission enjoyed full fiscal autonomy. (United Nations 2017a: 2)

These efforts highlight the need to reinforce the mandate of the CHRP, implementation of quasi-judicial processes and securing remedies for victims of human rights violations. Reflecting the Commission's concerns, Australia recommended during the UPR that the government "[p]rovide adequate resourcing to the Commission on Human Rights and allow it to investigate alleged extrajudicial killings (Australia)" amidst Duterte's highly problematic war on drugs (United Nations 2017b; 13). Such support is vital given the partisanship in Parliament that has led to pro-government MPs trashing the Commission for not denouncing violations of human rights by criminals and for being aligned with opposition political parties (Philippines House of Representatives, 2017). Beyond these criticisms of the Commission, it is fair to note that over the past two years the general human rights situation in the Philippines has been addressed by Parliament in House bills and resolutions concerning, inter alia, non-discrimination on the basis of SOGIE (2019), protection of human rights defenders (2019), anti-racial, ethnic and religious discrimination (2018), rights and welfare of workers (2018), anti-sexual harassment (2018), domestic violence (2018), reparations for victims of human rights violations (2018).

## Thailand

### *Protection Mandate*

Thailand's Commission was established through a post-coup Constitution of 1997 with operations beginning in 2001. Thailand's National Human Rights Commission (NHRCT) Act of 1999, provided in section 15, that the NHRCT had, inter alia, the powers and duties (1) to promote the respect for and the practice in compliance with human rights principles at domestic and international levels and (2) to examine and report the commission or omission of acts "which violate human rights or which do not comply with obligations under international treaties relating to human rights to which Thailand is a party" and "to propose appropriate remedial measures to the person or agency committing or omitting such acts for taking action." Failure to act by the offending party would lead to a proposal to the National Assembly regarding further action to redress (NHRCT Act B. E. 2542 1999). In performance of its duties the Commission could summon Governmental agencies and individuals to testify before its proceedings. Failure to comply with the terms of a summons by the Commission may lead to fines or imprisonment, under Sections 34 and 35 (NHRCT Act B.E. 2542 1999). The Government promoted the NHRCT as "fully exercising its power vested by the Constitution to advance the cause of human rights in the country, while fully respecting its independent character" (Abhisit 2009: 2).

Following the military coup of 22 May 2014, The National Council for Peace and Order (NCPO), which is the military junta that governed Thailand until 2019, promulgated Announcement No. 11/2557 on 22 May 2014 which repealed the Constitution of the Kingdom of Thailand B. E. 2550 (except for parts on the Monarchy, state organizations and other bodies established by the virtue of the 2007 Constitution to continue performing their duties). A consequence was that the NHRCT's powers and duties to propose matters and opinions to the Constitutional Court and the Administrative Court were annulled. Its powers to bring a case to the Court of Justice on behalf of the injured parties was also been terminated.

A merger of the National Human Rights Commission with the Ombudsman's office was on the table amidst failed draft constitutional talks in 2015. The proposed merger into one body to be called the Office of the Ombudsman and Human Rights Protection, however, ran counter to the Government's pledges, during its campaign for a seat on the Human Rights Council (2010–2013) to strengthen the protection of human rights by supporting the work of the NHRCT. A written submission by the NHRCT to the ruling Junta helped to preserve the Commission as it sought to manage its international reputation (ANNI 2016: 25).

Subsequently, the powers and duties of the National Human Rights Commission of Thailand were laid out in the Third National Master Plan on Human Rights. A consequent, 2017 NHRCT Organic Act, drafted without full public consultation contrary to Article 77 of the Constitution, elaborated on the provisions of Article 246 and 247 of the 2017 Constitution regarding the NHRCT. Section 26 of the 2017 NHRCT Organic Act provides for the following duties and responsibilities of the NHRCT:

1) To investigate and report on the accurate facts about human rights violations in all cases without delay and to recommend appropriate measures or guidelines for the prevention or to address of human rights abuses, including remedies for human rights abuse victims to the relevant public or private entities;
2) To prepare human rights situation assessment reports in the country and to submit the reports to the Parliament and the Cabinet. The reports shall also be made available to the public;
3) To recommend measures or guidelines for the promotion and protection of human rights to the Parliament, the Council of Ministers and relevant agencies. The NHRCT shall recommend law, regulation, and/or order amendments to comply with human rights principles;
4) To clarify and report the facts, without delay, in case of inaccurate or unjustified reporting of Thailand human rights situation; and
5) To promote every sector in the society to be aware of the importance of human rights. (ANNI 2017: 55)

A positive aspect of the NHRCT Organic Act 2017 is that it placed the role of the Office of the National Human Rights Commission under the guidance of the Commissioners collectively. Previously, under the 1999 NHRCT Act, the Office was as under the Parliament and the stewardship of the Office rested with the President of the NHRCT.

Nevertheless, there has been widespread disappointment over the performance of the NHRCT. The downgrade from A to B status, indicates clearly the lack of independence (Ashayagachat 2016). The 20th Constitution, approved by referendum on 7 August 2016 (with 59% voter turnout), provided for the retention of the NHRCT but with considerably reduced powers and independence. This Constitution also added a particularly onerous provision: a new duty for the NHRCT "to clarify and report the facts in case of inaccurate or unjustified reporting of Thailand human rights situation from civil society's reports and/or international bodies/organizations that criticise human rights in Thailand" (ANNI 2017: 54).

### *Protection Capacity*

The 2017 NHRCT Act provided for the Commission to conduct investigations and arrange reports to the National Assembly and the Council of Ministers on situations of violations of human rights and disseminate them to the public (Article 40). The Commission must then arrange a plan of operations to address the situation (Article 41) and make recommendations to the National Assembly, the Council of Ministers, or relevant agencies to proceed in accordance with this authority without delay (ANNI 2018: 90). This represents a significant climb-down from previous powers.

The investigative capacity of the NHRCT had appeared to come under serious threat even before the 2014 coup, when the then new Chairwoman, Amara Pongsapich, assumed office in 2009. The Hong-Kong-based Asian Human Rights Commission (AHRC) noted at the time that she "has effectively promised to make the national rights institution meaningless and irrelevant, other than as an obstacle to human rights" (Asian Human Rights Commission, 2009). The AHRC expressed concern over the Chairperson's statement, reproduced on AHRC's website, that "[t]he commission will not be acting as a law office, filing individual cases, but will create an environment for concerned agencies to work together" (Asian Human Rights Commission 2009). For the AHRC, while the NHRCT was supposed to have the power to file cases in court (section 257, para. 4 of the Constitution), the new chairperson seemed to be indicating "[t]hat she has no interest to exercise this power. Instead her commission will just 'create an environment'" (Asian Human Rights Commission 2009). A vigorous protective role for the NHRCT is not apparent from its actions, despite the Constitutional Court's ruling (No. 31/2548) of 2005, affirming that under the Constitution of Thailand the NHRCT had the powers and duties to inspect and prepare reports on acts or omissions which constituted violations of human rights or which were not in accordance with international obligations with respect to human rights to which Thailand was a party.

The NHRCT claimed in its report to the UPR in 2011 that the government was slow in enacting the law that would allow the National Human Rights Commission of Thailand (NHRCT) to discharge its additional functions prescribed by the 2007 Constitution. It argued that the draft law on NHRCT did not permit the NHRCT to disclose any information obtained during the carrying out of its functions and imposes a penalty for such disclosure. This restriction would severely affect the NHRCT's function as a monitoring body. It noted further, that Thailand was not adequately living up to its commitments under international core human rights and that there was a real lack of remedies to victims of human rights violations and a failure to bring perpetrators to justice. The NHRCT's credibility as a protective entity appeared to be seriously compromised as it had taken "no concrete action ... in the cases of many victims of human rights violations" to citizens and non-citizens (ANNI 2014: 39).

To be fair, before the proposed changes following the military coup of 2014, Thailand's NHRCT reported receiving some 666 complaints in 2012. It also reported examination of a total of "1,014 complaints in which 873 complaints are pending before 2011" (NHRCT 2012: 22). For 2014, it reported receiving some 689 complaints (ANNI 2015, Chapter on Thailand). To the extent that Thailand's NHRCT was "proactive" was linked to the political climate and ongoing tensions between rival political parties (ANNI 2014: 39). Statements, policy recommendations and legal recommendations emerged, but "few actions were taken by the NHRCT during a time when there was no political movement" (ANNI 2014: 39). Moreover, the legal and policy recommendations "lack proper analysis and focus only on changing the wording of the law" (ANNI 2014: 39).

The pre-military coup mandate of the NHRCT was under threat by the proposed merger of the National Human Rights Commission with the Ombudsman's office that was tabled in the draft constitution of 2015. This merger was sharply criticized by Human Rights Watch on several counts related to the proposed new rules, including: the lack of independence of 11 Commissioners to be selected "in closed an unaccountable vetting system by the Thai senate"; the requirement of "apparent knowledge and experiences in the protection of rights and liberties" and "having regard" only to the participation of civil society, which was not consulted; failure to recognize the different mandates of the NHRCT and the Ombudsman; and failure to heed past criticisms of lack of transparency and inclusiveness" (Human Rights Watch 2015). A technical note on the NHRCT of Thailand by the UN Office of the High Commissioner for Human Rights further noted that the proposed merger risked weakening the NHRCT (United Nations 2015: 2).

During prolonged uncertain constitutional situation in Thailand under military rule, the International Coordinating Committee monitoring the application of the Paris Principles by NHRIs downgraded the NHRCT from A to B status and the NHRCT's future protection role was uncertain.

It faced the prospect of a further downgrade. Continuing problems include the selection process of Commissioners. ANNI 2018 Report noted the presence of the President of the Senate on the Selection Committee, the same Senate that approves the list of Commissioners (ANNI 2018: 95). This situation epitomizes the situation of NHRIs in the region that are subject to the vicissitudes of national politics. Commissioners have been subjected to very difficult working conditions and internal political machinations as the Junta has sought to reign in the NHRCT.

The record of the third batch of Commissioners, who came into office on 20 November 2015, revealed a fragmented group in terms of appreciation of the NHRCT's role and functions. The process was neither in full conformity with the 2007 Constitution, nor in compliance with the Paris Principles. An additional concern was that many of the appointed Commissioners may not necessarily have the relevant competency in the field of human rights casting the ability of the Commission to perform impartially.

Interference by the Junta is rampant and the Chairperson of the Commission, a former Judge, has allegedly transformed it into a law enforcement agency as opposed to a human rights protection agency. The Chairperson's aloofness and unwillingness to consider public concerns has been noted. As the People's Empowerment Foundation, a Thai NGO, has noted: "It has tended to protect interests of the state rather than the people: excuses have been made by it in defense of the state instead of human rights principles" (ANNI 2016: 25). While concerns are expressed, they are not firmly rooted in human rights law and no real, tangible change has been made. Human rights violations are rampant. Moreover, human rights defenders have been subjected to persecution, including women human rights defenders (HRDs):

> Many of them have been killed, or disappeared, faced harassment and intimidation including sexual harassment in the past several years. Many also face criminal charges filed against them either by state agencies or private companies, particularly those working on land rights and natural resource extraction, as well as rights activists in Southern Thailand. (ANNI 2016: 6)

Public petitions to the Commission totaled 619 in 2017 since the Third Commission office, which clearly indicates the public's expectations of the NHRCT. In 2018, some 239 complaints were filed (NHRCT 2019). Of these cases before the Commission in financial year 2017, 885 were terminated, for a variety of reasons including that no-violation of human rights was found in 288 of the cases (ANNI 2018: 99).

The Commission addresses these cases in an overall situation of declining powers. The ANNI Report 2018, noted for example that the capacity of the Commission, prior to 2017, "to act on behalf of the aggrieved person in submitting charges to the Administrative Court or the Constitutional Court" for verdicts by the Administrative Court or the Constitutional Court regarding human rights violations by State officials, was. In addition, the Commission is now tasked with clarifying the accuracy of reports critical of Thailand's human rights situation. (ANNI 2018: 89) Overall,

> the NHRCT struggles to assert itself in a society where Government actions promote national security above human rights standards, where national leaders have a poor attitude towards human rights, and where officials and the public have no understanding of human rights. (ANNI 2018: 103)

## Timor-Leste

### *Protection Mandate*

Timor-Leste, which has applied for membership in ASEAN, has an Ombudsman for Human Rights and Justice (PDHJ), or "Provedor" in local language. In comparison to the other five NHRIs in the region, the PDHJ has a two-fold mandate in the areas of human rights and good governance. Globally, while the classical Ombudsman was seen as a mechanism for complaints about improper administration by public authorities, this institution has acquired a human rights protection function over the past four decades. Linda Rief has noted that a human rights Ombudsman has two functions: (1) promote and protect human rights of persons against the State and (2) monitor government administration for legality and fairness (Rief 2013). Human rights Ombudsmen today often operate in contexts where international human rights law has been incorporated into domestic law, as is the case of Timor-Leste which has ratified all core human rights conventions (Devereux 2015).

The Provedor of Timor-Leste was created in 2004, under section 27 of the Constitution of the Republic of Timor-Leste to provide for an independent Ombudsman with powers to investigate individual complaints against public bodies made by any natural or legal person. Law No. 7/2004 created the Office of the Ombudsman. Article 5.1 of the enabling law states that the PDHJ is empowered, among other things, to investigate violations of fundamental human rights, freedoms and guarantees, abuse of power, maladministration, illegality, manifest injustice and lack of due process, nepotism, collusion, influence peddling and corruptions. Interestingly, the PDHJ cannot be suspended during states of emergency or other exceptional circumstances (ANNI 2012: 35). This was evidenced during the 2006 crisis and 2008 State of Emergency where the PDHJ remained active and continued its investigations and monitoring.

Article 28(e) of the enabling law states that the Provedor may order a person to appear before him or her and has the power to "have access to any facilities, premises, documents, equipment, goods or information for inspection and interrogate any person to whom the complaint relates somehow" (ANNI 2010: 294). Article 48 prescribes fines for non-compliance, Article 49 provides for offences such as hindering the Office and threatening, intimidating or improperly influencing involved parties and provides for fines up to US$3000 and imprisonment for one year. The PDHJ can use formal notification procedures to summon State officials who must comply. It can investigate the exercise of judicial functions; challenge decisions issued by the Court or investigate a matter already before the court which has not yet been decided. The enabling law of 2004 provided that the Courts shall not arbitrarily interfere with, nor delay an investigation unless prima facie evidence places the investigation outside of the PDHJ's jurisdiction or if there is mala fide or conflict of interest (ANNI 2010: 291).

In Timor-Leste, the public may make complaints online, by phone, mobile service, or by directly visiting the central office in Dili or regional offices. A complaint may also be made orally and transcribed in writing later. If a complaint is investigated, recommendations about these complaints were to be forwarded to competent bodies. The complaints procedure of the Office of the Ombudsman (the Provedoria for Human Rights and Justice or "PDHJ") under Law No. 7/2004 provides that the Ombudsman must determine within 45 days whether a complaint will be investigated or dismiss it with reason. Once completed, the Ombudsman is required to provide a draft report to the parties on his or her key findings. A 15-day period is allowed for consideration. Any entity subject to a recommendation arising out of the investigation must comply and must inform the Ombudsman within 60 days on the status of implementation.

### *Protection Capacity*

As with other NHRIs in Southeast Asia, the ANNI report for 2017 noted Timor-Leste's challenges in realizing their full mandate ANNI 2017: 71), chief of which was the issue on consistent monitoring and follow up of investigations. Human rights actors highlighted the need for proactive monitoring and promotion of human rights by making public statements or declarations against any state action that act against the Constitution or in violation of human rights rather than wait for the public to lodge complaints.

For instance, in 2011, some 55 cases of human rights violations were investigated, though only three were closed. In 2014, some 97 complaints were filed, of which 57 were investigated and the rest declared outside of PDHJ's mandate (ANNI 2014: 60). An analysis of investigations by the PDHJ over six years (from 2007 to 2013), found that it only concluded 44 investigations of a total of 344 (ANNI 2014: 60). A low conclusion rate stems partly from a lack of professional and qualified human resources in the department of investigation (ANNI 2014: 60). By the end of 2015, the ANNI Report noted that the number of human rights cases investigated by the PDHJ has remained static (ANNI 2015). In 2016, improvements in the performance of the Provedor as it handled 198 complaints received, of which 113 related to good governance and 85 to human rights (ANNI 2017: 67). It concluded 169 cases in 2016 (ANNI 2017: 68). One may note the receipt of 189 complaints in 2017, of which 68 concerned human rights violations and the rest concerned good governance issues (ANNI 2018: 108).

While the Ombudsman has been positive in terms of the PDHJ's working relationship with public authorities, the Provedor is on record as having stated that "sometimes we face problems regarding our investigation when we want to get documents or information—sometimes they [public authorities] don't provide us with it" (ANNI 2010: 293). In addition, in joint police and military operations in 2014 and 2015 in the eastern part of the country, for example, monitoring and reporting by PDHJ was diminished by the fact that they rarely entered the areas most affected by the joint operation (ANNI 2015: 293). The PDHJ's only has legal power to recommend or propose remedies and reparations to victims of human rights violations to the Public Prosecutor. There was little by way of follow-up information regarding how many recommendations of the PDHJ have been adopted, and how many rejected (ANNI 2015), though the

2016 ANNI report provides some statistics. Partly, this is due to the lack of a mechanism for case monitoring and follow-up (ANNI 2017: 68) especially when cases related to crimes are referred to the public prosecutor for further investigation as well as limitations with respect to undertaking interventions in the judicial process which indicates the limitations of PDHJ's legal power to recommend or propose remedies and reparations to victims of human rights violations. The Provedor was urged to adopt a more proactive response in ANNI's 2016 report, especially in relation to violations committed by Timor-Leste's National Police (PNTL) and military forces (F-FDTL), which are alleged to have committed the most violations (ANNI 2016: 38, 2017: 68). The ANNI report noted that "The effectiveness of the Provedoria was put into question, as most of its reports and recommendation were not given due attention by the PNTL and the FFDTL" (ANNI 2016: 52).

Civil society organizations (CSOs) have been disappointed by the Provedor. While they submit complaints received from individuals to the Provedor, they remain disappointed over the Provedor's refusal to intervene in cases of harassment of human rights defenders and the forcible removal of Rohingya women, even while they were in the process of giving birth (ANNI 2016: 45).

Complainants referring cases to the Provedor have noted lack of response and communication. A Regular Human Rights Response Mechanism initiated by the UN in Timor-Leste, to foster communication between the Provedor and CSOs, has been resisted by locals who note that Timor-Leste is no longer dependent on the UN.

A major barrier that the Timorese general public faced was understanding of the human rights provision in national legislation as they were written in Portuguese even though the overwhelming majority of Timorese do not speak or understand Portuguese.

The ANNI Report for 2018, noted that despite broad powers given to the PDHJ, civil society continued to view its overall response as "ineffective and inefficient, claiming that it does not seriously address cases of human rights violations or complaints from individuals" (ANNI 2018: 110). The response of the PDHJ has been particularly questioned given that there were people who did not know the status of their complaints or cases. Also, according to civil society observation, the PDHJ in practice does not fully execute all of its constitutional competencies, such as requesting the Supreme Court of Justice to review the constitutionality, and unconstitutionality by omission, of legislation. This is a point that has been raised in previous ANNI reports (ANNI 2010, 2011, 2012, 2013, 2014, 2016, 2017).

Nevertheless, GANHRI's review of the PDHJ in 2018, led to a recommendation of "A" status while urging continued consultation with civil society, ensuring pluralism in the staffing of the office and formalization of an appointment process for the Deputy Ombudsman position (GANHRI 2018). In addition, PDHR faces limitations in terms of human and financial resources and facilities (ANNI 2018: 122). It is useful to recall the PDHJ's strategic plan for the period 2010–2020, which aimed to increase complaints coming from outside Dili, pay attention to public perceptions of the office and implement better systems for informing civil society about the progress of cases (PDHJ 2010). These will have to be assessed by 2020. The challenges faced by the PDHJ are reflected in the ANNI 2018 report which recommended, inter alia:

- Be more proactive in protecting and promoting human rights not only through monitoring and publishing reports, but also by making public statements or declarations against any action of state institutions or organs that violate human rights;
- Intervene in any and every situation where human rights violations occur regardless of citizenship, race, colour, religion, and ethnicity of victim; ...
- Actively follow-up and keep complainants informed on the processing of their cases or complaints, including cases that have been referred to other relevant institutions;
- Make publicly available all information and reports on human rights violations particularly on the official website of the PDHJ, not only its annual reports, but also thematic reports; ...
- Focus also on other human rights such as social, economic and cultural rights in order to hold the Government accountable to guarantee the rights of people to clean water, access to land, to good sanitation, education, etc. (ANNI 2018: 127)

## Analysis and Conclusion

From the review above all the three NHRIs surveyed here have legal mandates to perform investigative services into human rights abuses. However, the full realization of their mandates, the undertaking of quasi-judicial protection functions and the securing of remedies for victims of rights violations need improvement. For all three commonalities include (a) Dependence on political climate and leadership and often dependent in the respective countries; (b) the respective quasi-judicial investigative processes are either weak or lacking in the follow through that is necessary to address the issue of protection and justice, especially for parties in individual cases, impacting on the advancement of human rights consistent with international human rights standards; and (c) their weak capacities to secure resolutions or advance the cases of victims.

Wolman (2011) further notes and was taken up in the first section of the chapter of how NHRIs interact with the respective courts in their countries—namely collaboration; judicial training; participation in litigation; NHRJ advocacy of better human rights practices and rulings by the courts; NHRI defense of judicial independence; and interactions related to NHRI adjudication of human rights petitions—all of which make no mention of a hard protection approach to violations by the NHRIs. One can surmise that this has to do with capacity of the respective NHRIs, however on a broader context, it may be that Asian cultural value of play a role in minimizing a confrontational approach. This was pointed out by Bünte and Dressel (2017) who argued that the commitment of most Southeast Asian states to human rights is more tactical and notes the deep divide between ratified standards and actual rights practice.

Another major difference that likely reinforces the weaknesses of protection capacity of Southeast Asia's NHRIs is that unlike Europe Africa or the Americas, the Asia Pacific does not have a region-wide inter-government system such as treaties, courts, commissions or other institutions to protect and promote human rights. A platform for Southeast Asia's NHRIs to come together and strengthen their capacities and mandate would be a good starting point in lieu of the inter-government system. A regional cooperation platform for the enhancement of their capacities and fulfillment of their roles could be their participation to the Asia Pacific Forum of National Human Rights Institutions (APF or the Forum) which is a membership organization of National Human Rights Institutions (NHRIs) from across the Asia-Pacific region. As Byrnes et al. (2008) have noted, the APF may serve a "quasi-governmental horizontal network" that may push all regional NHRIs toward greater adherence to the Paris Principles. Within this network, NHRIs can cooperate closely on human rights issues of common concerns.

Overall, the actual practice of protection by the NHRIs featured in this chapter especially for Thailand and the Philippines cognizant of their current political leadership leaves a lot to be desired considering the intimate linkages between democracy, rule of law and human rights in the Southeast Asia region.

## References


Abhisit, V. Prime Minister of Thailand. 2009. *Thailand's Commitments, Voluntary Pledges and Contributions to the Promotion and Protection of Human Rights: Election to the Human Rights Council for the term 2010–1013*, Department of International Organizations, Ministry of Foreign Affairs, October 2009.

Ashayagachat, A. 2016. Thai rights agency downgraded by international body. Bangkok Post 28 January. Accessed on 2 February 2016. http://www.bangkokpost.com/news/general/843412/thai-rights-agency-downgraded-by-international-body.

ANNI Report (2015) *Report on the Performance and Establishment of National Human Rights Institutions in Asia*. Asia Pacific Forum of National Human Rights Institutions.

Asian NGO Network on National Human Rights Institutions (ANNI). 2010. *ANNI Report on the Performance and Establishment of National Human Rights Institutions in Asia*. Bangkok: Forum Asia. Available at https://forum-asia.org/2010/ANNI2010_TEXTONLY.pdf.

———. 2011. *ANNI Report on the Performance and Establishment of National Human Rights Institutions in Asia*. Bangkok: Forum Asia. Available at https://forum-asia.org/documents/ANNIReport2011.pdf.

———. 2012. *ANNI Report on the Performance and Establishment of National Human Rights Institutions in Asia*. Bangkok: Forum Asia. Available at https://www.forum-asia.org/?p=15570.

———. 2013. *ANNI Report on the Performance and Establishment of National Human Rights Institutions in Asia*. Bangkok: Forum Asia. Available at https://www.forum-asia.org/?p=16848.

———. 2014. *ANNI Report on the Performance and Establishment of National Human Rights Institutions in Asia*. Forum Asia and ANNI. Available at. https://www.forum-asia.org/uploads/books/2014/ANNI%202014%20FINAL.pdf

———. 2016. *ANNI Report on the Performance and Establishment of National Human Rights Institutions in Asia*. Forum Asia and ANNI. Available at https://www.forum-asia.org/?p=21790.

———. 2017. *ANNI Report on the Performance and Establishment of National Human Rights Institutions in Asia*. Forum Asia and ANNI. Available at https://www.forum-asia.org/?p=25246.

———. 2018. *ANNI Report on the Performance and Establishment of National Human Rights Institutions in Asia*. Forum Asia and ANNI. Available at https://www.forum-asia.org/?p=25246.

Asian Human Rights Commission (AHRC). 2009. Thailand: New NHRCT chief promises to ensure that human rights body is meaningless and irrelevant, August 20, 2009. AHRC-STM-174-2009.

Burdekin, Brian. 2007. *National Human Rights Institutions in the Asia-Pacific Region*. Martinus Nijhoff Publishers.

Bünte, M., and Dressel, B. (Ed.). 2017. Politics and Constitutions in Southeast Asia. London: Routledge.

Byrnes, Andrew C. and Durbach, Andrea and Renshaw, Catherine. 2008. Joining the Club: The Asia Pacific Forum of National Human Rights Institutions, the Paris Principles, and the Advancement of Human Rights Protection in the Region (May 26, 2008). *Australian Journal of Human Rights*, Vol. 14, No. 1, pp. 63–98, 2008; UNSW Law Research Paper No. 2008–39. Available at SSRN: https://ssrn.com/abstract=1397466.

Commission of Human Rights of the Philippines (CHRP). 2010. Annual Report for 2010.

———. 2017a. Statement of the Commission on Human Rights on the PHP 1,000 budget allocation of the House of Representatives for the Commission, Press Statement, 12 September. http://chr.gov.ph/wp-content/uploads/2018/01/12-Sep-2017-Statement-of-the-Commission-on-Human-Rights-on-the-PHP-1000-budget-allocation-of-the-House-of-Representatives-for-the-Commission.pdf.

———. 2017b. CHR concerns over President Duterte's Remarks against UN Special Rapporteur, Human Rights Defenders, Press Release, 31 August 2017.

Devereux, A. 2015. *Timor-Leste's Bill of Rights: A Preliminary History. Canberra*: ANU Press.

GANHRI. 2018. Sub-Committee on Accreditation Report. Report and Recommendations of the Session of the Sub-Committee on Accreditation (SCA) Geneva, 15–19 October 2018. Available at: https://nhri.ohchr.org/EN/AboutUs/GANHRIAccreditation/Documents/SCA%20Report%20October%202018-Eng%20FINAL%20.pdf.

Human Rights Watch. 2015. *Thailand: Keep Independent Rights Commission*, 3 February 2015. Available at http://www.hrw.org/news/2015/02/03/thailand-keep-independent-rights-commission.

Lorenzo, Johanna Aleria. 2011. Asian Rights, Asian Remedies: The ASEAN Intergovernmental Commission on Human Rights (AICHR) and the National Human Rights Institutions (NHRIs) February. Available at SSRN: https://ssrn.com/abstract=2694889 or https://doi.org/10.2139/ssrn.2694889.

Muntarbhorn, V. 2013. Unity in Connectivity?: Evolving Human Rights Mechanisms in the ASEAN Region. Martinus Nijhoff Publishers. See Brian Burdekin (2007), *National Human Rights Institutions in the Asia-Pacific Region*. Martinus Nijhoff Publishers.

———. 2014. The Southeast Asian System for Human Rights Protection in *Routledge Handbook of International Human Rights Law*, Scott Sheeran, Sir Nigel Rodley (Eds). London, Routledge, pp. 467–482

National Human Rights Commission ACT, B.E. 2542. 1999. Thailand.

National Human Rights Commission, Thailand (NHRCT). 2012. *Summary of the Human Rights Situations and Performance Report of the Year 2012*, Submitted to the Submitted to the Sub-Committee on Accreditation, International Coordination Committee.

———. 2019. Statistical Information on Complaints. Available at http://www.nhrc.or.th/NHRCT-Work/Statistical-information/Statistical-information-on-complaints/Yearly-(2010-Now).aspx.

Philippines House of Representatives. 2010. House Bill 2974, An Act Strengthening the Functional And Structural Organization Of The Commission On Human Rights, And For Other Purpose, First Regular Session, 15th congress, House of Representatives of the Philippines.

———. 2017. "Lawmakers to CHR: Denounce human rights abuses committed by criminals," Press Release, 08 August. Available at http://www.congress.gov.ph/press/details.php?pressid=10169&key=COMMISSION%20ON%20HUMAN%20RIGHTS

———. 2018. 18th Congress. Available at http://www.congress.gov.ph/search/.

Rief, L. 2013. *The Ombudsman, Good Governance and the International Human Rights System*. Springer, pp. 104–105.

United Nations. 2017a. Compilation on the Philippines Report of the Office of the United Nations High Commissioner for Human Rights, Human Rights Council Working Group on the Universal Periodic Review Twenty-seventh session 1–12 May 2017, A/HRC/WG.6/27/PHL/2. https://www.upr-info.org/sites/default/files/document/philippines/session_27_-_may_2017/a_hrc_wg.6_27_phl_2_e.pdf.

———. 2017b. Compilation on the Philippines Report of the Office of the United Nations High Commissioner for Human Rights, Human Rights Council Working Group on the Universal Periodic Review Twenty-seventh session 1–12 May 2017b. Report of the Working Group on the Universal Periodic Review: Philippines, Human Rights Council Thirty-sixth session 11–29 September 2017 Agenda item 6 Universal periodic review. 18 July. Doc. A/HRC/36/12.

UN OFFICE OF THE HIGH COMMISSIONER FOR HUMAN RIGHTS. 2015. Technical Note on the National Human Rights Commission of Thailand in the draft 2015 constitution. Available at https://bangkok.ohchr.org/files/OHCHR%20on%20NHRI%20150327.pdf.

Wolman, Andrew. 2011. National Human Rights Institutions and the Courts in the Asia-Pacific Region, Asia Pacific Law Review, Vol. 19, No. 2, pp. 237–251. https://doi.org/10.1080/10192557.2011.11788250.

CHAPTER 10

# Advocating for a National Human Rights Institution in Singapore

*James Gomez and Michelle D'cruz*

## Introduction

Singapore's long-standing political structure as a one-party dominant state has often raised the need for a separation of powers. Calls for independent checks and balances have come over the years from academia, civil society, media commentators, lawyers and opposition politicians. Yet the city-state's political system has stood at odds with the traditional notion that liberalism and economic development are connected (Reyes 2015). With a GDP of US$323.91 billion in 2017, Singapore is positioned as the 36th largest economy in the world (World Bank 2018). The People's Action Party (PAP), which has enjoyed one-party rule for over 50 years, is said to have "performance legitimacy" that its governance style is justified by a track record of economic development (Andrews 2015). Singapore's material prosperity has also resulted in a general population

J. Gomez (✉)
Asia Centre, Bangkok, Thailand
e-mail: james@asiacentre.co.th

M. D'cruz
Oxfam International, Nairobi, Kenya



J. Gomez, R. Ramcharan (eds.), *National Human Rights Institutions in Southeast Asia*,
https://doi.org/10.1007/978-981-15-1074-8_10

that is risk averse, unwilling to rock the boat and generally comfortable with the status quo.

The PAP views multiparty systems as fractious and potentially dangerous for Singapore as there is the possibility of parties courting voters along racial or class lines (Tan 2017). The PAP government has long disavowed the need for independent checks on the system, with first Prime Minister Lee Kuan Yew arguing that there was no need for more "political policemen" as long as the government was run in a clean, fair and meritocratic manner (Oon 2008). Lee Kuan Yew's son and Prime Minister Lee Hsien Loong, like his father the former Prime Minister, has also taken the position that Singapore does not have the necessary talent for "two A teams" summing the ruling party's position for a single party dominated system (Tan 2017). In 2019, Deputy Prime Minister Heng Swee Keat, who was at that time tipped to the next Prime Minister, in response to a media question if Singapore needs to have more political competition, said that an "adversarial political system" is not suitable for Singapore (Lai 2019). Others, such as Education Minister Ong Ke Yung, dubbed as one of the party's fourth-generation leaders, point to Singapore's small size as justification for one-party rule arguing that as a small country, Singapore's equilibrium is best found in a single party system (Yong 2017; Soezean 2017). Even those within the party like DPM Tharman Shanmugaratnam, who agrees that a lack of political competition could be disadvantageous in the long term, maintain that having a dominant player can be an asset (Tan 2017). Singapore government under the PAP's administration thus favours a moral conceptualisation of accountability, having a meritocratically elected elite negates the need for political accountability (Rodan and Hughes 2014).

The narrative of the PAP being the only party capable of ruling Singapore (Kennedy 2011) is built on an underlying ruling party articulated Asian Values and Confucian ethic that grounds governance in Singapore; "the concept of government by honourable men (junzi)" who are duty bound to do right by the people and who have the trust and respect of those they represent. This articulation of a political culture is largely consistent with the values the majority Chinese population observes and practices that discourage political competition and independent accountability (See Clammer 1985; Chua 1995; Gomez 2000). Law academic Thio characterises Singapore's human rights policy as being "informed by overriding state objectives and national development goals prioritising economic growth and social order," often justified by appeals to "Asian values" (Thio 2004). She argues that this form of cultural relativism argumentation is often used to shield against criticism, raise the counter point of cultural imperialism and present an alternative way to model and manage individual—societal relationships (Thio 2004). This stands in contrast to a government limited by checks and balances, which is seen as a Western idea (Parliament of Singapore 1991).

Advocates for democracy and independent checks and balances face significant restrictions on civil and political liberties and are constrained by a regulatory framework that is largely designed to stifle dissenting voices (Reyes 2015). In the early days the Internal Security Act was brandished against political opponents and those critical of the PAP, and one high profile victim was Nobel Peace Prize nominee Dr Chia Thye Poh who was detained for 32 years as a political prisoner (AFP 2015). After the last round up of political opponents in 1987, the government transitioned towards using defamation and bankruptcy laws as a tool for disenfranchising and delegitimising opponents. Civil society activists, bloggers and academics who are critical of the ruling regime and its leaders are often be subject to legal sanctions. This is in addition to an array of legislation, such as the Societies Act, Political Donations Act, Public Order Act and others that curb the effective operation of dissent in the city-state. Narrative around Singaporean politics is controlled by a complaint local mainstream press which often carries uncritically negative reports of activists. The Freedom House annual report on civil and political liberties classifies Singapore as only Partly Free, with the media categorised as Not Free (Freedom House 2016).

In this political environment where the notion of independent checks and balances are rejected by the ruling party and advocates are penalised, how can calls for independent institutions like a human rights commission be realistically implemented? Starting in 2011 when Singapore first went through the Universal Periodic Review (UPR) and later for the second time in 2016, these "calls" have moved onto the United Nations platform. Over two UPR cycles, member states and other stakeholders have raised the issue of independent institutions, in particular the need for a national human rights institution (NHRI). This chapter fills a gap in the literature on NHRIs in Southeast Asia, notably on the reasons for the absence of an NHRI in ASEAN's one-party-dominated state such as Singapore. It looks at the how the discourse on NHRIs in Singapore has developed historically around the idea of an Ombudsman to provide oversight of parliament and the legislative process as well as the more recent discourse around national human rights institutions. It then reviews the recommendations for the establishment of a Singaporean NHRI in the UN Human Rights Council's Universal Periodic Review (UPR) during the 2011 and 2016 cycles. The review is based on key documents submitted to the UPR process; these include the national report, a compilation of UN information, summary of stakeholders' information and the outcome documents. Additionally, the paper also takes onboard information received via an online survey conducted with Singapore activist respondents. The findings suggest that firstly the government remains unwilling to establish independent institutions or embrace a system of independent checks and balances as would be required in establishing an NHRI. Secondly, while the UPR continues to be an important platform for placing international pressure on the state on the issue of NHRIs, CSOs, however, have not sustained their advocacy of the issue across both cycles. Thirdly, patterns of CSO engagement with the UPR reveal that a minimum advocacy on NHRIs is in line with a broader pattern of not-engaging on hard political issues. This points to a need for sustained and pointed advocacy both locally and internationally if momentum is sought for establishing an NHRI in Singapore. Otherwise, there is a risk that the calls to set up an Ombudsman, to reel in increasing lapses in the civil service, might the option the PAP government will be willing to implement. Should this happen it will fall far short of what is needed to deal broadly with human rights violations in Singapore.

## Discourse on NHRIs in Singapore

The discourse on the establishment of NHRIs in Singapore can be linked to the establishment of NHRIs in the region beginning with the Philippines in 1987 and most recently Myanmar in 2011. Of the ten ASEAN countries plus Timor-Leste, five currently have NHRIs, Philippines, Indonesia, Malaysia, Thailand, Myanmar and Timor-Leste. Literature on the establishment of NHRIs in Asia suggest that many have emerged as a result of international and domestic pressure (Cardenas 2004), that the establishment of an NHRI was part of the political transition towards a more democratic regime or as a response to signal that a new institution has been established to monitor and deter the significant human rights abuses that had taken in previous regimes (Gomez and Ramcharan 2016). We see examples in the Philippines where the commission was established by President Cory Aquino in the aftermath of gross violations committed during the Marcos dictatorship; in Thailand, it was established through the post-coup Constitution of 1997 (Gomez and Ramcharan 2016). The NHRIs in Indonesia, Malaysia and Myanmar followed waves of political liberalisation (Gomez and Ramcharan 2016). It should be noted that in times of regression in democratic space, as seen in the case of Malaysia, Philippines and Thailand, NHRIs are less effective due to its inability to perform their mandates. A comparative work by Gary Rodan contrasted the creation of Suhakam in Malaysia with the absence of independent human rights accountability mechanisms in Singapore. He pointed to the space created through conflicts within capitalism in Malaysia versus a singular elite in Singapore that leaves no room for such an accountability mechanism (Rodan 2009). This lack of contestation may also explain the absence of NHRIs in Brunei, Cambodia, Laos and Vietnam, where there is a similar lack of contestation and dominance of the State by one party, a sultanate or one man. While this is self-evident in the case of Brunei's monarchical political system, a similar situation exists in Hun Sen's Cambodia and in Communist Laos and Vietnam, both one-party states with a tight grip over their societies (See Gomez and Ramcharan 2014).

In the Singapore context, demands for an NHRI have been rather piecemeal and disparate in the absence of strong internal demand or external pressure. Calls for an Ombudsman began as early as 1967, when a Constitutional Commission recommended that an Ombudsman be set up to serve as an independent check on the public sector, with wide investigative powers and autonomy to publish findings (The Straits Times 1967). While the recommendation was not rejected, the government response was that it was not a suitable time to set up such an institution, pointing to factors such as the high level of illiteracy and a lack of understanding of citizenship rights and obligations among the population with Law Minister E.W. Barker noting that the Ombudsman might be "flooded by complaints by people who do not know what are the limits of his jurisdiction" (The Straits Times 1967). Between the late 1970s and the early 2000s, the matter was raised in parliament on different occasions by opposition party member JB Jeyaretnam and nominated members of Parliament Geoffrey Abisheganadan and Shrinwas Rai (George 2011b). PAP backbenchers have on occasion taken up the issue, in 1994 K. Shanmugam then backbencher and current Law Minister, responded to the government position that existing channels were sufficient by arguing that the existing channels relied very much on the system to operate correctly. In 1999 Prof. Tommy Koh then director of the Institute of Policy Studies argued that Singapore's survival depended on the restructuring of existing institutions and setting up new ones like an Ombudsman. In a 2008 exchange Professor Koh asked then Minister Mentor Lee Kuan Yew, if he saw Singapore's democratic system evolving to include a human rights commission or Ombudsman, to which Lee responded that it was a matter for the next generation of leaders to decide. In 2013, Professor Koh again reiterated his belief that an Ombudsman would be an effective safeguard particularly when there was no recourse to judicial review (Tan 2013).

Outside of parliament and politics, there have also been calls by civil society, academics, lawyers, media commentators and members of the general public. On Human Rights Day in 2007, three local lawyers petitioned the Law Society of Singapore to, among other things, strengthen its independence, increase its involvement in human rights and urge the government to set up an NHRI (The Online Citizen 2007). In response, then Law Society president Michael Hwang stated that the establishment of an NHRI had nothing to do with the Law Society but was a matter under the purview of the government (The Straits Times 2008). Commentaries in the media have also argued in favour of an Ombudsman (George 2011a; Agarwal 2016) that can serve as independent entity through which people can raise complaints against public agencies. Following Singapore's first UPR, the Singapore Unity Project—a joint civil society initiative comprising civil society groups and individuals that seeks to strengthen civil society collaboration—released a statement calling on the government to establish an NHRI among other measures (Singapore Unity Project 2011). Following the second UPR in 2016, a member of the public wrote a letter to the press that a human rights commission that is independent from the state would an important first step for Singapore to ensure government accountability (Kuah 2016).

While there have been calls in Singapore to establish an NHRI, the city-state has not experienced the momentum that paved the way for the setting up NHRIs in the other ASEAN member states, whether in the form of internal waves of political liberalisation or as a response to international pressure over gross human rights violations in the country. There have been some intermittent calls for an Ombudsman but the discourse on this has not developed very much since the first mentions in 1966 beyond it being an oversight mechanism of the public service. There has also been little external pressure via the UN on Singapore to set up an NHRI as the city-state is not a party to the core international human rights instruments like the ICCPR and ICESCR. With the advent of the UPR there now is an international platform on which a broad spectrum of human rights concerns, not limited to specific treaty obligations, can be addressed.

## UPR and NHRI

The articulation for a Singaporean NHRI entered into the UN system in the first cycle of the UPR. Singapore's lack of an NHRI was raised in the UN report and Stakeholder summary, with civil society highlighting that there were no plans or discussion to establish one from the government. An analysis of the submissions reveals the discourse on NHRIs was raised in just three of the eighteen Stakeholder submissions for Singapore and that the matter was only taken up by local civil society organisations, with a total of nine organisations and independent civil society members participating in these submissions. The content of the submissions also did not exclusively focus on a national human rights institution but also more generally on the need for independent institutions (UN Human Rights Council 2011). There were different lines of reasoning offered from practical and managerial justifications for an NHRI to suggestions that Singapore needed to keep up with external and regional developments. The Singapore Institute of International Affairs took the position that an NHRI could serve as focal point for human rights and could provide input to ASEAN- and UN-related human rights mechanisms while a coalition submission by Solidarity for Migrant Workers, HOME, TWC2 and Migrant Voices noted that other ASEAN countries already had NHRIs in place (UN Human Rights Council 2011). More general calls for independent checks took the form of a call for an independent commission on equal opportunities that would be tasked with tackling racial discrimination and inequality as well as calls for an independent elections commission (UN Human Rights Council 2011).

During the review, Singapore received seven recommendations from Timor-Leste, Thailand, Poland, Egypt, Canada, Moldova and South Africa to establish an NHRI. In response, the government noted that UN member countries have different approaches to NHRIs and that Singapore preferred "a decentralized, but interlocking and mutually reinforcing system of human rights protection" (UN Human Rights Council 2016). Presumably, this means all parts of the government and society working together to achieve the fulfilment of rights or, put another way, an appeal to keep matters as they are.

In 2016, the civil society stakeholders did not raise the issue of NHRIs; the only reference to creating an independent institution was MARUAH's call for an independent elections commission (UN Human Rights Council 2015). In the UN report, the Committee on the Elimination of Discrimination Against Women noted their regret that Singapore had yet to establish an NHRI to further women's human rights. During the review Singapore received six recommendations calling for the establishment of a national human rights institution (FIDH 2016), these came from Greece, Uganda, Nepal, Poland, Timor-Leste, Malaysia, Republic of Korea and Costa Rica. Notably Poland and Timor-Leste were the only countries to maintain their efforts in the second UPR at recommending the establishment of an NHRI. Another point to note from the second cycle was that some countries supported Singapore's direction of having an Inter-Ministerial Committee on Human Rights,[1] with Colombia welcoming its establishment, Barbados suggesting that Singapore strengthen this institution and Paraguay recommending that Singapore continues with this institution following up on recommendations. During the review Indonesia encouraged Singapore to strengthen their national human rights institutions in line with the Paris Principles but did not make a specific recommendation on this issue. Singapore maintained its response that it was committed to the rule of law and had "interlocking legislation, institutions and mechanisms in place to protect and promote human rights" (UN Human Rights Council 2016). It raised the examples of meet-the-people sessions with MPs and the Inter-Ministerial Committee on Human Rights engaging with civil society and monitoring the implementation of human rights.

Thus when we examine the discourse on NHRIs in the UPR across both cycles, we see that the issue is very much on the periphery for the UN reporting bodies and civil society stakeholders and in the discourse among states during the review. The Singapore state's approach of defining and articulating its approach to human rights governance across both cycles has allowed it to shape much of the discourse and avoid focus on independent institutions. This has led Ambassador Chan Heng Chee who led Singapore's delegation to the UPR claim that many countries endorsed Singapore's pragmatic approach to human rights (Channel News Asia 2016). The subsequent media narrative in the local press was that

[1] The Inter-Ministerial Committee on Human Rights in an inter-government agency that coordinates the Singapore government's engagement with the UPR.

Singapore's approach to human rights was well received and endorsed (Channel News Asia 2016). This is in line with previous research on Singapore and the UPR which revealed that the UPR was an effective platform for advocacy on selected issues such as migrant workers, LGBTI and the death penalty, but was less effective on hard political issues relating to fundamental freedoms, civil and political liberties and independent institutions (Gomez and D'cruz 2017). Notably on the issues where there has been traction, we see that civil society has done a commendable job of maintaining the spotlight on the issue across both cycles, reiterating the importance of the issue with multiple submissions and groups participating in joint and individual submissions on the topic, and demonstrating nuance and intersectionality in their advocacy for the issue. The low level of uptake and lack of sustained advocacy on NHRIs in the UPR by civil society suggests that it is not given the same level of priority as other issues. The political realities and constraints on civil society in Singapore also go some way to explaining the lack of pressure and demand for independent institutions. An analysis of civil society participation in the first cycle noted that while the process spurred coalition building, there remained challenges such as competition between groups disagreement on how strong a stand to take on contentious issues and the apparent need to maintain a distinction between civil and political society which would prevent broader coalitions (Ortmann 2012).

Nevertheless following the second cycle, local civil society organisations were effective in critiquing the government's lack of commitment to human rights and offering a counter narrative in the local media (Han 2016). However, by late 2018, the government began to take action against civil society activists including taking legal actions against them for comments and posts shared over social media (The Economist 2018). By 2019 Singapore introduced legislation against "fake news" which is widely seen as measures to curb dissent against the regime (The Guardian 2019).

## Challenges of NHRI Advocacy

Overall there are several factors that contribute to the lack of independent institutions in Singapore, these include the nature of the political system, insufficient internal demand and lack of external pressure. Collectively, these present the key challenges towards advocating for the establishment of an NHRI in Singapore.

On the nature of the political system, we must question whether the one-party state structure sits well with having an independent checks. With the Singapore governmental system having been built around the PAP, Lee Kuan Yew and carefully chosen elites, provide little opportunities for accountability. Studies on Singapore have noted that neither of the two cornerstones of the Singapore system, state driven capitalism and the idea of a society operating on the basis of meritocracy, embrace ideas of institutionalising political rights or freedoms (Rodan and Hughes 2014). Rather the type of accountability the system propagates is a moral accountability as previously discussed. When asked about the prospects of an NHRI or Ombudsman in 2008, then Minister Mentor Lee Kuan Yew stated "The ultimate objective is clean, corruption-free, capable, effective, meritocratic, fair government. As long as we remove malpractices, I don't see the need for more political policing" (quoted in Rodan and Hughes 2014). The Worker's Party's Pritam Singh called the PAP's approach a system of "ownself check ownself" a phrase in local parlance that has since been popularised (Singh 2015). Singh's comments were in reference to Singapore's second PM Goh Chok Tong's comment that, the notion of checks and balances were a "seductive lie" the opposition used to attempt to sway voters and that the integrity of the PAP allowed them to be their own check (Philomin 2015). Yet, the issue of accountability, independence, transparency continue to dog the Singapore political landscape. Dr. Tan Cheng Bock, a former PAP stalwart and widely expected to lead an opposition coalition against the PAP, cited these as reasons when he explained why he set up a new opposition political party (Mohan 2019).

Following the UPR there was some discussion on Singapore's approach to human rights and the need for an NHRI. For instance, a letter to the press which noted an NHRI would "institutionalise the state's commitment to human rights and aid in the promotion and protection of citizens' human rights" and would be a first step in cementing public and civil society involvement in human rights promotion and protection (Kuah 2016). However, civil society has yet to articulate a clear argument and strategy for an NHRI. This can be attributed to the fact that most NGOs in Singapore tend to be issue oriented, focusing on their specific niche be it migrant worker rights, abolition of the death penalty, women's rights or LGBTI rights. It is also worth noting that the authors' online semi-structured interviews conducted with Singaporean civil society activists on their experiences over the two UPR cycles revealed that many did not know of the existence of the Inter-Ministerial Committee or were unclear about the role and function of the Committee prior to the state publicising it during the UPR review. Inter-Ministerial Committee has been misunderstood both by the UN member states and the general public that it might be the start or possible nucleus of an NHRI. In fact, in its present form the Committee is nothing more than a coordinating mechanism for the government to respond to and engage with the UPR process.

There are also significant operational, financial and legal hurdles for organisations that advocate for civil and political rights. Groups that advocate for civil and political rights as well as the promotion of democracy can be gazetted as "political associations, which places significant restrictions on their ability to attract funding. Such groups as run the risk of negative campaigning by government aligned academics, civil servants, diplomats, politicians, supporters and online trolls as being supported by "foreign powers". This acts as a deterrent for groups to actively engage on these issues. Even for organisations like MARUAH, a civil society organization engaged on human rights which was deemed a 'political association', there is a recognition of the political reality in which it operates." Ms. Braema Mathi, then MARUAH president conceded in 2012 that establishing an NHRI in Singapore remained a "distant objective" and that MARUAH would strategically focus its efforts on violations under the Internal Security Act in an attempt to gather public support and push the government to act (Rodan and Hughes 2014).

Externally there has been little pressure on Singapore to establish an NHRI compared that faced by other countries that have established NHRI due to external pressure on internal human rights abuses. Regionally, we also see that the ASEAN human rights regime which Singapore is a part of, has demonstrated a resistance to the liberal democratic rights tradition, with bodies like the ASEAN Intergovernmental Commission on Human Rights remaining highly elitist, made up of primarily government aligned appointees and focused on rights promotion. This regional, conservative climate lends support to the non-establishment of a Singaporean NHRI. Thus none of the push factors seems to be sending Singapore on the path of developing an NHRI.

Nevertheless there are undercurrents of resentment, very much arising as a response to the rumblings of domestic dissatisfaction around political accountability and increasing instances of corruption in the civil service. In terms of political accountability, when current Prime Minister Lee Hsien Loong articulated his principles of governance in 2004; leadership, being able to remain relevant, to reward work and correspondingly work for reward and to ensure everyone has a stake and opportunities (Loong 2004). However, academics studying the statement noted that accountability was not included (Rodan and Hughes 2014). Fast forward to 2016, after the PAP saw its vote share increase to 69.9% following a watershed 2011 election that saw the opposition win a group representative constituency (GRC) for the first time, there was a noticeable change in tone. This time PM Lee set out five guiding principles of Singapore's political system with a strong focus on governance; ensuring high-quality government, keeping politics open and contestable, maintaining governmental accountability; upholding a multiracial society and a system with in-built stabilisers. The discussion on the need for checks and balances, independent institutions and the separation of powers between the arms of the State continues in Singapore following the appointment of former PAP MP, Hri Kumar Nair as Deputy Attorney General (The Online Citizen 2017). In terms of corruption, since 2011 almost yearly there have been recorded instances of corruption and bribery in different government agencies. There was also some dissatisfaction over the role of the Corrupt Practices Investigation Bureau. While Singapore continues to score yearly on international corruption perception indexes, on the ground there is increasing dissatisfaction over regular reportage of corruption among civil servants and staff of government linked companies. This explains the increased calls around setting up an Ombudsman which still falls short of what Singapore needs—an NHRI.

## Conclusion

It remains to be seen how the new accountability driven guiding principles will impact Singapore's political landscape. It is highly likely that any efforts at creating a checking mechanism will be very state-centric with circumscribed authority, much like the Presidential Council for Minority Rights. The unelected council which includes members of the judiciary and government is tasked with reviewing Parliamentary bills to ensure there is no discrimination against any racial or religious community and is allowed to refer any bill they find wanting back to Parliament for reconsideration. The discourse around the development of an NHRI from as early as the 1966 Constitutional Commission envisaged the role as an independent check on parliament, something that might bolster the responsibility and accountability of ministers to parliament and the government as a whole. This is somewhat different from the idea of a national human rights institution as we know today; however, the discourse around the establishment of NHRIs continues to circle back to ideas of bureaucratic oversight over parliament and proposed legislation as opposed to an NHRI separate from the government, with the ability to take up complaints, with powers of investigation, adequate resources and the political will to address human rights issues, that is, an institution in line with the Paris Principles. The government likewise seems more comfortable with bureaucratic checks and independent institutions with circumscribed powers or very specific areas of focus and a limited ability to act, like the President's Council for Minority Rights. The unelected council which includes members of the judiciary and government is tasked with reviewing Parliamentary bills to ensure there is no discrimination against any racial or religious community and is allowed to refer any bill they find wanting back to Parliament for reconsideration. Given that at present the discussion circles around the idea of the Ombudsman as a complaint's mechanism against concerns against public agencies or a bureaucratic check, it is unlikely something that is far wider to encompass human rights abuses and a quasi-judicial functions that is in line with the Paris Principles would materialise. The push for an NHRI in line with Paris Principles must thus come from civil society. The lack of engagement on the issue through existing platforms like the UPR suggests that local civil society organisations have a long way to go to build up their advocacy efforts and articulate a clear position on NHRIs, a submission focused specifically on NHRIs would be a good starting point for Singapore's third UPR cycle. Otherwise, Singapore might end up with an institution which falls far short of international human rights standards but merely ticks the box of having a weak and constrained mechanism if the present government gives into calls for an Ombudsman.

## References

Andrews, Sally. 2015. "Soft" Repression: The Struggle for Democracy in Singapore. *The Diplomat*, 6 February, at: http://thediplomat.com/2015/02/soft-repression-the-struggle-for-democracy-in-singapore/.

AFP. 2015. Nobel Gesture: Singapore's Longest-Held Political Prisoner Chia Thye Poh Nominated for Peace Prize, October 3, at: http://www.scmp.com/news/asia/southeast-asia/article/1863749/nobel-gesture-singapores-longest-held-political-prisoner.

Agarwal, Chirag. 2016. How an Ombudsman Could Benefit Singapore. *Today*, July 13, at: https://www.todayonline.com/singapore/how-ombudsman-could-benefit-singapore.
Cardenas, S. 2004. *Adaptive states: the proliferation of National Human Rights institutions*. Carr Center for Human Rights Policy Working Paper T-01-04, at: http://content.knowledgeplex.org/kp2/cache/kp/24.pdf.
Channel News Asia. 2016. Singapore's Pragmatic Approach to Human Rights Endorsed by Many: Ambassador-at-Large', January 28, at: http://www.channelnewsasia.com/news/singapore/singapore-s-pragmatic/2467014.html.
Chua, Beng-Huat. 1995. *Communitarian Ideology and Democracy in Singapore*. Routledge: London, pp. 237.
Clammer, John. 1985. *Singapore: Ideology. Society, Culture*. Chopmen Publishers: Singapore, pp. 170.
FIDH. 2016. Government's Response to UN Review a Major Setback for Human Rights, June 24, at: https://www.fidh.org/en/region/asia/singapore/government-s-response-to-un-review-a-major-setback-for-human-rights.
Freedom House. 2016. *Freedom in the World 2016: Anxious Dictators, Wavering Democracies: Global Freedom under Pressure*, at: https://freedomhouse.org/sites/default/files/FH_FITW_Report_2016.pdf.
George, Cherian. 2011a. Relieving the Weight of Democratic Expectations. *Yahoo! News*, August 22, at: https://sg.news.yahoo.com/relieving-the-weight-of-democratic-expectations.html.
———. 2011b. The Presidential Election 2011: The Weight of Democratic Expectations, 20 August, at: https://www.airconditionednation.com/2011/08/20/presidential-election-2011/.
Gomez, James. 2000. *Self-Censorship: Singapore's Shame*. Think Centre: Singapore, pp. 98.
Gomez, James, and Robin Ramcharan. 2014. Introduction: Democracy and Human Rights in Southeast Asia. *Journal of Current Southeast Asian Affairs*. Volume 33, Issue 3, pp. 3–17.
———. 2016. The "protection" capacity of National Human Rights Institutions in Southeast Asia, Southeast Asia City Research Centre, Working Paper Series, No. 172, University of Hong Kong, February, at: https://www.cityu.edu.hk/searc/Resources/Paper/16021610_172%20-%20WP%20-%20Dr%20Gomez.pdf.
Gomez, James, and Michelle D'cruz. 2017. Singapore's Universal Periodic Review: Civil Society Trends and Themes. *The Universal Periodic Review of Southeast Asia: Civil Society Perspectives*. Palgrave Macmillan and SIRD: Malaysia, pp. 115–136.
Han, Kristen. 2016. Singapore Civil Society Responds to Universal Periodic Review. *The Online Citizen*, January 29, at: http://www.theonlinecitizen.com/2016/01/29/singapore-civil-society-responds-to-universal-periodic-review/.

Kennedy, Alex. 2011. Singapore Leadership Admits Mistakes as It Faces Strongest Electoral Challenge in Five Years. *Associated Press*, May 5, at: https://lkyspp.nus.edu.sg/ips/wp-content/uploads/sites/2/2013/04/AP_Singapore-leadership-admits-mistakes_050511.pdf.

Kuah, Alison. 2016. Singapore Needs Independent Human Rights Commission, *The Straits Times* (Letters in Print), February 13, at: https://www.straitstimes.com/forum/letters-on-the-web/singapore-needs-independent-human-rights-commission.

Lai, Linette. 2019. Adversarial politics not good for Singapore: Heng Swee Keat, *The Straits Times*, July 29, at: https://www.straitstimes.com/singapore/adversarial-politics-not-good-for-singapore-heng-swee-keat.

Lee Hsien Loong. 2004. Singapore's Four Principles of Governance. Speech delivered at the opening of the Commonwealth Association of Public Administration and Management (CAPAM) Biennial Conference, at: https://wpqr4.adb.org/lotusquickr/cop-mfdr/PageLibrary482571AE005630C2.nsf/0/5554DBE9192524BC48257BD4000CDDCB/$file/Day%201b%20-%20Winston%20Tan_Handout%20on%20POG-PM_Lee_Singapore_Four_Principles_Governance.pdf.

Mohan, Matthew. 2019. Tan Cheng Bock says new party will be 'unifying alternative' for Singapore. *Channel News Asia*, July 26, at: https://www.channelnewsasia.com/news/singapore/tan-cheng-bock-psp-progress-singapore-party-alternative-11755736.

Oon, Clarissa. 2008. Major Task to Find Next 'A Team' from Small Talent Pool—MM: Two-Party System Not Viable as There's Not Enough Top Talent. *The Straits Times*, February 2, at: https://maruah.org/2008/02/05/a-human-rights-commission-for-singapore/.

Ortmann, Stephen. 2012. Policy Advocacy in a Competitive Authoritarian Regime: The Growth of Civil Society and Agenda Setting in Singapore. *Administration & Society*. September 1, Volume 44, Issue 6, pp. 13–25.

Parliament of Singapore. 1991. *White Paper on Shared Values*, at: https://www.academia.edu/1740666/White_paper_on_shared_values_1991_.

Philomin, Laura Elizabeth. 2015. Check and Balance a Seductive Lie: ESM Goh. *The Straits Times*, August 27, at: http://www.todayonline.com/singapore/check-and-balance-seductive-lie-esm-goh.

Reyes, Sebastian. 2015. Singapore's Stubborn Authoritarianism. *Harvard Political Review*, September 29, at: http://harvardpolitics.com/world/singapores-stubborn-authoritarianism/.

Rodan, Gary. 2009. Accountability and Authoritarianism: Human Rights in Malaysia and Singapore. *Journal of Contemporary Asia*. Volume 39, Issue 2, pp. 180–203.

Rodan, Garry, and Hughes, Caroline. 2014. *The Politics of Accountability in Southeast Asia: The Dominance of Moral Ideologies*. Oxford: Oxford University Press. pp. 256.

Singapore Unity Project. 2011. Advancing Human Rights in Singapore. December 10, at: http://www.thinkcentre.org/article.php?id=3104.

Singh, Pritam. 2015. Rally Speech—Hougang. September 2, at: http://www.wp.sg/pritam-singhs-rally-speech-hougang-rally-2-sep/.

Soezean, Martha. 2017. Ong Ye Kung: Singapore's One Party System, A Result of Free and Fair Election. *The Online Citizen*, January 24, at: https://www.theonlinecitizen.com/2017/01/24/ong-ye-kung-singapores-one-party-system-a-result-of-free-and-fair-election/.

Tan, Jeanette. 2013. Ambassador-at-large Tommy Koh Still Wants an Ombudsman for Singapore. *Yahoo! News*, October 31, at: https://sg.news.yahoo.com/ambassador-at-large-tommy-koh-still-wants-an-ombudsman-for-singapore-075242414.html.

Tan, Weizhen. 2017. Multi-Party Political System Could Ruin Singapore: Ong Ye Kung. *TodayOnline*, January 24, at: http://www.todayonline.com/singapore/multi-party-political-system-could-ruin-spore-ong-ye-kung.

The Guardian. 2019. Singapore fake news law a 'disaster' for freedom of speech, says rights group. May 9, at: https://www.theguardian.com/world/2019/may/09/singapore-fake-news-law-a-disaster-for-freedom-of-speech-says-rights-group.

The Online Citizen. 2007. Lawyers Petition Law Society of Singapore, December 10, at: https://www.theonlinecitizen.com/2007/12/10/lawyers-petition-law-society-of-singapore/.

The Economist. 2018. Mild Social-Media Posts Scandalise Singapore's Judges, October 13, at: https://www.economist.com/asia/2018/10/13/mild-social-media-posts-scandalise-singapores-judges.

The Straits Times. 2008. Law Society President Says Singapore Lawyers Apathetic About Public Law. March 18, at: http://forums.vrzone.com/chit-chatting/250817-news-law-society-president-says-singapore-lawyers-apathetic-about-public-law.html.

———. 1967. Ombudsman when the time is opportune—Barker, 13, March 18, at: http://eresources.nlb.gov.sg/newspapers/Digitised/Article/straitstimes19670318-1.2.97.

The Online Citizen. 2017. Newspaper Said No Space to Publish Sylvia Lim's Comments on Appointment of a Former PAP MP as Deputy AG. February 17, at: http://www.theonlinecitizen.com/2017/02/17/newspaper-said-no-space-to-publish-sylvia-lims-comments-on-appointment-of-former-pap-mp-as-deputy-ag/.

Thio, Li-ann. 2004. Pragmatism and Realism Do Not Mean Abdication': A Critical and Empirical Inquiry into Singapore's Engagement with International Human Rights Law. *Singapore Yearbook of International Law*. Volume 8, pp. 41–91, at: http://www.commonlii.org/sg/journals/SGYrBkIntLaw/2004/4.html.

UN Human Rights Council. 2011. *Summary of stakeholders' information*, February 21, A/HRC/WG.6/11/SGP/3.

———. 2015. *Summary of stakeholders' information*, November 6, A/HRC/WG.6/24/SGP/3.

———. 2016. *Report of the Working Group on the Universal Periodic Review—Singapore—Addendum Views on conclusions and/or recommendations, voluntary commitments and replies presented by the State under review*. June 13, A/HRC/32/17/Add.1.

World Bank. 2018. *Gross Domestic Product*, at: http://databank.worldbank.org/data/download/GDP.pdf.

Yong, Charissa. 2017. One-Party Rule 'May be Way for S'pore to Succeed': Ong Ke Yung. *The Straits Times*, January 24, at: http://www.straitstimes.com/politics/one-party-rule-may-be-way-for-spore-to-succeed.

PART III

# Thematic Perspectives on NHRI in Southeast Asia

CHAPTER 11

# Mental Health and Human Rights: The Role of Komnas HAM

*Kimberly Clair*

## Introduction

The Indonesian National Human Rights Commission (Komnas HAM) was established in 1993[1] with 'the function of monitoring, mediation, public awareness, and research on human rights, including implementation of international human rights norms in Indonesia' (Komnas HAM 2016a: 2). Although the institution's early years focused on criticizing police and military activities (Eldridge 2002: 145), it has also supported the rights of marginalized groups through research, public discussions, training sessions and partnerships with civil society organizations and other government bodies. For Herbert (2008: 462), these activities are 'part of the process of educating the public, government and civil society on human rights issues'.

[1] Jeff Herbert (2008: 461) notes that Komnas HAM 'was actually established prior to the legislation by Presidential Decree No 50 of June 1993, as a governmental auxiliary body' and has been referred to as 'Komnas HAM I' prior to Law No. 39/1999 and 'Komnas HAM II' post-1999.

K. Clair (✉)
University of California, Los Angeles, Los Angeles, CA, USA
e-mail: kstwarog@ucla.edu



J. Gomez, R. Ramcharan (eds.), *National Human Rights Institutions in Southeast Asia*,
https://doi.org/10.1007/978-981-15-1074-8_11

Komnas HAM took on a more active role in supporting the rights of persons with disabilities with the development of the United Nation's Convention on the Rights of Persons with Disabilities (CRPD), which represents the 'first comprehensive and legally binding international framework for promoting the rights of people with mental and psychosocial disabilities' (Drew et al. 2011: 1665). Komnas HAM supported Indonesia's decision to sign the convention in 2007 and pushed for ratification, which was achieved in 2011. For Suharto et al. (2016: 694–695), Indonesia's ratification of the CRPD 'reaffirmed the spirit on advocacy of the rights of people with disabilities' and has helped bring about 'a gradual shift in the societal tendency towards recognising and utilising the unique abilities of people with impairments' (2016: 695). In 2009, Komnas HAM met with disability activist groups to discuss appropriate, non-stigmatizing terminology for referring to persons with disabilities within official documents.[2] These meetings resulted in a Memorandum of Understanding (2010) that promoted *penyandang disibilitas* as the most preferable term (Edwards 2014: 4).

In the early 2000s, disability rights activists called for the amendment of Law No. 4/1997 on Persons with Disabilities,[3] which contained provisions they believed conflicted with the CRPD.[4] Komnas HAM contributed revisions, which eventually informed Law No. 8/2016 on Persons with Disabilities (Ibid.: 5). However, this law has also been criticized for its failure to 'fully comply' (Human Rights Watch 2017) with the UN CRPD. Other laws and policies directly violate the human rights of individuals with psychosocial disabilities, such as a regional election law, which bars persons with permanent mental illness from participating in elections (Irmansyah 2017), and interdiction provisions, which deny persons with mental illness the right to make their own legal decisions (Colbran 2010: 48). Disability rights activists have also criticized the 2014 Mental Health Act, which 'allows a family member or guardian to admit a child or an adult with a psychosocial disability without their consent to a mental

[2] Nursyamsi et al. (2015: 44–45) note that debate over proper terminology 'is still ongoing'.

[3] Edwards (2014: 4) takes issue with the translation of Law No. 4/1997 on 'Persons with Disabilities', claiming that 'a more accurate translation of the legislation—the title of which refers to *penyandang cacat*—is "Law No 4 of 1997 on the Handicapped"'.

[4] For example, Law No. 4/1997 is seen to promote a 'charity-based' model of disability instead of the more commonly accepted 'social model'. See Edwards (2014) and Colbran (2010) for specific criticisms of Law No. 4/1997.

health or a social care institution and without any judicial review' (Reese 2016).

To combat these and other forms of discrimination against persons with psychosocial disabilities, Komnas HAM has urged the Indonesian government to ratify the Optional Protocol to the Convention on the Rights of Persons with Disabilities (OP CRPD), which will 'strengthen the implementation and monitoring of the CRPD' (Nainggolan et al. 2016: 8–9). The OP CRPD will allow individuals to directly petition the international OP-CRPD Committee, which is comprised 92-member states, to investigate violations of their rights. In this way, the OP CRPD grants persons with disabilities 'alternative channels' for seeking justice (ibid.: 6).

## Komnas HAM's Limitations

Beyond issuing legal recommendations, Komnas HAM processes complaints, publishes new research and partners with civil society organizations to protect the human rights of persons with psychosocial disabilities. Nevertheless, the institution remains hampered by its inability to enforce anti-discrimination laws and by widespread confusion about disability rights, mental health issues and human rights violations. Such confusion has the potential to undermine Komnas HAM's advocacy efforts. The following section outlines these limitations in greater detail.

### *Lack of Enforcement*

Since its inception, Komnas HAM has been critiqued for its inability to enforce the law. The institution's responses to complaints are not legally binding, leading some to perceive Komnas HAM as 'toothless' (Edwards 2014: 9). For Eldridge (2002: 147), 'perceptions of powerlessness weaken public credibility and confidence in approaching [the institution]. These largely stem from false expectations that Komnas HAM can enforce its own recommendations'. Others have suggested that the call for a separate National Disabilities Commission (Komisi Nasional Disabilitas), which would to oversee the implementation of Law No. 8/2016 on Persons with Disabilities as well as the CRPD, suggests 'skepticism' towards Komnas HAM's contributions to disability rights advocacy (Pusat Studi Hukum dan Kebijakan Indonesia 2014; Edwards 2014: 9). The creation of a National Disabilities Commission is included in Law No. 8/2016 on

Persons with Disabilities and designed to 'ensure "the implementation of respect, protection and fulfilment of rights of Persons with disabilities"' (Pusat Studi Hukum dan Kebijakan Indonesia 2016). However, the presidential regulation required to establish the Commission has not yet been issued, causing disability rights activists to publicly demand swifter action (Fransisca 2017).

In the absence of robust legal powers, Komnas HAM has often relied on media publicity to draw attention to human rights violations and 'exert pressure on individuals or groups to cooperate with its inquiries' (Herbert 2008: 463). In May of 2016, Komnas HAM Commissioner Siane Indriani used this tactic to shine a spotlight on cases of *pasung*—the practice of restraining persons with severe mental illness, either by confining them within rooms, cages or huts or restricting their limbs with chains or wooden stocks (Stratford et al. 2014: 72). *Pasung*, which is typically a last resort for families whose relatives pose a danger to themselves or others, is considered a violation of human rights within the Indonesian Constitution (1945), Law No 39/1999 ('Human Rights' Law), and Law No 36/2009 ('Health' Law), which states, 'Patients with mental disorders who are abandoned, left to wander about, or who threaten the safety of themselves and/or others, and/or disturb public order and/or public safety are obligated to receive treatment and care at health-care facilities' (Pramesti 2014). Indriani visited several families in East Java who had restrained their relatives and spoke to reporters at *Tempo* and *Harian Jogja* to advocate for the use of medical treatment, greater access to mental health facilities and reduced stigma towards individuals and families affected by mental illness (Harian Jogja 2016; Nugroho 2016).

Despite these efforts to promote the rights of persons with psychosocial disabilities through media platforms, Komnas HAM acknowledges that 'people with disabilities in Indonesia still experience various forms of human rights violations and their cases cannot be resolved effectively by existing national mechanisms in Indonesia. The state does not act to provide effective solutions' (Nainggolan et al. 2016: viii). The U.S. Department of State (2016) has found that the Indonesian government has ignored and 'often avoided' adopting recommendations submitted by Komnas HAM and other agencies, such as Komnas Perempuan. For Komnas HAM to be effective, Hsien-Li argues, the Indonesian government must not 'obstruct' the institution (2011: 89–90): 'Real powers and adequate resources must be given [to Komnas HAM] such that the proper functioning of its mandate—educating the public about human rights and encouragement on the ratification of UN human rights treaties, as well as reporting and rectifying Indonesian rights practices in line with the Constitution, *Pancasila*, and UN treaties Indonesia has acceded to—can be carried out'.

### *Lack of Clarity*

Komnas HAM's advocacy efforts are also weakened by what Edwards refers to as 'widespread ignorance about people with disabilities in Indonesian society' (2014: 11). Misconceptions about what constitutes a 'disability' or a 'human rights violation' undermine the institution's efforts to promote human rights literacy and may interfere with current complaint reporting procedures and data collection. Unfortunately, inconsistencies within Komnas HAM's own publications may contribute to this confusion.

Article 1 of the United Nation's Convention on the Rights of Persons with Disabilities defines 'persons with disabilities' as 'those who have long-term physical, mental, intellectual or sensory impairments which in interaction with various barriers may hinder their full and effective participation in society on an equal basis with others' (Drew et al. 2011: 1665). In this formation, psychosocial impairment is included within, and considered a specific type of, disability. This same construction emerges within Komnas HAM's 'Position Paper' (Nainggolan et al. 2016: 1–2), which further elaborates on the differences among physical, mental, intellectual and sensory forms of impairment'. Similarly, in their recent Submission to the United Nations/3rd Universal Periodic Review (Komnas HAM 2016: 4–5), a discussion of *pasung* and other forms of discrimination faced by 'persons with mental disabilities' appears under the sub-heading, 'Persons with Disabilities', suggesting that psychosocial impairment is included within the broader category of 'disability'.

In other publications, however, 'disability' refers specifically to physical impairments and does not include experiences of mental illness. A 2015 edition of *Suar*, a Komnas HAM newsletter 'distributed to civil society, educational institutions, religious groups, the military, police, and government agencies' (Herbert 2008: 462), was dedicated exclusively to issues concerning 'persons with disabilities' (*penyandang disabilitas*) but contained no articles on mental health issues. This construction, which separates psychosocial impairment from physical disability, is consistent with popular understandings of the term, '*penyandang disabilitas*', which, according to Suharto et al. (2016: 693), 'focuses on physical deficits rather than acknowledging the varied abilities'.

The lack of clarity surrounding the definition and classification of various disabilities directly impacts the quality and availability of assistance for persons with either or both mental and physical impairments. In some cases, individuals with vision impairments have been required to submit verification of their ability to make independent decisions—a process typically reserved for individuals with psychosocial impairments rather than visual/sensory disabilities (Colbran 2010: 49; Edwards 2014: 11). For Edwards (2014: 11–12), such confusion is not 'limited to the uneducated'; in fact, 'The apparent ignorance about people with disabilities evinced by members of the legal profession may be another reason why the formal rights which do clearly exist for people with disabilities in Indonesian law are largely unenforced, in that the very people who are supposed to advocate on behalf of people with disabilities may not really understand the issues'.

Ambiguous constructions of 'disability' and 'persons with disabilities' have also compromised data collection efforts by producing unreliable demographic estimates. In 2012, the National Socioeconomic Survey (Susenas) estimated approximately 2,126,000 individuals living with a disability in Indonesia, or 2.45 percent of the total population (Nainggolan et al. 2016: 2). The World Health Organization puts this figure closer to 10 percent, a discrepancy Edwards attributes to 'differing understandings about the basic issue of what constitutes a disability' (2014: 11). The Indonesian Centre for Law and Policy Studies views such discrepancies as an obstacle to mental health advocacy, since '[a] thoroughly valid inventory is essential for the basis of policy making' (Pusat Studi Hukum dan Kebijakan Indonesia 2014).

Such confusion impacts Komnas HAM's data collection efforts as well. The institution's monthly reports[5] offer information about the groups and individuals who have submitted complaints, using classifications such as 'Corporation', 'LGBT individual', 'Person with Disabilities' (*Penyandang Disabilitas*) and 'Disabilities Organization' (*Kelompok Penyandang Disabilitas*). Because these classification schemas do not address whether persons with psychosocial disabilities are included in the category, 'penyandang disibilitas', it is impossible to draw any definitive conclusions about

[5] These reports can be accessed at: https://www.komnasham.go.id/index.php/data-pengaduan/.

such individuals' complaint reporting practices. Nonetheless, current data suggests that Komnas HAM's reporting mechanisms remain underutilized by this group. In 2015, Komnas HAM received a total of 8249 complaints, only two of which were submitted by individuals with disabilities and four from disabilities organizations. In 2016, individuals with disabilities submitted four complaints and disabilities organizations submitted only one out of a total of 7188 complaints. These dramatically low numbers support one of three possibilities: reporting mechanisms are not accessible to persons with disabilities; confusion about what constitutes a human rights violation against persons with disabilities persists; persons with disabilities are disinclined to report violations of their rights to Komnas HAM. For Drew et al. (2011: 1672), 'Part of the reason why violations continue unabated is that they are unreported. Legal mechanisms therefore need to be in place to enable and encourage people with mental and psychosocial disabilities, their family members, friends, and advocates to report any human rights violations freely and securely'.

The scope and variety of discrimination faced by persons with disabilities may contribute to lingering confusion about what constitutes a human rights violation against such individuals. In a 2016 Position Paper (Nainggolan et al. 2016: 3), Komnas HAM lists 'discrimination, stigmatization, harassment, expulsion, ridicule, assault, rape, violence, and murder' as examples of human rights violations against persons with mental illness and notes that such violations can occur with respect to employment, education, public services, transportation, participation in elections and physical abuse. Persons with disabilities continue to be regarded as 'unhealthy people' (ibid.: 4–5), 'unproductive citizens' (Reese 2016), or 'spiritually deficient' individuals (U.S. Department of State 2016) and may be further dehumanized through stigmatizing language. Although the term '*penyandang cacat*', which translates literally as 'persons with defects' (Suharto et al. 2016: 699) has been replaced by '*penyandang disabilitas*' in official documents, terms like '*orang gila* (mad person), *gelo* (crazy), *edan* (crazy), and *otack miring* (unstable brain) are still common and exacerbate stigma' (Reese 2016). The U.S. Department of State (2016) found that stigma has a direct impact on the utilization of resources, as 'persons with disabilities commonly failed to pursue the accommodations to which they are entitled'. In this way, ongoing stigma towards persons with physical and/or psychosocial disabilities disrupts advocacy efforts.

In recent years, Komnas HAM has taken steps to improve complaint reporting and increase public literacy of human rights within specific communities throughout Indonesia. Their April 2017 report (Komnas HAM 2017: 7) includes plans to hold 'proactive complaint consultation and procurement in the region' of East Java by opening a new complaint post, holding a focus group discussion and developing a radio talk show. Their May 2016 report (Komnas HAM 2016: 14–15) describes similar activities implemented in the Gunung Sitoli region of Nias. However, such efforts tend to have a general focus and do not directly address misconceptions towards mental illness or disability rights.

### *Lack of Coordination*

As a national institution with limited powers of enforcement, Komnas HAM may be most influential through its regional offices, which can respond to the unique needs of Indonesia's provinces. Herbert notes, 'Regional centers are generally established around existing local human rights networks and draw heavily on the input and knowledge of the local sector. All centers work hard to build dynamic links with local government, civil society and educational institutions' (2008: 465). At present, Komnas HAM has offices in Aceh, West Sumatra, West Kalimantan, Central Sulawesi, Maluku and Papua.

Nevertheless, an uneven distribution of power within these regional offices may negatively impact advocacy for the rights of persons with psychosocial disabilities. Herbert explains, 'Regional representatives are to some extent personality-driven… The personal networks, previous vocations, and level of skills in advocacy, mediation and campaigning of individual commissioners tend to influence the overall strategies adopted by each regional center in responding to regional human rights issues, alongside the strength and effectiveness of their relationships with regional government' (Ibid.: 466). This pattern suggests that discrimination against persons with psychosocial disabilities will not be addressed unless the representatives themselves prioritize mental health. The specific interests and training of individual Commissioners also impact the procedure for reviewing and responding to complaints. According to Colbran (2010: 27), 'Most complaints are directed personally to one of the Commissioners who is himself blind. He responds directly, rather than submitting the complaints through Komnas HAM's formal complaint mechanism procedure'.

Protecting the human rights of persons with psychosocial disabilities demands coordinated action among mental health professionals, social workers, human rights advocates and community members. Both national and regional officials must commit to protecting the rights of persons with psychosocial disabilities not merely through legislation, but through stigma reduction, accurate data collection and research methods and a commitment to making mental health resources more affordable and accessible. Similarly, Komnas HAM must adopt a comprehensive approach to mental health advocacy rather than assign unequal responsibility to regional representatives. In this way, Komnas HAM representatives can help build a wider network of support for individuals who have experienced human rights violations as a result of mental illness.

## Beyond *Pasung*: Developing a Comprehensive Approach to Mental Health Advocacy

With lingering stigma towards persons with disabilities, 'widespread ignorance' (Edwards 2014: 11) about disability-related issues, unreliable data and inconsistent attention devoted to disability rights with Komnas HAM's regional offices, it is unsurprising that approaches to mental health advocacy continue to be disjointed and disaggregated. Lata Mani (2013: 121) describes disaggregation as 'the separation of an interconnected whole into its component parts. It follows that when this whole is disaggregated, the relations of multiplicity and relationality of which it is comprised are also taken apart and remade'. Indonesia's recent efforts to protect the human rights of individuals who have been chained, shackled or confined due to mental illness presents a clear example of such a 'disaggregated' approach.

Although *pasung* has been banned in Indonesia since 1977, the past decade has seen a more concentrated effort to view the practice as a human rights violation and reduce the total number of cases throughout Indonesia. In 2010, Aceh was first province to launch a 'Bebas Pasung' ('Free Pasung') program, which aimed to release and provide medical treatment to the 200 individuals reported to be in physical restraint (Irmansyah et al. 2009). The Ministry of Health developed a similar program in 2011 called, 'Menuju Indonesia Bebas Pasung' ('Towards a Shackle-Free Indonesia'), which has been implemented on a regional level (Stratford et al. 2014: 72). A recent report (Reese 2016) found that 'about 20 out of Indonesia's 34 provinces—including Central Java, West Nusa Tenggara, East Java, Jambi, Yogyakarta, and Aceh have a functional *pasung*-free initiative'. Initially, the national campaign bore the name 'Stop Pasung', as efforts focused on eliminating the practice 'from the whole of Indonesia' (Puteh et al. 2011: 4). The name was later changed to 'Free Pasung'.

In theory, the Bebas Pasung program aims to do more than merely 'free' individuals from restraint. Through coordination with government officials, social services, community mental health workers and community leaders, the campaign strives to reduce the stigma associated with mental illness, raise awareness about effective forms of treatment, and improve Indonesians' access to mental health care. However, the emphasis on 'stopping' or 'eliminating' *pasung* has discouraged a long-term, comprehensive approach that devotes equal attention to follow-up care. In a recent New York Times article (Emont 2016), Dr. Nova Riyanti Yusuf, a psychiatrist, former chairwoman and well-known advocate for persons with mental illness, reflected on the limitations of such an approach.

During her time in Parliament, Ms. Nova worked to convince lawmakers of the dire situation of the mental health system. She led lawmakers on a trip to Lombok, an underdeveloped island east of Bali, where the mentally ill were chained to sheds by family members who did not know what else to do with them. 'The male parliamentarians were so eager to remove the person from his chains', she remembered. But then 'the family began crying. After he was released the family didn't know what came next'. The point, she explained to her colleagues, was that there was no clear next step, as Indonesia did not have an established system for mental health care.

Regional initiatives, such as Makpasol[6] and e-pasung, have also prioritized identifying and documenting cases of *pasung* and have devoted less attention to creating additional opportunities for follow-up care. According to Dr. Azhari Cahyadi Nurdin and Dr. Agung Wiretno Putro, who designed Makpasol, the website offers 'a database for pasung cases' that serves West Nusa Tenggara Province.[7] Community members, social workers and government officials can report cases of *pasung* through the site's online submission form. Once these reports are verified by Mutiara Sukma Mental Hospital, a team of community mental health workers is sent to

[6] Makpasol is an abbreviation of 'Masyarakat Aktif Klik Pasung Online', or 'Active Society/Community Clicks Pasung Online'. For more information, see: http://www.makpasol.ntbprov.go.id/.

[7] Email correspondence with author, 3 April 2017.

release individuals from *pasung* and deliver appropriate medical services. The site also contains a counter that estimates the number of *pasung* cases in each region. Although Makpasol includes an FAQ page that addresses misconceptions about mental illness, surveys designed to encourage early detection, links to articles and other resources on mental health and a consultation page allowing visitors to submit queries anonymously to a psychiatrist, it is clear that, at least at this stage, the site functions primarily to address current cases of *pasung*.

The e-pasung program represents a similar initiative. First launched in Surabaya in May of 2016, 'e-pasung' refers to the use of smartphone applications as data collection technology that, in conjunction with educational campaigns and affordable treatment, may expedite symptom assessment and strengthen community mental health networks. In East Java, e-pasung has been praised for offering mental health workers a fast and reliable means of reporting new cases of *pasung*, organizing existing cases into an accessible database and continually monitoring individuals who have been shackled to prevent 'relapse', that is, the family's resumption of *pasung* after a relative has received medical treatment (Fajerial 2016). According to Dr. Sukesi, the Head of Social Services in East Java, e-pasung has helped reduce the number of pasung cases from 729 in early 2016 to 712 cases in July 2016 (Budiawan 2016). However, the success of e-pasung has been measured by the number of individuals that community mental health workers have identified, released from confinement, and brought to local hospitals for medical treatment. There are no complementary efforts to determine whether the use of e-pasung has increased public awareness of mental health and human rights, strengthened relationships between community members and mental health workers or improved resource allocation in targeted areas.

For this reason, Makpasol and e-pasung offer a disaggregated approach to mental health advocacy, placing undue emphasis on eliminating existing cases of *pasung* without sufficiently addressing the multiple, intersecting factors that cause families to rely on *pasung* in the first place. For Chapman (2009: 108), this represents a challenge for human rights advocates more broadly, as 'the narrow and sometimes excessively legalistic understanding of the right to health held by many in the human rights community does not accord sufficient importance to the role of the social determinants of health'. The social determinants underlying families' reliance on *pasung* include persistent stigma toward persons with psychosocial disabilities and 'inaccessible, unaffordable, ineffective psychiatric treatment services' (Puteh et al. 2011: 5).

Without an effective stigma-reduction program, for example, individuals who have been released from *pasung* and received medical treatment may face difficulties with community re-integration. Reese (2016) explains, 'Even those who are rescued return to *pasung* once they return to the community due to a lack of follow-up and access to community-based support and mental health care services, and continued stigma in the community'. Mamnuaha et al. (2016: 24) also stress the importance of 'community integration' within the recovery process: 'Patients striving to free themselves from the confines of the illness and developing a personal identity is meaningful, where they are able to carry out their role in the community'.

A comprehensive approach to mental health must also increase the availability and accessibility of mental health resources. Of Indonesia's thirty-four provinces, eight are without a mental hospital and three have no psychiatrists (Reese 2016). Even when mental health facilities are available, negative perceptions of psychiatrists and hospitalization can cause an under-utilization of such resources. For Suripto and Alfiah (2017), 'The large number of people with severe mental disorders who did not receive medical treatment is due to factors such as lack of funds and families' and community members' lack of knowledge about the symptoms of mental disorders'. Families may also avoid hospitalization due to a preference for spiritual and traditional healers (Reese 2016).

Further, although Makpasol and e-pasung may improve coordination among community health workers, human rights activists and government officials in the long-term, these initiatives rely on technologies that are not necessarily accessible to low-income families, individuals in geographically remote areas or persons with psychosocial disabilities themselves. Instead, these initiatives are geared towards community members with smartphones and internet access who are aware that *pasung* constitutes a human rights violation. These factors merely increase the likelihood that the Makpasol and e-pasung initiatives will function primarily to identify and respond to cases of *pasung* rather than provide a comprehensive mental health resource for the greater community.

The Bebas Pasung campaign also represents a disaggregated approach to mental health advocacy by shining a spotlight on the most extreme human rights violation against persons with severe mental illness without connecting *pasung* to broader discussions of discrimination against persons with psychosocial disabilities. In recent years, *pasung* has dominated both international and national discussion of mental health and human rights in Indonesia. For example, in both the 2016 and 2017 Human Rights Watch Country Reports on Indonesia, the section devoted to 'Disability Rights' focuses entirely on *pasung* as an ongoing human rights violation. Within Indonesian news, stories of individuals who have been released from restraint or confinement are a regular feature. Such reports emphasize the violence of *pasung*, with photographs focused on grimy shackles and chains. In video footage, government officials, psychologists or social workers are shown heroically sawing through chain links or locks to free the *pasung* 'victims'. These stories, and the Bebas Pasung campaign, suggest that mental health advocacy depends primarily on the protection of individual's 'negative' rights—that is, the right *not* to be restrained—and devotes considerably less attention to the protection of individuals' and communities' 'positive' rights, such as the right to affordable, accessible mental health care. Moreover, the campaign divorces *pasung* from other experiences of psychosocial disability, suggesting that only individuals who have been restrained deserve media attention and social resources. In this way, the Bebas Pasung campaign offers a disaggregated approach to mental health and may exacerbate widespread confusion surrounding mental health, disability and human rights in Indonesia.

## Conclusion

Komnas HAM has guided Indonesia towards laws, policies and campaigns designed to improve the lives of persons affected by mental illness. The government's ratification of the Convention on the Rights of Persons with Disabilities (2011), the passage of the Mental Health Act (2014) and the enactment of Law No. 8 on Persons with Disabilities (2016) represent critical first steps towards strengthening legal protections and addressing existing discrimination against persons with mental illness. However, these actions must be more than just 'window dressing' and must represent 'a serious commitment to implement respect for human rights in practice' (Hafner-Burton and Tsutsui 2005: 1378). Although Komnas HAM lacks the power to enforce mental health legislation, the institution can continue to protect the human rights of individuals and families affected by psychosocial disabilities through research, education and advocacy.

Specifically, Komnas HAM should offer clarification with regards to terminology used to refer to persons with psychosocial disabilities within its publications and reports. Such clarification is needed to improve research on complaint reporting practices and increase the accessibility of complaint reporting mechanisms. Second, Komnas HAM can bolster its outreach and education efforts by integrating comprehensive discussions of mental health into workshops and training sessions that focus more generally on human rights. Including persons with psychosocial disabilities as both consultants and instructors in such workshops can help reduce stigma within the community and address misconceptions surrounding disabilities, discrimination and human rights.

Finally, Komnas HAM should strive to provide consistent mental health advocacy throughout Indonesia so that regional offices do not adopt a 'personality-driven' agenda dictated by the concerns of individual representatives. Through partnerships with community mental health organizations and disability rights activists, Komnas HAM's regional offices can offer mental health resources that address the specific needs and values of the community. In all these efforts, Komnas HAM must adopt an inclusive approach to protecting the 'positive' rights of persons with psychosocial disabilities (including the right to health, the right to participate in government elections, and the right to independent decision-making) while also responding to, and striving to prevent, human rights violations. Such an approach will prove beneficial both to individuals with psychosocial disabilities and to Indonesian society.

## References

Budiawan, A. 2016. 'E-pasung kurangi kasus pemasungan di Jatim' [E-pasung reduces cases of shackling in East Java], *Aktual*, 6 August. Available at: http://www.aktual.com/e-pasung-kurangi-kasus-pemasungan-jatim/.

Chapman, A. 2009. Globalization, human rights and the social determinants of health, *Bioethics*, Vol 23, Issue 2, Pgs. 91–111.

Colbran, N. 2010. Access to justice for persons with disabilities in Indonesia: background assessment report, *International Labour Organization*. Available at: http://www.ilo.org/jakarta/whatwedo/publications/WCMS_160337/lang%2D%2Den/index.htm.

Drew, N. et al. 2011. Human rights violations of persons with mental and psychosocial disabilities: an unresolved global crisis, *The Lancet*, Vol 378, Pgs. 1664–1675.

Edwards, N. 2014. Disability rights in Indonesia? Problems with ratification of the United Nations Convention on the Rights of Persons with Disabilities, *Australian Journal of Asian Law*, Vol 15, Issue 1, Pgs. 1–15.

Eldridge, Philip J. 2002. *The Politics of Human Rights in Southeast Asia*, London: Routledge.

Emont, J. 2016. Fighting for Indonesia's mentally ill, and counting toilets and progress, *The New York Times*, 21 October. Available at: https://www.nytimes.com/2016/10/22/world/asia/fighting-for-indonesias-mentally-ill-and-counting-toilets-as-progress.html?mcubz=0.

Fajerial, Edwin. 2016. 'E-pasung untuk pantau penderita sakit jiwa di Jawa Timur' [E-pasung to monitor persons with mental illness in East Java], *Tempo*, 20 May. Available at: https://m.tempo.co/read/news/2016/05/20/173772739/e-pasung-untuk-pantau-penderita-sakit-jiwa-di-jawa-timur.

Fransisca, M. 2017. 'Aksi penyandang disabilitas tuntut bentuk komisi nasional disabilitas' [Persons with disabilities demand action on forming a National Disabilities Commission], *Tempo*, 18 May. Available at: https://video.tempo.co/read/2017/05/18/6787/aksi-penyandang-disabilitas-tuntut-bentuk-komisi-nasional-disabilitas.

Hafner-Burton, Emilie M. and Kiyoteru Tsutsui. 2005. Human rights in a globalizing world: the paradox of empty promises, *American Journal of Sociology*, Vol 110, Issue 5, Pgs. 1373–1411.

Harian Jogja. 2016. 'Komnas HAM: setop pemasungan terhadap penderita sakit jiwa' [Indonesian National Human Rights Commission: stop shackling persons with mental illness], *Harian Jogja* [Jogyakarta Daily], 20 May. Available at: http://m.harianjogja.com/baca/2016/05/20/korban-pasung-komnas-ham-setop-pemasungan-terhadap-penderita-sakit-jiwa-721060.

Herbert, J. 2008. 'The legal framework of human rights in Indonesia', in Timothy Lindsey (ed), *Indonesia: Law and Society*, 2nd ed., New South Wales: The Federation Press, Pgs. 456–482.

Hsien-Li T. 2011. *The ASEAN Intergovernmental Commission on Human Rights*, New York: Cambridge University Press.

Human Rights Watch. 2017. World Report 2017: Indonesia, Events of 2016. Available at: https://www.hrw.org/world-report/2017/country-chapters/indonesia.

Irmansyah, I. 2017. Orang dengan gangguan jiwa berhak dan mampu memilih [Persons with mental illness have the right and ability to vote], 5 May. Available at: http://pdskji.org/article_det-33-orang-dengan-gangguan-jiwa-berhak-dan-mampu-memilih.html.

Irmansyah, I., Y.A. Prasetyo and Harry Minas. 2009. Human rights of persons with mental illness in Indonesia: more than legislation is needed, *International Journal of Mental Health Systems*, Vol 3, Issue 14, Pgs. 1–10.

Komnas HAM. 2016a. Submission to the United Nations: 3rd Universal Periodic Review, Jakarta Pusat, Indonesia: Komisi Hak Asasi Manusia [The Indonesian National Human Rights Commission]: 1–13.

———. 2016b. Laporan pengaduan bulan May 2016 [Monthly complain report, May 2016]. Available at: https://www.komnasham.go.id/files/20160508-laporan-data-pengaduan-mei-2016-$V5K0YM.pdf.

———. 2017. Laporan pengaduan bulan April 2017 [Monthly complain report, April 2017]. Available at: https://www.komnasham.go.id/files/20170507-laporan-pengaduan-bulan-april%2D%2D$XJ8.pdf.

Mamnuaha et al. 2016. Literature review of mental health recovery in Indonesia, *Journal of Nursing and Health Care*, Vol 3, Issue 2, Pgs. 20–25. Available at: http://dl6.globalstf.org/index.php/jnhc/article/viewFile/1584/1612.

Mani, L. 2013. *The Integral Nature of Things: Critical Reflections on the Present*, New Delhi: Routledge.

Nainggolan, Yossa. et al. 2016. Kertas posisi: mendorong pengesahan Optional Protocol to the Convention on the Rights of Persons with Disabilities [Position paper to encourage ratification of the Optional Protocol to the Convention on the Rights of Persons with Disabilities], Komisi Hak Asasi Manusia [The Indonesian National Human Rights Commission]: 1–40.

Nugroho, N. 2016. Komnas HAM investigasi pemasungan orang gila di jatim [Indonesian National Human Rights Commission investigates the shackling of crazy people in East Java], *Tempo*, 17 May. Available at: https://nasional.tempo.co/read/news/2016/05/17/058771735/komnas-ham-investigasi-pemasungan-orang-gila-di-jatim#IYZfPzxHe6bDQ938.97.

Nursyamsi et al. 2015. Kerangka hukum disibilitas di Indonesia: menuju Indonesia ramah disibilitas [Legal framework of disability in Indonesia: toward a disability-friendly Indonesia], Pusat Studi Hukum dan Kebijakan Indonesia [Indonesian Centre for the Study of Law and Policy]: Pgs. 1–98.

Pramesti, Tir Jata Ayu. 2014. Klinik: hak asasi penderita gangguan jiwa [Clinic: the human rights of persons with mental illness], 7 January. Available at: http://www.hukumonline.com/klinik/detail/lt52c808d73d54f/hak-asasi-penderita-gangguan-jiwa.

Pusat Studi Hukum dan Kebijakan Indonesia [Indonesian Centre for the Study of Law and Policy]. 2014. 'Siaran pers: 7 catatan Untuk RUU Penyandang Disabilitas' [Press release: 7 notes on the Persons with Disabilities Bill]. Available at: http://www.pshk.or.id/wp-content/uploads/2015/09/Siaran-Pers-11-Maret-2014-Catatan-untuk-RUU-Penyandang-Disabilitas.pdf.

———. 2016. Komisi Nasional Disabilitas: implementasi UU Penyandang Disabilitas [National Disabilities Commission: implementing the Persons with Disabilities Bill]. Available at http://www.pshk.or.id/id/berita/aktivitas/komisi-nasional-disabilitas-implementasi-uu-penyandang-disabilitas/.

Puteh, Ibrahim, M. Marthoenis and Harry Minas. 2011. *Aceh Free Pasung*: Releasing the mentally ill from physical restraint, *International Journal of Mental Health Systems*, Vol 5, Issue 10, Pgs. 1–5.

Reese, A.S. 2016. Living in hell: abuses against people with psychosocial disabilities in Indonesia, *Human Rights Watch*. Available at: https://www.hrw.org/report/2016/03/21/living-hell/abuses-against-people-psychosocial-disabilities-indonesia.

Stratford et al. 2014. Introducing recovery-oriented practice in Indonesia: the Sukambumi project—an innovative mental health programme, *Asia Pacific Journal of Social Work and Development*, Vol 24, Issues 1–2, Pgs. 71–81.

Suharto, Suharto, Pim Kuipers and Pat Dorsett. 2016. Disability terminology and the emergence of 'diffability' in Indonesia, *Disability and Society*, Vol 31, Issue 5, Pgs. 693–712.

Suripto and Siti Alfiah. 2017. Indonesia bebas pasung 2017: Pemodelan inovasi pemerintah daerah menuju bebas pasung [Shackle-free Indonesia 2017: an innovative model from regional governments towards a pasung-free Indonesia], *National Innovation Administration*. Available at: http://inovasi.lan.go.id/uploads/download/1472810970_INDONESIA-BEBAS-PASUNG-2017%2D%2D-Pemodelan-Inovasi-Pemerintah-Daerah-menuju-bebas-pasung.pdf.

U.S. Department of State. 2016. Country reports on human rights practices for 2016: Indonesia. Available at: https://www.state.gov/j/drl/rls/hrrpt/humanrightsreport/index.htm?year=2016&dlid=265338.

CHAPTER 12

# Bridging Gaps and Hopes: Malaysia's National Human Rights Commission and Rights Related to SOGIESC

*Henry Koh*

## Introduction

This chapter argues that Malaysia's National Human Rights Institution, known in Malay as *Suruhanjaya Hak Asasi Manusia Malaysia* (SUHAKAM) has progressed in a positive direction albeit in a limited manner with regard to the protection of the rights related to sexual orientation, gender identity, and expression of sex characteristics (SOGIESC). Overall, however, for a country that has achieved impressive economic development, Malaysia's human rights record has not similarly developed, especially with

SOGIESC is an acronym for sexual orientation, gender identity, and expression of sex characteristics.

This chapter was written when the author served with Fortify Rights.

H. Koh (✉)
Global Fund Malaysia Representative, Kuala Lumpur, Malaysia





J. Gomez, R. Ramcharan (eds.), *National Human Rights Institutions in Southeast Asia*,
https://doi.org/10.1007/978-981-15-1074-8_12

regard to SOGIESC. SUHAKAM's mandate compels it to do more to advocate for the advancement of SOGIESC rights.[1]

The issue of lesbian, gay, bisexual, transgender, and intersex (LGBTI) rights remains polarizing in Malaysia. Sexual minorities face discrimination and violations of their fundamental human rights. Malaysian authorities have failed to enforce protective laws or protect the rights of LGBTI persons, and high levels of anti-LGBTI stigma pose significant challenges to LGBTI individuals in their efforts to claim their rights. Moreover, the government's failure to promote and protect rights related to SOGIESC impedes prevention of sexually transmitted diseases, including HIV, as stigma and criminalization impacts a person's ability to take charge of their personal health or access health services when needed.

Since the advent of the 2006 Yogyakarta Principles—a set of human rights principles relating to SOGIESC intended to provide guidance on preventing violations and protecting the rights of LGBTI people[2]—there are a growing number of initiatives from National Human Rights Institutions (NHRIs) in Southeast Asia to tackle rights violations and discrimination faced by people of diverse SOGIESC.[3] In comparison with NHRIs in other Southeast Asian nations, Malaysia's National Human Rights Institution, known in Malay as *Suruhanjaya Hak Asasi Manusia Malaysia* (SUHAKAM), has at times struggled to take up SOGIESC initiatives due to political and cultural impediments, but SUHAKAM has shown signs of significant improvement in this area.

Following a brief overview of SOGIESC rights, this chapter analyses SUHAKAM's efforts to respond to SOGIESC issues, discusses the challenges the rights body faces, and provides recommendations for expanding SOGIESC rights in Malaysia. The chapter draws on primary documents, notably NHRI reports and policy statements, and on Fortify Rights' first-hand experience with interaction interviews with a staff member and officers of SUHAKAM.

[1] Malaysia was ranked 13th by the World Bank's Commission on Growth and Development among countries with an average increase in Gross Domestic Product (GDP) of more than 7 per cent per year for 25 consecutive years or more.# This demonstrates that Malaysia can grow and change in ways intended to benefit society and the region.

[2] International Commission of Jurists and International Service for Human Rights (2006) *Yogyakarta Principles: Preamble.*

[3] Asia Pacific Forum, UNDP Asia Pacific (2016) Promoting and Protecting Human Rights in relation to Sexual Orientation, Gender Identity and Sex Characteristics, Thailand.

## Understanding SOGIESC

SOGIESC are the fundamental identifiers of a person's personality or identity. Scholars and human rights experts agree that the freedom to self-define one's SOGIESC is one of the most basic aspects of self-determination, dignity, and freedom.[4] Sexual or gender identification is intrinsic to every person's identity, regardless of whether that identification manifests in physical or other ways.

The United Nations (UN) treaty monitoring bodies have spoken out many times against violations of a person's right to physical and bodily integrity, self-determination, and autonomy. For example, the Concluding Observations from the Committee on the Rights of the Child,[5] the Committee on Economic, the Committee on Social and Cultural Rights,[6] and the Committee on the Rights of Persons with Disabilities[7] have provided detailed recommendations about the treatment of sexual minorities.

In recent years, a consensus has emerged on using the term "sex characteristics," expanding the original terminology from SOGI (sexual orientation and gender identity) to SOGIESC (sexual orientation, gender identity, and sex characteristics). This shift is intended for the protection and inclusion of intersex individuals.[8] Susan Ryan, Age Discrimination Commissioner at the Australian Human Rights Commission, explained the importance of using correct terminology to describe a person's identity or characteristics:

> I want to acknowledge that terminology can have a profound impact on a person's identity, self-worth and inherent dignity. The use of inclusive and acceptable terminology empowers individuals and enables visibility of important issues. The [Australian Human Rights] Commission supports the right of people to identify their sexual orientation, sex and gender as they choose. The Commission also recognizes that terminology is strongly contested.[9]

[4] International Commission of Jurists and International Service for Human Rights (2006) *Yogyakarta Principles: Principle 3.*

[5] Committee on the Rights of the Child, (2015) *Concluding Observations: CRC/C/CHE/CO/2–4, para. 43b*, Switzerland.

[6] Committee on Economic, Social and Cultural Rights, (2011) *Concluding Observations E/C.12/DEU/CO/5, para. 26*, Germany.

[7] Committee on the Rights of Persons with Disabilities (2015) *Concluding Observations: CRPD/C/DEU/ CO/1, paras. 37–38*, Germany.

[8] International Lesbian and Gay Association (2015) *How to be a Great Intersex Ally: A Toolkit for NGOs and Decision Makers*, p. 23, Switzerland.

[9] Presentation to the Homosexual Histories Conference (2014)—*Pride History Group, November 2014; at* www.humanrights.gov.au/news/speeches/homosexual-histories-conference-2014-pride-history-group-0.

## SUHAKAM AND SOGIESC

SUHAKAM'S emerging/slow progression on SOGIESC rights, as discussed below, must be seen in the context of problems afflicting this body. Civil society groups in Malaysia, particularly those working on HIV/AIDS, SOGIESC, and human rights issues, fear that the propagation of repulsive attitudes towards SOGIESC diversity will lead to increased hate crimes[10] in Malaysia. Concerned organizations have forwarded such concerns regarding LGBTI issues to SUHAKAM, putting SUHAKAM in a critical position to bridge the gap between the government and civil society.[11]

SUHAKAM was established through the Human Rights Commission of Malaysia (SUHAKAM) Act 1999. The Act provides a broad mandate to advise the Government in human rights matters and establishes a commission comprised a maximum of 20 members.[12] Under the Paris Principles—the guidelines for the establishment and effective operations of NHRIs in line with international standards[13]—an NHRI should be able to operate with independence from political direction or interference.[14] However, SUHAKAM fails to meet the international standards set by the Paris Principles due to its lack of independence. For example, SUHAKAM's Commissioners are appointed by the *Yang di-Pertuan Agong* (King of Malaysia) on the recommendation of the Prime Minister and funded under the discretion of the Ministry of Finance on an annual basis.[15] Under the Paris Principles, the funding of NHRIs should "not be subject to financial control which might affect its independence." Control of SUHAKAM's budget by the Ministry of Finance is problematic as demon-

[10] Justice For Sisters (2017) *Brief Media Analysis*, https://justiceforsisters.wordpress.com/2017/03/01/brief-media-analysis-sameeras-case-justiceformeera/; 76 Crimes (2017) *Malaysian group teaches how to report on trans people*, https://76crimes.com/2017/04/28/malaysian-group-teaches-how-to-report-on-trans-people/.

[11] SUHAKAM (2013) *Report of the Complaints and Inquiries Working Group: LGBT*, Malaysia.

[12] Laws of Malaysia (1999) *Act 597: Human Rights Commission of Malaysia Act, Section 5(1)*.

[13] OHCHR (1993) *Principles relating to the Status of National Institutions (The Paris Principles), Adopted by General Assembly Resolution 48/134 of 20 December 1993*, Switzerland.

[14] United Nations Commission on Human Rights resolution 1992/54 and General Assembly resolution 48/134.

[15] Laws of Malaysia (1999) *Act 597: Human Rights Commission of Malaysia Act, Section 5(2), 19(1)*.

strated in November 2015 when the Ministry reduced SUHAKAM's budget by almost 50 per cent for 2016. During that same year, the Asian NGO Network on National Human Rights Institutions recommended an increase in SUHAKAM's budget to ensure the effectiveness of the Commission.[16]

SUHAKAM's lack of independence as well as political and societal pressures potentially limits its ability to fully promote LGBTI rights and protect LGBTI persons. SUHAKAM did not prioritize LGBTI issues in its early work due to an apparent adherence to "cultural" and "religious" relativism. For example, in 2009, after attending the Asia Pacific Forum Workshop on how NHRIs can engage the Yogyakarta Principles in their mandates, SUHAKAM stated:

> Within the Malaysian context, SUHAKAM emphasised that the position of Islam as the official religion of the Federation, together with the whole society's religious, moral and cultural sensitivity, must be given due respect in determining the extent of LGBT rights as well as the non-LGBT. Liberal steps taken by some States may not work for others, as cultural and religious diversity significantly mould the society's standard of tolerance and acceptance towards certain practices and actions. Article 29(2) of the UDHR also recognises cultural diversity of a society in the application of human rights principles. The State-legislated Syariah laws, applicable to Muslims, lay down certain prohibitions based on Islamic moral values, preserving teachings of Islam. Once again, such restrictions are not violation of human rights and whether in the context Syariah laws or the public law, no rights are absolute. The prohibitions are with purposes and do not infringe any basic rights of the LGBT as human beings.[17]

More recently, SUHAKAM adopted a cautious approach to engaging in LGBTI-related work, which may be viewed as a strategic method to support the work of LGBTI activist organizations and slowly chip away at cultural and other factors resulting in violations of LGBTI rights. This lack of prioritization is evident in SUHAKAM's annual reports. While SUHAKAM's annual reports highlight many critical violations of human

[16] ANNI, FORUM-ASIA (2016) *Report on the Performance and Establishment of National Human Rights Institutions in Asia*, p. 14.

[17] SUHAKAM's Interventions at the Workshop on the Role of the NHRs in the Implementation of The Jogjakarta Principles (2009), www.asiapacificforum.net/issues/sexual_orientation/downloads/apf-regional-workshop-may-2009/Malaysia.doc.

rights in the country that require immediate action by the state, LBGTI violations are mentioned in only 4 of 17 total reports by SUHAKAM.[18]

By 2016, SUHAKAM made progress and suggested that LGBTI rights should not be trumped by cultural and religious intolerance. Then Chairperson of SUHAKAM, Tan Sri Hasmy Agam described LGBTI rights as a challenging issue that the Malaysian society will need to deal with seriously and carefully. He said:

> This is a highly sensitive issue in Malaysia, which must be handled with great care and prudence so as not to affect the progression of human rights agenda in the country. A national discussion must be had to understand and promote a degree of tolerance towards the (LGBTI) community. The Commission will continue to handle this challenge through greater dialogue and engagement with the parties concerned in the hope that over time, there would be greater understanding or tolerance resulting in fewer, if not zero incidence of harassment and intimidation and better respect for personal liberties and privacy. I must admit this is one of the most difficult issues to be handled by the Commission, with no easy solution in sight.[19]

SUHAKAM Officer Nurul Hasanah confirmed to Fortify Rights that the current Commissioners are now more concerned or at least emphatic towards SOGIESC issues:

> SUHAKAM started looking into LGBT issues back in 2010–2011, when the then Commissioner Datuk Khaw Lake Tee brought up the discussion with the other commissioners after attending forums on SOGIESC rights. In 2014, when Human Rights Watch published their "I am Scared to be A Woman" report, SUHAKAM was asked to hold a public inquiry into the violations of transgender persons. However, the Commission decided that the lack of complaints from the transgender community did not serve as a strong ground for the inquiry. This is understandably so, as the transgender community would not dare to come forward to SUHAKAM—seeing the Commission as another government body. The institutionalisation of religious laws is causing the situation to regress, making it difficult for SUHAKAM to confidently work on SOGIESC issues.[20]

[18] SUHAKAM Publications: *(2010) Annual Report*, pp. 16 & 67; *(2011) Annual Report*, p. 76; *(2015) Annual Report*, pp. 44–45, 107 & 144; *(2016) Annual Report*, p. 27; Malaysia.

[19] The Malaysian Insider (3 January 2016) www.themalaysianinsider.com/malaysia/article/were-turning-back-human-rights-clock-if-nsc-bill-becomes-law-says-hasmy.

[20] Fortify Rights interview with Ms. Nurul Hasanah, SUHAKAM Officer, 25 May 2017, Malaysia.

Recognizing the challenging environment in Malaysia about SOGIESC issues, discussed below, SUHAKAM has undertaken several commendable initiatives in recent years to address specific SOGIESC-related concerns and rights violations. For example, in 2014, SUHAKAM adopted the right to health in prison as one of its two thematic priority areas,[21] and through its work on ensuring that the conditions of confinement in Malaysia are constitutional and consistent with rights to health, safety and human dignity, SUHAKAM established a monitoring program that included examining the treatment of transgender people in detention. This work led to calls to ensure that inmates with diverse gender identity are placed in the same cell, separate from other inmates.[22] SUHAKAM highlighted the outcome of its monitoring in its 2015 Annual Report, finding that there is no standard policy or basic ethical standards when it comes to treating transgender prisoners.[23]

SUHAKAM has carried forward its work to ensure the treatment and conditions of detention for transgender prisoners are in line with international standards. For example, on 30 May 2017, SUHAKAM demanded the Prisons Department to set up a "standard operation procedure" (SOP) on the treatment of transgender prisoners to ensure their safety, and that they are treated fairly and lawfully.[24] This recommendation stemmed from SUHAKAM's finding in its 2017 publication *The Right to Health in Prison: Results of A Nationwide Survey and Report* that transgender people are at substantially high risk of assault or self-harm in the Malaysian prison environment.[25] SUHAKAM found:

> [T]here is no standardised policy concerning the placement of transgender persons in prisons. As it stands, decisions over whether to send a prisoner (prisoners) to male or female prisons depend on their legally recognised gender, which is determined through their birth certificate or identity card.[26]

[21] SUHAKAM (2014) *Areas of Work: Right to Health in Prison*, Malaysia.

[22] Ibid., p. 13.

[23] SUHAKAM (2015) *Annual Report, Chapter 1: Report of the Policy, Law and Complaints Group, Right to Health in Prison*, pp. 21–22, Malaysia.

[24] Free Malaysia Today (30 May 2017) *SUHAKAM calls for SOP on transgender prisoners*, http://www.freemalaysiatoday.com/category/nation/2017/05/30/suhakam-calls-for-sop-on-transgender-prisoners/, Malaysia.

[25] SUHAKAM (2017) *The Right to Health in Prison: Results of A Nationwide Survey and Report*, Malaysia.

[26] SUHAKAM (2017) *The Right to Health in Prison: Results of A Nationwide Survey and Report*, p. 78, Malaysia.

As a result, SUHAKAM recommended that prison authorities produce a policy framework outlining how transgender prisoners could be assured of their safety within the prison environment and consider training selected staff to address their special needs in prisons.[27]

SUHAKAM also monitored court proceedings involving SOGIESC issues. Although the Commission will not formally intervene in court proceedings, it will monitor cases of concern,[28] which indicates cases that raise important human rights concerns.[29] For example, in 2015 SUHAKAM monitored a case concerning the validity of Section 66 of the Syariah Criminal (Negeri Sembilan) Enactment 1992 that criminalizes any male person who "wears women's clothing" or "poses as a woman."[30]

On 27 January 2015, during the leave proceedings in the case of *Mohd Juzaili bin Mohd Khamis v Kerajaan Negeri Sembilan*, where a transwoman was charged under the same discriminative state legislation, SUHAKAM attended the leave proceedings as an observer, in accordance with its commitment that "all human beings, regardless of their sexual orientation, should be able to enjoy the full range of human rights without exception.[31]" The Federal Court granted leave to appeal and SUHAKAM continued to monitor the case and attended the hearing on the merits in August 2015 as an observer.[32] However, the Federal Court in October 2015 unanimously overturned the decision by the Court of Appeal on a technical ground—that the legal challenge to the constitutionality of any law should be made directly to the Federal Court as the matter would involve an interpretation of the Federal Constitution.[33] As a result, the law still stands.

Considering the sensitivities surrounding LGBTI issues in Malaysia, SUHAKAM has strategically adopted a step-by-step approach to meet with various stakeholders, including religious leaders and civil society

[27] SUHAKAM (2017) *The Right to Health in Prison: Results of A Nationwide Survey and Report*, p. 82, Malaysia.

[28] Ibid., p. 8.

[29] Paris Principles (1991) *Principle 6.3: Monitoring functions.*

[30] Syariah Justice Department (1992) *Syariah Criminal (Negeri Sembilan) Enactment 1992, Section 66*, Malaysia.

[31] SUHAKAM (2012) *Annual Report*, p. 110, Malaysia.

[32] APF (2015) *SUHAKAM in Briefing document for the workshop on the role of National Human Rights Institutions in promoting and protecting the rights of LGBTI in Asia and the Pacific*, pp. 15–16.

[33] Human Rights Watch (2015) *Malaysia: Court Ruling Sets Back Transgender Rights.*

groups, to gain an understanding of the different perspectives on SOGIESC. For example, in August 2010, SUHAKAM organized a meeting with various Islamic groups in order to gain better understanding of the Islamic perspective on SOGIESC issues, such as same-sex intercourse, cross-dressing, imitation of the opposite gender, and gender reassignment.[34] The participants also discussed the application of the principles of non-discrimination under the Federal Constitution with regards to LGBTI people.

In November 2010, SUHAKAM also met with LGBTI individuals and civil society groups with the objective of engaging directly with members of the LGBTI community to comprehend the challenges and violations that they face.[35] SUHAKAM also discussed violations against sexual minorities during a roundtable discussion on "Gender Equality: Unaddressed Women's Rights Issues" organized with the Selangor Community Awareness Organisation (EMPOWER).[36] In January 2015, SUHAKAM further engaged civil society groups to discuss issues related to Section 66 of the Syariah Criminal (Negeri Sembilan) Enactment 1992 (concerning prohibition of males posing as females) and other related issues affecting the criminalization and marginalization of LGBTI people.[37]

SUHAKAM has demonstrated a continued commitment to engage on SOGIESC issues despite social, political, and religious challenges in Malaysia. For example, in 2016, the Commission agreed to undertake a baseline study to obtain information on discrimination faced by transgender persons in the country. The Commission interviewed 100 respondents, including transwomen and transmen, and held structured interview sessions whereby respondents gave detailed information on matters of their personal backgrounds as well as related to their rights to employment, health care, education, housing, and dignity.[38] The research is expected to be completed within the next year.[39] SUHAKAM Officer Lau Sor Pian, who oversees the project, told Fortify Rights:

[34] SUHAKAM (2010) *Annual Report*, Malaysia.

[35] Ibid., p. 15.

[36] SUHAKAM (2011) *Annual Report*, Malaysia.

[37] SUHAKAM (2015) *Annual Report*, Malaysia.

[38] SUHAKAM (2016) *Annual Report, Chapter 1: Research on Transgender*, p. 27, Malaysia.

[39] Fortify Rights interview with Ms. Lau Sor Pian, SUHAKAM Officer, 25 May 2017, Malaysia.

> The research is targeted to be completed by next year. Due to resources and budget restraints, we are only able to focus the study in Kuala Lumpur and Selangor. Clearly, there is a gap to be addressed as this pioneer study will not reflect the situation of transgender people across the country. Nonetheless, it is important for the Commission to make the report public to raise awareness on the dire need to address transgender rights.[40]

This dire need arises from societal norms and politics that also seriously constrain SUHAKAM'S work on SOGIESC.

## Limitations on SUHAKAM: Societal Norms, Legal and Cultural Attitudes Towards SOGIESC

In Malaysia, intolerance towards issues related to SOGIESC is reflected in the predominant use of anti-LGBTI legislation.[41] In a multicultural and ethnically diverse society that is largely socially conservative, Malaysia's strong religious and faith traditions have neglected such diversity[42]; leaving and allowing LGBTI people to be ostracized or punished. In the last few decades, attacks on LGBTI people are largely happening in the context of Malaysia's emerging politicization of Islam.[43] This has manifested, for example, in medical diagnoses that referred to sexual orientation and gender variations as illnesses that could or should be cured or fixed.[44] Such approaches are inconsistent with medical science, medical ethics, and international human rights standards.[45]

There is a deeply rooted sociological assumption in Malaysia that individuals are born either male or female and are then attracted to a person

[40] Fortify Rights interview with Ms. Lau Sor Pian, SUHAKAM Officer, 25 May 2017, Malaysia.

[41] UNDP (2016) *Leave no one behind: Advancing social, economic, cultural, and political inclusion of LGBTI people in Asia and the Pacific*, Thailand.

[42] Mohd Izwan bin Md Yusof, Muhd Najib bin Abdul Kadir, Mazlan bin Ibrahim & Tengku Intan Zarina (2014) *Malaysian Muslim Gay and Lesbian Community's Perspective on The Concept Of Domestic Partnership and Marriage In The Quran.*

[43] Thi Thu Huong Dang (2005) *A Comparative Analysis of the Strategies the New Order and UMNO Regimes in Indonesia and Malaysia adopted to deal with Islam in 1965–1998.*

[44] APTN, USAID, UNDP, WHO (2010) *Blueprint for the Provision of Comprehensive Care for Trans People and Trans Communities in Asia and the Pacific.*

[45] WHO (2014) *Proposed declassification of disease categories related to sexual orientation in the International Statistical Classification of Diseases and Related Health Problems (ICD-11)*, United States of America.

of "the opposite" sex. For example, someone born with what is considered to be a "male body" is expected to grow up and identify as a man, have a masculine gender expression, and be solely attracted to women. Similarly, someone born with a "female body" is expected to identify as a woman, be feminine, and only be attracted to men.[46]

Such flawed expectations fail to reflect the lived realities of LGBTI people in Malaysia—or anywhere, for that matter—or uphold their fundamental human rights to dignity, equality, and freedom.[47] These rigid stereotypes perpetuate gender inequalities. When false distinctions determine heterosexuality as superior (heteronormativity), they contribute to the pervasive marginalization and discrimination of LGBTI people.

Ironically, anthropological studies show that diverse sexual minorities, including the third gender (*hijra*), were accepted as societal norms during the era of ancient Malay Sultanates empire.[48] Anthropologist Michael Peletz documented historical texts from the fifteenth to nineteenth centuries that testified to the existence of "androgynous" royal priests or courtiers, both male and female at that time:

The evidence indicates the existence in the Malay Peninsula in the late pre-modern and modern era of a pre-Islamic class of male-bodied priests or courtiers, referred to by the term "*sida-sida*" ... who were said to be involved in "androgynous behavior," such as wearing women's clothes and possibly performing tasks generally undertaken by women.[49]

The criminalization of LGBTI people (especially towards men who have sex with men) under federal laws did not take place in British Malaya[50]—when the Malay Peninsula States were still part of the British colony—until 1936,[51] when British colonial authorities introduced the nineteenth century Indian Penal Code in all 42 then British colonies.[52] In Section 377, British Malaya criminalized sexual acts between homosexuals

[46] Theresa W. Devasahayam (2009) *Gender Trends in Southeast Asia: Women Now, Women in the Future*.

[47] Asia Pacific Forum, UNDP Asia Pacific (2016) *Promoting and Protecting Human Rights in relation to Sexual Orientation, Gender Identity and Sex Characteristics*, Thailand.

[48] Michael Peletz, (2009) *Gender Pluralism: Southeast Asia Since Early Modern Times*, pp. 58–59, New York.

[49] Ibid., p. 4.

[50] Osborne, Milton (2000) *Southeast Asia: An Introductory History. Allen & Unwin*, UK.

[51] Vanja Hamzic (2015) *Sexual & Gender Diversity in the Muslim World: History, Law and Vernacular Knowledge*.

[52] Cheong-Wing Chan, Barry Wright and Stanley Yeo (2011) *Codification, Macaulay and the Indian Penal Code: The Legacies and Modern Challenges of Criminal Law Reform*, UK.

with a maximum sentence of up to 20 years in prison. This provision remains in Malaysia's current Penal Code (Act 574).[53]

Criminalization under Syariah laws towards sexual minorities also did not take place in Malaysia until the 1980s. In 1968, the National Council of Islamic Affairs was established at the behest of the Conference of Rulers—a council comprising the nine rulers of the Malay states, and the governors or *Yang di-Pertua Negeri* of the other four states out of the 14 states in Malaysia. It was established under Article 38 of the Constitution of Malaysia and is the only such institution in the world—in recognizing the need for a national body to streamline the development and advancement of Islamic affairs. In 1982, the Fatwa Committee under the Council learned about sex reassignment surgeries (SRS) for transgender people that were carried out at the University of Malaya Hospital. The committee immediately issued a *fatwa*—an Islamic legal pronouncement, issued by experts in religious law such as a Mufti or Imam, pertaining to a specific issue, usually at the request of an individual or judge to resolve an issue where Islamic jurisprudence is unclear[54]—banning the SRS.[55] Although the Fatwa Committee has no legal authority, the hospital's SRS facilities shut down in 1983 due to such pressure.[56]

The issuance of Islamic *fatwas* led to development of Syariah Criminal Offences Enactments in all 14 states[57] in Malaysia and the Federal Syariah Criminal Offences Act 1997—religious legislation that criminalizes the activities of sexual minorities. In 1996, the restructuring of Syariah courts throughout Malaysia took place to establish the Syariah Judiciary Department and Courts in all states.[58] More recently in 2008, the Fatwa Committee issued a ruling prohibiting "tomboy behaviour" in an apparent attempt to prevent lesbianism among Muslims.[59] The Syariah Criminal Enactments/Acts had already criminalized sexual acts between two

[53] Laws of Malaysia (1976) *Act 574: Penal Code, S377*, Malaysia.

[54] Yew-Foong Hui (2013) *Encountering Islam: The Politics of Religious Identities in Southeast Asia*, p. 129, Malaysia.

[55] Yik Koon Teh (2001) *Mak Nyahs (Male Transsexuals) in Malaysia: The Influence of Culture and Religion on their Identity*, Malaysia.

[56] JAKIM (1982) *Fatwa Issued by the National Fatwa Council Prohibiting Sex Reassignment Surgery*, Malaysia.

[57] Syariah Judiciary Department Malaysia (JKSM): http://www.jksm.gov.my/, Malaysia.

[58] Syariah Courts (Criminal Jurisdiction) Act 1985, Malaysia.

[59] The Star (2008) *Fatwa on Tomboys*, http://www.thestar.com.my/news/nation/2008/10/24/fatwa-on-tomboys/, Malaysia.

females.[60] However, it is important to note that while Muslims in Malaysia are subjected to both federal criminal laws and state-level Syariah enactments, non-Muslims in Malaysia are only subjected to the federal criminal laws.[61]

Intolerance towards SOGIESC diversity in Malaysia escalated prior to the turn of the millennia when anti-LGBTI legislation became pervasive in the country's dualistic legal system. Moreover, local media outlets singled out transgender identities in anti-LGBTI discourses, derogating LGBTI persons as suffering from a social illness.[62]

The attitude of the Malaysian government towards LGBTI persons has also been largely and consistently negative. For example, in 2005, the Royal Malaysian Navy Chief Mohd Anwar Moh Nor stated that the Navy would never "condone unnatural sex acts" and accept homosexuals into its fold.[63]

On 18 August 2015, during an Islamic conference in Selangor, Prime Minister Najib Razak pledged that his administration would not defend human rights issues that are not within the "context of Islam," citing LGBTI advocates as an example:

> Although universal human rights have been defined, we still define human rights in the country in the context of Islam and the Syariah (law). And even if we cannot defend human rights at an international level, we must defend it in the Islamic context. Liberal groups like LGBT advocates are trying to dominate most of the country's population. These groups are hiding behind the façade of human rights to approve their acts, which deviate from Islamic teaching.[64]

[60] Tan Beng Hui (2008) *Moral and Sexual Offences in Malaysia: The Role and Impact of the Syariah Criminal Offences Enactments. Paper presented at the Second Conference of the Kartini Network, Bali*, Indonesia.

[61] Laws of Malaysia (1965) *Act 355: Syariah Courts (Criminal Jurisdiction) Act, section 2*, http://www.agc.gov.my/Akta/Vol.%208/Act%20355.pdf, Malaysia.

[62] International Federation of Journalists (2015) *Country Report: "Media and Gender in Malaysia" Part of the IFJ Media and Gender in Asia-Pacific Research Project*, http://www.ifj.org/uploads/media/MALAYSIA.pdf.

[63] Today Online (2005) *No Homosexuals in Malaysian Navy, Says Chief, 25 February 2005.*

[64] The Washington Blade (2015) *Malaysia Prime Minister: Government Will Not Defend LGBT Rights*, http://www.washingtonblade.com/2015/08/21/malaysian-prime-minister-government-will-not-defend-lgbt-rights/, Malaysia.

The Malaysian Prime Minister further added that the country would only uphold human rights within the confines of Islam—in line with the Islamic teaching of balance and *wasatiyyah* (moderation).[65]

Dismayed by the narrow approach of the government, the then SUHAKAM chairperson Tan Sri Hasmy Agam said in a press statement:

> The commission therefore regrets the many myths and misunderstandings that have sprung up on the concept of human rights, and, the construal and superficial understanding of human rights in Malaysia. The commission calls on the government to emulate the best practices of other Muslim countries about the advancement of human rights. The challenges of promoting and protecting human rights in Malaysia does not end with the adoption of a declaration or the establishment of a human rights commission.[66]

It is not surprising that during the UN's Universal Periodic Review (UPR) of Malaysia[67] in 2008 and 2013, the Government of Malaysia refused to accept any of the recommendations made about SOGIESC issues.[68]

## The Way Forward for SUHAKAM

SUHAKAM has an indispensable role to play in promoting SOGIESC rights in Malaysia and regionally. As an authority mandated to promote and protect all human rights and identify specific groups at risk of human rights violations, SUHAKAM should continue to include LGBTI persons as a priority group to monitor. It must be a bastion of resistance to corrosive pressure from political and conservative religious factions who are committed to dismissing SOGIESC rights.

[65] Malay Mail Online (2015) *Najib: Putrajaya will defend human rights, but only in the context of Islam*, http://www.themalaymailonline.com/malaysia/article/najib-putrajaya-will-defend-human-rights-but-only-in-the-context-of-islam, Malaysia.

[66] SUHAKAM (20 August 2015) *Press Release: SUHAKAM Opines that Fundamental Rights and Universal Freedoms are an Integral Part of Islam*, Malaysia.

[67] UN Human Rights Council (2009–2013) *Human Rights Bodies: UPR—Malaysia*, http://www.lan.ohchr.org/EN/HRBodies/UPR/Pages/MYSession17.aspx, Switzerland.

[68] UN Human Rights Council (2013) *Report of the Working Group on the UPR—Malaysia*, https://documents-dds-ny.un.org/doc/UNDOC/GEN/G13/188/48/PDF/G1318848.pdf?OpenElement, Switzerland.

SUHAKAM can leverage regional engagement by working with SOGIESC dedicated groups like the ASEAN SOGIE Caucus (ACS),[69] which has fostered partnerships between ASEAN LGBTI civil society and NHRIs since its establishment in 2011. This would enable SUHAKAM to engage in research, advocacy, and educational experiences and develop positive working relationships with other NHRIs on SOGIESC issues in Southeast Asia.

On a domestic level, SUHAKAM can engage in strategic dialogue with law enforcement officers, government agencies and service providers, members of the judiciary, and religious leaders to develop and implement policies and programmes for the protection and welfare of LGBTI people.

As the power of media can make either a positive or a detrimental impact, SUHAKAM's engagement with and education of local media outlets on SOGIESC issues is vital to ensure proper use of terminology and non-derogatory terms and work with them in raising awareness of sexual minorities' rights.

SUHAKAM has the capacity to establish a special committee or inquiry to investigate abuse of power and violence against LGBTI persons by the public, law enforcement officers, and other government agencies.

## Conclusion

This chapter has demonstrated, that despite some progress, SUHAKAM's work is seriously limited by impeding factors such as the its lack of autonomy and resources, and its sensitivity to societal and cultural values. Hence, it is not immune to political pressures given the challenge of maintaining its independence.

To take forward SOGIESC rights, in line with its current research into discriminatory practices against the transgender community in Malaysia, SUHAKAM can usefully broaden its research to evaluate Malaysia's existing laws and practices in relation to protections for LGBTI persons. Based on this analysis, SUHAKAM should work with the government to amend and bring problematic laws in line with international standards. SUHAKAM can fulfil its role by pushing the Government of Malaysia to become a signatory of the Yogyakarta Principles 2006.

[69] Statement of Representatives of (2011) *ASEAN Civil Society Conference/ASEAN People's Forum to the Informal Meeting Between ASEAN Leaders and Civil Society*, Indonesia.

## References

76 Crimes. 2017. *Malaysian group teaches how to report on trans people*, https://76crimes.com/2017/04/28/malaysian-group-teaches-how-to-report-on-trans-people/.

APTN, USAID, UNDP, WHO. 2010. *Blueprint for the Provision of Comprehensive Care for Trans People and Trans Communities in Asia and the Pacific.*

ASEAN People's Forum. 2011. Statement of Representatives to the *ASEAN Civil Society Conference/ASEAN People's Forum to the Informal Meeting Between ASEAN Leaders and Civil Society*, Indonesia.

Asia Pacific Forum. 2015. *SUHAKAM in Briefing document for the workshop on the role of National Human Rights Institutions in promoting and protecting the rights of LGBTI in Asia and the Pacific*, pp. 15–16.

———. 2016. *Promoting and Protecting Human Rights in relation to Sexual Orientation, Gender Identity and Sex Characteristics*, Thailand.

Asian NGO Network on National Human Rights Institutions (ANNI). 2016. *Report on the Performance and Establishment of National Human Rights Institutions in Asia*, Bangkok: Forum Asia, p. 14.

Australian Human Rights Commission. 2014. *Pride History Group*, Presentation to the Homosexual Histories Conference. Available at www.humanrights.gov.au/news/speeches/homosexual-histories-conference-2014-pride-history-group-0.

Cheong-Wing, C, Barry, W, and Stanley Y. 2011. *Codification, Macaulay and the Indian Penal Code: The Legacies and Modern Challenges of Criminal Law Reform*, UK.

Committee on Economic, Social and Cultural Rights. 2011. *Concluding Observations E/C.12/DEU/CO/5*, para. 26, Germany.

Committee on the Rights of the Child. 2015. *Concluding Observations: CRC/C/CHE/CO/2–4.* Switzerland, para. 43b.

Committee on the Rights of Persons with Disabilities. 2015. *Concluding Observations: CRPD/C/DEU/CO/1.* Germany, paras. 37–38.

Devasahayam, T. 2009. *Gender Trends in Southeast Asia: Women Now, Women in the Future.*

Fortify Rights interview with Ms. Nurul Hasanah and Ms. Lau Sor Pian, SUHAKAM Officer, 10–12pm, 25 May 2017, Malaysia.

Free Malaysia Today. 2017. *SUHAKAM calls for SOP on transgender prisoners*, 30 May 2017, Malaysia. Available at http://www.freemalaysiatoday.com/category/nation/2017/05/30/suhakam-calls-for-sop-on-transgender-prisoners/.

Government of Malaysia, Laws of Malaysia. 1965. Act 355: Syariah Courts (Criminal Jurisdiction) Act, Section 2, Malaysia. Available at http://www.agc.gov.my/Akta/Vol.%208/Act%20355.pdf.

———. 1976. *Act 574: Penal Code, S377*, Malaysia.
———. 1999a. *Act 597: Human Rights Commission of Malaysia Act, Section 5(1).*
———. 1999b. *Act 597: Human Rights Commission of Malaysia Act, Section 5(2), 19(1).*
Human Rights Watch. 2015. *Malaysia: Court Ruling Sets Back Transgender Rights.*
International Commission of Jurists and International Service for Human Rights. 2006a. *Yogyakarta Principles: Preamble.*
———. 2006b. *Yogyakarta Principles: Principle 3.*
International Federation of Journalists. 2015. *Country Report: "Media and Gender in Malaysia" Part of the IFJ Media and Gender in Asia-Pacific Research Project.* Available at http://www.ifj.org/uploads/media/MALAYSIA.pdf.
International Lesbian and Gay Association. 2015. *How to be a Great Intersex Ally: A Toolkit for NGOs and Decision Makers*, p. 23, Switzerland.
Jabatan Kemajuan Islam Malaysia (JAKIM). 1982. *Fatwa Issued by the National Fatwa Council Prohibiting Sex Reassignment Surgery*, Malaysia.
Justice For Sisters. 2017. *Brief Media Analysis*, https://justiceforsisters.wordpress.com/2017/03/01/brief-media-analysis-sameeras-case-justiceformeera/.
Malay Mail Online. 2015. *Najib: Putrajaya will defend human rights, but only in the context of Islam*, Malaysia. Available at http://www.themalaymailonline.com/malaysia/article/najib-putrajaya-will-defend-human-rights-but-only-in-the-context-of-islam.
Mohd Izwan bin Md Yusof, Muhd Najib bin Abdul Kadir, Mazlan bin Ibrahim & Tengku Intan Zarina. 2014. *Malaysian Muslim Gay and Lesbian Community's Perspective on The Concept Of Domestic Partnership and Marriage In The Quran*, Malaysia.
Osborne, M. 2000. *Southeast Asia: An Introductory History. Allen & Unwin*, UK.
Paris Principles. 1991. *Principle 6.3: Monitoring functions.*
Peletz, M. 2009. *Gender Pluralism: Southeast Asia Since Early Modern Times*, New York, pp. 58–59.
Singapore Misuse of Drugs (Amendment) Act 2012.
Suruhanjaya Hak Asasi Manusia Malaysia (SUHAKAM). 2009. SUHAKAM's Interventions at the Workshop on the Role of the NHRs in the Implementation of the Jogjakarta Principles. Available at www.asiapacificforum.net/issues/sexual_orientation/downloads/apf-regional-workshop-may-2009/Malaysia.doc.
———. 2010. *Annual Report*, Malaysia pgs 16 and 67.
———. 2011. *Annual Report*, Malaysia, pg 76.
———. 2012. *Annual Report*, Malaysia, p. 110.
———. 2013. *Report of the Complaints and Inquiries Working Group: LGBT*, Malaysia.
———. 2014. *Areas of Work: Right to Health in Prison*, Malaysia.
———. 2015a. *Annual Report, Chapter 1: Report of the Policy, Law and Complaints Group, Right to Health in Prison*, Malaysia, pgs 21–22.

———. 2015b. *Annual Report*, Malaysia, pgs 44–45; pgs 107 and 144.

———. 2015c. *Press Release: SUHAKAM Opines that Fundamental Rights and Universal Freedoms are an Integral Part of Islam*, 20 August 2015, Malaysia.

———. 2016a. *Annual Report, Chapter 1: Research on Transgender*, Malaysia, p. 27.

———. 2016b. *Annual Report*, Malaysia, pg 27.

———. 2017. *The Right to Health in Prison: Results of A Nationwide Survey and Report*, Malaysia p. 78–82.

Syariah Courts (Criminal Jurisdiction) Act 1985, Malaysia.

Syariah Judiciary Department Malaysia (JKSM). Available at http://www.jksm.gov.my/.

Syariah Justice Department. 1992. *Syariah Criminal (Negeri Sembilan) Enactment 1992, Section 66*, Malaysia.

Tan Beng Hui. 2008. *Moral and Sexual Offences in Malaysia: The Role and Impact of the Syariah Criminal Offences Enactments. Paper presented at the Second Conference of the Kartini Network, Bali*, Indonesia.

The Malaysian Insider. 2016. 3rd January, Malaysia. Available at www.themalaysianinsider.com/malaysia/article/were-turning-back-human-rights-clock-if-nsc-bill-becomes-law-says-hasmy.

The Star. 2008. *Fatwa on Tomboy*, Malaysia. Available at http://www.thestar.com.my/news/nation/2008/10/24/fatwa-on-tomboys/.

The Washington Blade. 2015. *Malaysia Prime Minister: Government Will Not Defend LGBT Rights*, Malaysia. Available at http://www.washingtonblade.com/2015/08/21/malaysian-prime-minister-government-will-not-defend-lgbt-rights/.

Thi Thu Huong Dang. 2005. *A Comparative Analysis of the Strategies the New Order and UMNO Regimes in Indonesia and Malaysia adopted to deal with Islam in 1965–1998*.

Today Online. 2005. *No Homosexuals in Malaysian Navy, Says Chief*, 25 February 2005.

United Nations Commission on Human Rights Resolution. 1992/54 and General Assembly resolution 48/134.

United Nations Development Programme, Asia Pacific Forum, Asia Pacific. 2016. *Promoting and Protecting Human Rights in relation to Sexual Orientation, Gender Identity and Sex Characteristics*, Thailand.

United Nations Human Rights Council. 2013. *Report of the Working Group on the UPR – Malaysia*, Switzerland. Available at https://documents-dds-ny.un.org/doc/UNDOC/GEN/G13/188/48/PDF/G1318848.pdf?OpenElement.

United Nations Office of the High Commissioner of Human Rights. 1993. *Principles relating to the Status of National Institutions (The Paris Principles), Adopted by General Assembly Resolution 48/134 of 20 December 1993*, Switzerland.

Vanja H. 2015. *Sexual & Gender Diversity in the Muslim World: History, Law and Vernacular Knowledge.*

WHO. 2014. *Proposed declassification of disease categories related to sexual orientation in the International Statistical Classification of Diseases and Related Health Problems (ICD-11)*, United States of America.

Yew-Foong Hui. 2013. *Encountering Islam: The Politics of Religious Identities in Southeast Asia*, p. 129, Malaysia.

Yik Koon Teh. 2001. *Mak Nyahs (Male Transsexuals) in Malaysia: The Influence of Culture and Religion on their Identity*, Malaysia.

CHAPTER 13

# Komnas HAM and the Land Rights of Indigenous Peoples: National Inquiry as a New Mechanism for the Settlement of Disputes

*Isnenningtyas Yulianti*

## Introduction

This chapter demonstrates the capacity of Komnas HAM to address complaints of violation of the ownership rights of indigenous peoples who were deprived of their property by third parties. Komnas Ham has been criticized for not handling cases effectively. By examining its capacity to do this, this chapter also informs us about Komnas HAM's contribution to the fulfillment of economic, social and cultural rights (ESCRs) embedded in a community, especially the indigenous peoples for whom land is not only a source of livelihood but integral to their spirituality and identity. It is the "home" and/or also a "Mother". The role of this Commission, which scrutinizes all policies related to ESCRs, is to ensure the enjoyment of the ESCRs and to contribute to the progressive realization of such rights.

This chapter examines Komnas HAM's handling of claims of violations of land rights of indigenous peoples in Indonesia. It outlines the new

I. Yulianti (✉)
Komnas HAM, Jakarta Pusat, Indonesia



J. Gomez, R. Ramcharan (eds.), *National Human Rights Institutions in Southeast Asia*,
https://doi.org/10.1007/978-981-15-1074-8_13

mechanism of National Inquiry used by Komnas HAM in dealing with land rights for indigenous peoples.

It uses a qualitative methodology to look at the norms and tasks of the Commission in the handling of cases by Komnas HAM. It is based on the primary documents emanating from legislative sources and from the Commission itself. This chapter employs a desk study approach and literature study conducted at Komnas HAM by the author, who works with this institution. The data were collected from Complaint data and National Inquiry data which were carried out by Komnas HAM. In 2014–2015 Komnas HAM implemented a National Inquiry to settle various cases of indigenous peoples in Indonesia. In this study, the authors also conducted interviews with various parties including officers in the complaints, monitoring, mediation and researchers who actively participated in the National Inquiry.

The focus here on Komnas HAM's role in the protection of land rights of indigenous peoples is not only topical but has received no attention in academic literature at the time of writing. Some academic papers highlight the role of Komnas ham as an institution. The first book on Komnas HAM was written by Cornelis Lay et al. titled, *Komnas HAM 1993–1997 The Struggle in Authoritarianism*. It examined Komnas HAM since its formation in 1993, which was a period of strong authoritarianism. Many people doubted the establishment of Komnas HAM because of the way it was established by President Suharto. Yet, Komnas HAM was able to show remarkable achievement, as noted by Inosentius in this volume. With all the limitations faced, Komnas HAM has been able to build collective energy in developing independence from State control. It was able to build a remarkable public reputation (Lay et al. 2002a). A second book by Cornelis Lay et al. titled *Komnas HAM 1998–2001, The Struggle in the Political Transition* covered the transition period (Lay et al. 2002b). In this period Komnas HAM was not able to handle cases of violations of human rights properly. Some cases of human rights violations such as the Maluku, Sampit and Semanggi tragedies have not been resolved (See Lindsey 2008).[1] Generally, Komnas HAM fell into internal conflict throughout 2000–2001.

[1] The role of Komnas HAM in the protection of human rights was discussed in a thesis entitled, *The Role of National Commission on Human Rights in the Enforcement of Human Rights in Indonesia*, written by R. Agus Supriyanto for master degree program law. The thesis

Jeff Herbert (2008) provided a useful overview of the legal powers and functions of Komnas Ham, in which he noted the "inquiry and examination function" that seeks to determine whether a violation has taken place and a "pre-trial inquirer function" introduced under Law 26 of 2000, also known as the "pro justicia inquiry" which is a series of actions aimed at determining whether gross violations of human rights have taken place (Herbert 2008: 467).

Beyond the above works, Komnas HAM's handling of the death penalty was treated by Matthew Grose, in *The Komnas HAM and Death Penalty: Assessing the Role of the National Human Rights Commission in the Death Penalty Debate in Indonesia*, focused on the death penalty in Indonesia and the role and position of Komnas HAM.[2]

The Danish Institute for Human Rights study referred to earlier in this book, notes three studies on Komnas Ham between 1996 and 2017, all providing general overviews (See Stokke 2007; Setiawan 2013, 2016). This chapter, therefore, provides a unique scoping of Komnas HAM's engagement on indigenous rights cases.

It proceeds, first, with a discussion of the mandate of Komnas HAM, followed by a brief overview of the situation of indigenous land rights in Indonesia and finally the Commission's research on indigenous rights. It then examines cases relating to indigenous peoples who have complained to Komnas HAM.

## The Mandate of Komnas HAM

As a state institution, Komnas HAM has a mandate to encourage the protection, fulfillment and enforcement of human rights in Indonesia. Komnas HAM handles cases based on Law No. 39 of 1999 and it makes recommendations after examining each case.

These recommendations are addressed to the relevant parties directly related to the case. However, sometimes the recommendations do not result in justice for the victim. Komnas HAM Recommendations are not legally binding on the perpetrator, which leads to difficulties for victims and does not encourage further settlement of cases.

mentions the role of Komnas HAM in upholding Ham within the framework of Law No. 39 of 1999 on Human Rights and Law Number 26 Year 2000 on Human Rights Courts.

[2] Resulting from a thesis for the School of Language, Cultures and Linguistics, Monash University.

Komnas HAM works are based on Law Number 39 of 1999 on Human Rights. Articles 75 to 103 regulate the work of Komnas HAM. It is tasked with the protection, fulfillment and enforcement of human rights in Indonesia. Komnas HAM has four mandates which are: research studies, public awareness, monitoring and mediation.

To carry out its research mandate, Komnas HAM may conduct studies and research on various international human rights instruments with the aim of providing suggestions on the possibility of accession or ratification. Komnas HAM may also undertake a review and research of legislation to provide recommendations on the establishment, amendment and revocation of human rights-related legislation.[3] Komnas HAM may also cooperate with other national, regional and international parties in the field of human rights.[4]

To carry out its education and public awareness mandate,[5] Komnas HAM can disseminate insight into human rights to the people of Indonesia. Komnas HAM can also make efforts to improve community awareness about human rights through formal and non-formal education institutions and various other groups. In order to carry out the mandate, Komnas HAM can also cooperate with other parties as well as research and studies.

To carry out Komnas HAM's functions in monitoring and investigation,[6] it is authorized to observe the implementation of human rights in the preparation of reports of observations. Komnas Ham is also authorized to investigate events that arise in a society where human rights violations are suspected. Furthermore, Komnas HAM may also call the complainant or the victim or the complained party to be questioned and hear his or her statements and witnesses. Komnas HAM can also conduct a review of the scene and other places deemed necessary.

To carry out the mediation function,[7] Komnas HAM can make peace on both sides. The settlement of cases may be done through consultation, negotiation, mediation, conciliation and expert judgment. Komnas HAM is also authorized to advise the parties to resolve disputes through the courts. Furthermore, Komnas HAM is authorized to submit a recommen-

[3] Ibid., Article 89 paragraph 1.

[4] Ibid.

[5] Ibid., Article 89 paragraph 2.

[6] Ibid., Article 89 paragraph 3.

[7] Ibid., Article 89 paragraph 4.

dation on a case of human rights violations to the government and the People's Legislative Council for follow-up.

However, the public felt that the case handling mechanism in Komnas HAM as regulated by Law number 39 of 1999 has not been effective in enforcing human rights in Indonesia. In addition, the authority possessed by Komnas HAM is felt to be very weak because it can only provide recommendations that are not legally binding (Patra 2012: 209–217). So far, the mediation mechanism is the only resort that can facilitate a victim's case up to the point of suggested agreement between the parties, the victims and the perpetrator. The recommendations of Komnas HAM do not have legal obligations for the parties who receive them. Therefore, a number of complaints to Komnas HAM cannot find resolution as per the requests by the complainants, especially those concerning civil law (Kholis 2012: 4). The pattern of settlement through the mediation mechanism can be an effective resolution of cases, especially civil cases that involve violations of ESCRs. The outcome of the agreement can be registered with the court and each party must comply. However, in reality some parties ignore the outcome of the agreement.[8] It should be mentioned that not all letters of recommendations or letters handling cases issued by Mediation Sub Commission receive responses. This is partly because not all letters need or request for a response from related parties.

## Komnas HAM Research on Indigenous Peoples' Rights

Komnas HAM has conducted various studies on the rights of indigenous peoples, which are produced in the framework of enforcing, fulfilling and protecting communities and indigenous peoples. Those studies concerned the inventory of indigenous and tribal peoples in Indonesia, as well as land rights in Indonesia. Some studies conducted by the Komnas HAM on indigenous peoples are on the rights of indigenous peoples in general, but the contribution of Komnas HAM in the protection of indigenous peoples has not been studied. In 2005, Komnas HAM conducted a study on the urgency of agrarian reform and recommendations with respect to the idea of establishing KNUPKA and alternative institutional mechanisms specifi-

[8] See Article Mediasi Relokasi Gagal, Warga Dadap Gebrak Meja dan Keluar dari Komnas HAM https://news.detik.com/berita/3242895/mediasi-relokasi-gagal-warga-dadap-gebrak-meja-dan-keluar-dari-komnas-ham.

cally solving agrarian cases (Setiawan 2005). Furthermore, in 2006, Komnas HAM also conducted a study on the structural relations of indigenous peoples in the perspective of human rights.

Komnas HAM has been handling various cases of indigenous peoples, such as the Orang Rimba Jambi and Padumaan Sipituhuta in North Sumatra. However, these cases continue to recur, and complaints to Komnas HAM continue because there are no settlements that guarantee the protection of and rights for the victims.

So, has Komnas HAM achieved a new breakthrough in handling such cases, which is long overdue? What are the steps of Komnas HAM in providing protection and enforcement of the rights of indigenous peoples in the context of indemnification? Hereafter we examine the situation of indigenous peoples' land rights and Komnas HAM's handling of the matter.

## *Land Grabbing, Exclusion and Human Rights*

Land grabbing or current land grabs often occur in different parts of the world. Global studies show that in recent years, indigenous peoples have been deprived of between 20 and 80 million hectares of land, although it is difficult to ascertain because most of the deals are made secretly. Africa appears to be a prime target for this large-scale investment, but numerous similar reports have come from all over the developing world. A total of some 134 million hectares of deals have been reported, of which 34 million hectares have been cross-referenced. The next largest target is Asia with 29 million hectares (Anseeuw and Wily 2012: 4).

The land grabbing phenomenon occurs in several countries, especially those in the Global South. There are several factors that encourage the expropriation of land. These factors can be analyzed in from various perspectives: finance, food, energy and the global climate crisis. The 2007–2008 global food crisis, which has pushed up food prices, created political and economic momentum for land acquisition. Likewise, climate change and the energy crisis created an urgent need to find land for renewable energy crop production (Bolin 2011).

Large-scale plantation trends and concentrated contract farming in pockets of chronic poverty are issues that have been discussed for a long time in agrarian studies and are well documented (Little and Wats 2011). While the general assumption in the World Bank environment is that Foreign Direct Investment flows to areas with good governance and clearly defined property rights, research conducted by the World Bank itself confirms that capital flows into areas where labor and the right to land is uncertain and not protected by the legislation and the government (Li 2011: 283). When wages are low, capitalist exploitation and profit maximization are high. Under these conditions, large-scale land use projects become very problematic when displacing communities and depriving them of their most valuable assets and resilience, their land (de Schutter 2011: 209–206).

What happened to indigenous peoples is exclusion from their "ulayat" or what is termed as "ancient" lands. According to Byrne, social exclusion can be interpreted as a process that prevents or inhibits individuals, families, or groups from the resources needed to participate in social, economic and political activities in a community intact (Byrne 2005).

In their book, *Powers of Exclusion: Land dilemmas in Southeast Asia* (2011), Derek Hall, Philip Hirsch and Tania Li show four power factors that exclude others from access to land in Southeast Asia: (1) regulation, legitimate regulations of the state; (2) coercion by force, whether by state or non-state actors; (3) the market, which limits access to land through price mechanisms and provides incentives for claims to more individualistic lands; (4) legitimacy, that is, various forms of moral justification, such as claims of hereditary rights, scientific considerations, economic rationality and government claims to regulate. The four aspects of power describe the reality of indigenous peoples being removed from their lands, especially through countries and corporations based on natural resources dredging.

The use of force to eliminate access it occurs in six removal processes: (1) the regularization of land rights through government programs on land registration, formalization and peace; (2) space expansion and intensification through conservation of forests by suppressing agricultural activity; (3) new boom crop in the form of monoculture crop expansion leading to massive land conversion; (4) land conversion after use for agriculture; (5) processes arising from agrarian formations within the village involving ropes and village neighbors (intimate exclusions); and (6) mobilization of groups to maintain their access to land.

The UN Declaration of the Rights of Indigenous Peoples (UNDRIP) takes note of the fact that indigenous peoples have long experienced oppression and appropriation of their land, for which the rights of indigenous peoples to their lands, territories and customs must be recognized and respected:

*Concerned* that indigenous peoples have suffered from historic injustice as a result of, inter alia, their colonization and dispossession of their lands, territories and resources, thus preventing them from exercising, in particular, their right to development in accordance with their own needs and interest

*Recognizing* the urgent need to respect and promote the inherent rights of indigenous peoples which derive from their political, economic and social structure and from their cultures, spiritual traditions, histories and philosophies, especially their rights to their lands, territories and resources

## Land Grabbing and the Threat to Indigenous Peoples' Way of Life in Indonesia

In Indonesia, the threat of land grabbing by industry, plantation companies and even by the State is omnipresent. The largest land area recently required in the development project is the Food Estate program. Food Estate is a food industry program created in response to hunger in the world. Food Estate is intended as a world food barn program to ensure world food stock. Instead of being able to provide world food stocks, it has proven to be a disaster in terms of the loss of indigenous peoples' lands. Food estate development is inseparable from the MP3EI program. In this Masterplan, the government is targeting Merauke and Kalimantan as food granaries. Merauke's land area is 1.2 million hectares (Ministry of Economic Affairs 2011: 159).

In 2010, the Government of Indonesia inaugurated the Merauke Food and Energy Plantation development project in an integrated or more popular way as Merauke Integrated Food and Energy Estate (MIFEE).[9] The Food Estate aims to strive for food security for Indonesia. This program was triggered by a global food crisis, and in Indonesia specifically it occurred due to unstable prices affecting the price of other basic necessities. For that purpose, the Government proclaimed a food security program through Food Estate and made Merauke and Papua areas for big projects. The program has been institutionalized with the issuance of Presidential Instruction No. 5 Year 2008 on the Focus of the Economic Program of 2008–2009 including the arrangement of Food Investment Scale Area or Food Estate. Furthermore, the government also issued

[9] About MIFEE see R. Yando Zakaria, Emilianus Ola Kleden, Y.L. Franky (2011), *MIFEE Tak Terjangkau Angan Malind (Mifee Not Reacheable of Malind People)*, Pusaka Foundation, Jakarta.

Government Regulation No. 18 of 2010 on Cultivation of Plants, used as a legal umbrella for the mega Food Estate project.

The Food Estate requires large areas of land; an estimated millions of hectares of land is needed for this food estate program. Certainly, many people will lose their land, especially indigenous peoples as the government is projecting hundreds of thousands of hectares for this mega project. This kind of land grabbing has triggered agrarian conflicts around the country.

Besides Papua and Merauke, which are used as food estate development projects and energy estates, the Government is also developing a Food estate in East Kalimantan (McCarthy and Krystof 2015). Thousands of hectares of land have been allocated for this program. In East Kalimantan or precisely in Bulungan, the food estate program was targeted to be implemented in the delta area of mangrove and wetlands. However, the absence of land in East Kalimantan caused the project to be moved to West Kalimantan. A food estate has been developed in West Kalimantan by printing new paddy fields and optimizing the land which all reach 250 ha (Ibid.). Indigenous peoples in Papua and Kalimantan will become the direct victims of this program.

In addition to the above issues, indigenous peoples also face various criminalization issues as they can no longer take food from their customary forests. The state has appropriated the resources. The process of state control over forests takes place through at least three territorial stages. First, the state claims that all land, deemed to be non-land owned by any other person, belongs to the state (Siscawati 2014: 7). At this stage, the state intends to derive revenue from the extraction of natural resources. Second, the state establishes land boundaries which are declared as state property to emphasize control by the state on forests. Once the limit is set, the forest becomes closed and the state forbids anyone to access the area including the forest resources contained therein. Third, the state divides the forest into various functions based on criteria. This program is a zoning of a region to set the type of activity allowed in it (Ibid.).

As a result, indigenous peoples living in forests have been criminalized even though they are the owners of ancestral lands (Rahman and Siscawati 2014). Indigenous peoples who have experienced criminalization are the Semende Appeal in Kaur district, Bengkulu, customary law community of Marga Tungkal Ulu in Musi District, Palembang, customary law community of Turungan Baji in Sinjai District, South Sulawesi, customary law community of Golo Lebo in East Manggarai district, Flores-NTT, Talang

Mamak customary law community in Indragiri Hulu Regency, Riau, and Tana Ai customary law community in Sikka Regency, Flores-NTT (AMAN 2014).

Law No. 41 of 1999 on Forestry uses the term "forest management" to describe the management of forest resources. Limitations of Forest Management under Law No. 41 of 1999 place forest resources at the national level.[10] In the law, forests are divided into two categories, namely, Forest rights and State Forests. The customary forest within the law is still included in state forests.

The issuance of the decision of the Constitutional Court, Number 35/PUU-X/2012 on 16 May 2013 has approved the application of judicial review or review of some provisions in Law No. 41 of 1999. Through the decision of the Constitutional Court, a customary forest is no longer a State forest. The verdict establishes the existence of the "customary forest" which is an integral part of the customary territory. Conflicts have occurred because customary forests that are part of customary territory were included or claimed as State forest areas either in its function as forest conservation, forest protection or production forest. Komnas HAM recorded increased cases of complaints after the issuance of the Constitutional Court decision number 35. This is due to the weakness of the decision because the Law on customary law community has not been approved. There is also a lack of willingness by the government to follow up on the decision. Post-MK 35, there are a lot of cases that have gone to Komnas HAM because many cannot be established into customary forest. Prior to Decision of the Constitutional Court 35, the customary territory established through the product of local law only covered 15,199.16 hectares and customary forest area 10,097.31 hectares. After three years of Constitutional Court leading to MK 35, the total area of land has increased to 197,541,85 hectares and customary forests of 6451.74 hectares. So, until 2016, the area of customary territory which was established through legal products totaled an area of 212,741 hectares and customary forests totaled an area of 16,549 hectares (Yance 2017).

[10] Forest Resources Management and Utilization Handbook on Ecosystems Land Payment Mechanism, in Indigenous Forest (2015), The Alliance of Indigenous Peoples of the Archipelago (AMAN) p. 5.

### *Remedies for Land Grab Under International Law*

In seeking to resolve cases, Komnas HAM can only provide recommendations as a final form in the settlement of a case if there is no indication of gross human rights violations. In some cases, the settlement does not bring justice to the victim. In this manner, Komnas HAM sought to innovate and to provide a breakthrough in the settlement of cases. The principle of remedy becomes the most important thing that is endeavored by Komnas HAM for the settlement of cases. For some indigenous peoples, indemnification or reimbursement is a highly anticipated aspect especially for justice for victims. The compensation is not only limited to material replacement, but also the restoration of their dignity as human beings when the state has taken it primarily for cases of land grabbing with violence or criminalization of indigenous peoples on suspicion of looting forest products.

UNDRIP provides, as have other human rights laws, that indigenous peoples are entitled to justice in a fair and independent process. Article 27 of the UNDRIP states:

> States shall establish and implement, in conjunction with indigenous peoples concerned, a fair, independent, impartial, open and transparent process, giving due recognition to indigenous peoples' laws, traditions, customs and land tenure systems, to recognize and adjudicate the rights of indigenous peoples pertaining to their lands, territories and resources, including those which were traditionally owned or otherwise occupied or used. Indigenous peoples shall have the right to participate in this process

The UNDRIP also provides for the principle of remedy for victims as referred to in Article 28 paragraph 1 of the UNDRIP: "Indigenous peoples have the right to redress, by means of which it can be restored, for the lands, territories and Resources which they have taken to be confiscated, taken, occupied, used or damaged without their free, prior and informed consent".

If the land is taken under an agreement, UNDRIP provides that the state must also consider fair remedies for indigenous peoples.[11] "Unless otherwise freely agreed upon by the peoples concerned, the compensation shall take the form of lands, territories and resources equal in quality, size and legal status of monetary compensation or other appropriate redress".

[11] Article 28 Paragraph 1 UNDRIP.

Article 29, UNDRIP also stipulates the state's role in taking measures in the protection of indigenous peoples' lands or customary law[12] or "adat". It states:

> Indigenous peoples have the right to the restoration and protection of the environment and the productive capacity of their lands, territories and natural resources. Countries will establish and implement assistance programs for indigenous peoples such as conservation and protection, without discrimination.

In its submission to the third cycle of the UPR in 2017, Komnas HAM recommendations on indigenous peoples, namely that

> 23. ... (1) The Government should prepare a comprehensive program for indigenous communities and their land rights issues in a timely manner, 32 (2) Government and Parliament should expedite the Bill on Recognition and Protection of Indigenous Peoples Rights approval process, based on human rights principles, including clauses on remedies for a variety of continuing human rights violations; (3) Establish an independent institution for the promotion and protection of the rights of indigenous peoples, (4) Government should adopt a uniform definition and terminology by using the term "indigenous people" as the translation of the term "masyarakat hukum adat" and vice versa. (Komnas HAM 2017)

## Komnas HAM and Indigenous Peoples' Land Rights

As Komnas HAM's research has indicated, human rights violations originated from several actions and events, including the annexation and expropriation of customary land and loss of indigenous peoples' resources. Based on Komnas HAM's complaints files, the number of complaints related to indigenous people is as follows: In 2013, there were 1123 case files and in 2014 this increased to 2483 case files of which 20 percent were agrarian. Agrarian issues were one of the most reported issues to Komnas HAM in addition to police violence and employment issues. In 2012–2014, agrarian cases were the highest-ranking cases in Komnas HAM for four consecutive years. The highest number of human rights violation in agrarian case according to Komnas HAM report in 2012 concerns land grabbing and seizing, amounting to 622. The number concerns half of all

[12] Ibid., paragraph 2 UNDRIP.

acts that lead to human rights violations in agrarian case (51 percent) (Annual Report Komnas HAM 2012).

Komnas HAM also succeeded in identifying perpetrators who allegedly committed human rights violations. The corporate sector was ranked first as perpetrator of agrarian cases, which amounted to 558. Local government actions led to as many as 167 cases, National Land Agency as many as 156 cases, armed forces (TNI) 66 cases, police 34 cases, courts 29 cases, state 24 cases, and among individuals 179 cases (Komnas HAM 2012).

The following table shows cases of human rights violations related to agrarian issues that Komnas HAM received in 2012 based on Komnas HAM complaints data (Fig. 13.1).

The potential for conflicts and case-load of Komnas HAM are expected to increase if one looks at the data from the Ministry of Forestry and the Environment (2009): 31,957 villages were incorporated into state forest areas. In fact, about 71.06 percent of the people in the village depend on forest resources (Komnas Ham, National Inquiry Report 2016: 2). Community complaints files received by Komnas HAM in 2012–2014 concerned 117 files in 2012, 113 complaint files by 2013 and 213 files by 2014. By 2014 there had been a twofold increase in the number of

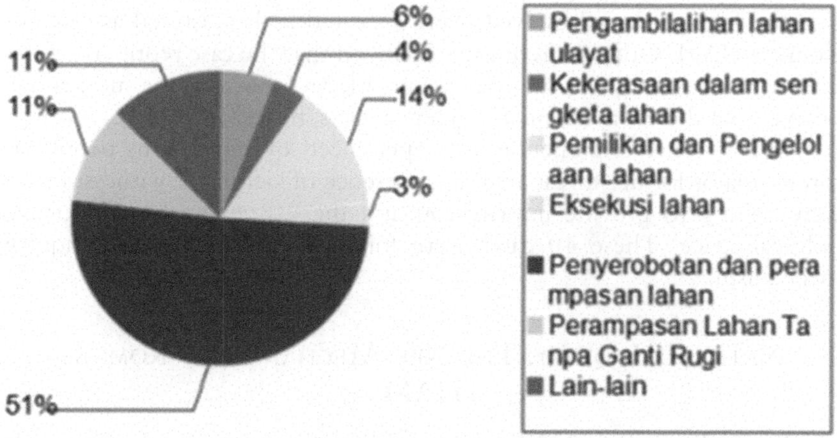


**Fig. 13.1** Complaint data 2012. (Source: Yossa Nainggolan, Tito Febismanto, Laporan Penelitian *Indikasi Pola Pelanggaran HAM Hak Masyarakat Adat dan Harapan Korban, Studi 40 Kasus Masyarakat Adat di kawasan Hutan*, Komnas HAM 2015 (unpublished) p. 4)

complaints filed. The increase is due to post decision of MK 35 of 2012. Most of the indigenous peoples' cases were registered by Alliance of Indigenous peoples of Nusantara (AMAN) to Komnas HAM. The MK-35's 2012 ruling provides an opportunity for indigenous and tribal peoples to reclaim their forests and customary territories.

Among the various cases of indigenous peoples which are reported to Komnas HAM, some cannot be traced as indigenous peoples' cases due to the codification of Komnas HAM based on rights and incoming cases, not the complainants. In the complaints administration system at Komnas HAM there is no special code for indigenous cases; the code refers to the complainant (individual or community), the unified actor and the type of case only. So for incoming cases, some cannot be identified as indigenous cases. Furthermore, when a complainant who is an indigenous person is incidentally accompanied by a legal counsel, the latter reporter or lawyer is recorded. Further data are needed on the total number of indigenous cases reported to Komnas HAM.

In order to resolve these cases, Komnas HAM carried out a study on *Indications of Pattern of Rights Violations of Indigenous* people in 2015. Komnas HAM selected 40 cases of violations of indigenous rights (Komnas HAM, National Inquiry Report 2016). Those cases were based on complaints that were reported to Komnas HAM with the precondition that the case had not been resolved, were repeated and registered as cases in Komnas HAM. Other prerequisites included that the case represented the diversity and breadth of massive, systematic violations of the indigenous people; that there was adequate evidence, facts, history, literature, research results and other documentation; experienced by indigenous people in forest area or former forest area; the presence of victims or witnesses who were willing to provide information and the existence of a supportive political space. These 40 cases were followed up by National Inquiry mechanism.

## National Inquiry: The New Mechanism of Komnas HAM

Until now Komnas HAM has not handled various cases of indigenous peoples properly, and the public has been waiting for their action. The latter is pressing considering the land rights cases comprise a very large group of cases reported to Komnas HAM, and it is a key part of Komnas HAM's work to address the rights of vulnerable groups. Komnas HAM has been looking for a new strategy to handle cases. Komnas HAM considers that the series of cases cannot be resolved one by one. Therefore, it is necessary to consider a new mechanism in handling cases in Komnas HAM, especially those related to land rights and the rights of indigenous peoples. In 2014–2015 Komnas HAM conducted National Inquiry activities on indigenous issues. This Inquiry is carried out not only as a handling of various cases that receive by Komnas HAM but also cases of indigenous peoples.

A National Inquiry is a thorough investigation or systematic study of the problem of human rights that is systemic and massive involving community participation. Unlike most other investigations, this model should be implemented in a transparent and public manner. The work involves tracking general evidence of witnesses and experts, directed toward a thorough investigation to discover the systematic pattern of human rights abuses. It requires a wide range of expertise within the institution, which includes researchers, educators and people with experience in the field of development of regional wisdom in Indonesia.

The National Inquiry is a method and an event conducted by Komnas HAM to develop efforts to solve widespread and systemic human rights violations. This method is conducted as a more comprehensive case solution. This effort is also carried out as a case handling model that is not only the completion of the case, but also serves as an educational tool and campaign.[13]

The steps taken by Komnas HAM for the National Inquiry were: choosing themes, formulating background and scope, identifying and consulting stakeholders, formulating objectives and terms of reference inquiry, resource mobilization, research and evidence collection, public hearings, public campaigns and media engagement. From thousands of cases of dispute, Komnas HAM then selected 40 cases related to indigenous peoples of forest areas in seven areas, namely Sumatra, Java, Kalimantan, Sulawesi, Maluku, Bali and Nusa Tenggara, and Papua. The cases are mostly acute and have taken place since the New Order era, have continued, even expanded (Fig. 13.2).

[13] On National Inquiries, see Asia Pacific Forum of National Human Rights Institutions and Raoul Wallenberg Institute of Human Rights and Humanitarian Law (2012). *Manual on Conducting a National Inquiry into Systemic Patterns of Human Rights Violations.*

Komnas HAM's inquiry team consisted not only of the internal elements of Komnas HAM, but also consists of various other parties. The institutions involved in this Inquiry are the Witness and Victim Protection Agency, the relevant ministries, community organizations, academics (universities), and mass media, both electronic and printed.

Komnas HAM realized that research and evidence collection is an important step in the National Inquiry. So, it prepared three research designs, namely, reviewing allegations of human rights violations, ethnographic research of indigenous peoples living in forest areas, and policy research in forestry and indigenous communities. This research was done together with Sajogjo Institute.

Another step in the inquiry process was to do a Public Recognition List, which is a method that provides a forum for listening to victims, government, corporations and other related parties. This method has become a common forum for victims to share their experiences (Komnas Ham, National Inquiry 2016: 15).

Based on the results of the study, and the study of the case, Komnas HAM found the root cause of human rights violations against indigenous peoples. Komnas HAM considers that the absence of recognition as indigenous people affects the uncertainty of their legal status, thus making it unlawful for their customary territory and security of their customary

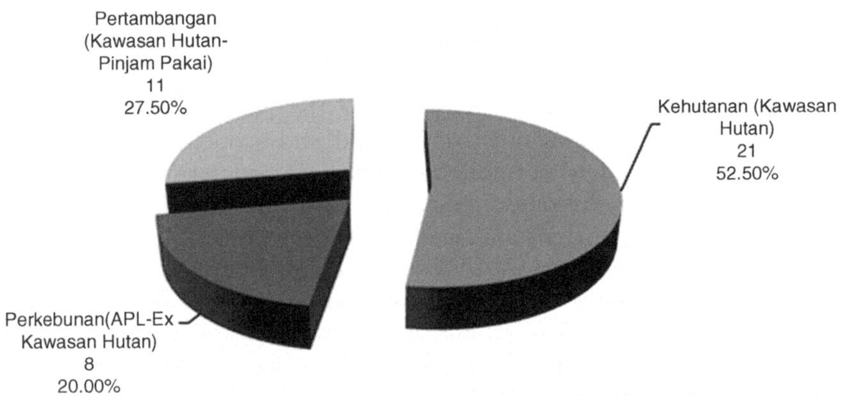


**Fig. 13.2** National Inquiry database by sector. (Source: Yossa Nainggolan, Tito Febismanto, Laporan Penelitian (2015) *Indikasi Pola Pelanggaran HAM Hak Masyarakat Adat dan Harapan Korban, Studi 40 Kasus Masyarakat Adat di kawasan Hutan*, Komnas HAM 2015 (unpublished) p. 47)

territories. The second issue is that it simplifies the existence of indigenous peoples and their rights over forest areas and resources only to the extent of administrative matters or legality. This simplification results in the abandonment of indigenous peoples' rights to its territory in the forest area directly or indirectly (Komnas Ham, National Inquiry 2016: 15).

The National Inquiry as a whole generated some recommendations based on remedial principles and is submitted to a number of related institutions. The recommendations asked a number of related ministries, the House of Representatives, the President to take immediate steps in providing protection and compliance with indigenous and tribal peoples. General recommendations were given as follows:

1. Governments needs to pursue reconciliation efforts among communities to resolve horizontal conflicts due to different views on corporate presence and overlapping customary land claims.
2. The settlement of long-standing land rights conflicts should be carried out in a peaceful manner based on the principles of respect and protection of human rights and the rights of indigenous peoples.
3. Indigenous peoples and/or its citizens who are victims of human rights violations need to receive remedies so as to prevent the recurrence of similar human rights violations.
4. Remedies made immediately as compensation (reparation) in the form of:

   (a) Restitution given by the corporation or institution that can be considered as responsible for the occurrence of human rights violations to the customary law community both physically, mentally and economically;
   (b) The compensation is granted by the state if the party responsible for the restitution is unable to provide compensation;
   (c) Rehabilitation (restoration of the original condition) in the form of restoration of freedom, resettlement, land restoration and repair of other life infrastructure damaged by land reclamation;
   (d) Sense of justice in the form of effective action to stop and prevent continuing violations. Investigation of events suspected of human rights violations. Public apology for human rights violations. Provision of legal and administrative sanctions against perpetrators. (Komnas HAM, National Inquiry 2016: 81)

### *Equal and Effective Justice Access*

After the National Inquiry, the Government of Indonesia has taken steps to provide recognition, protection and fulfillment of indigenous peoples' rights. On 30 December 2016, President Joko Widodo submitted a Decision Letter of Acknowledgment of Customary Forest to nine Customary Law Community (indigenous people) spread in several areas in the country. He stated on 25 October 2017, "Today, we reiterate the recognition of customary forests as a whole, there are 9 customary law groups and we formalize the recognition of their customary forests with an area of 3341 hectares" (KBR 2017) (Table 13.1).

National Inquiry is the opening of communication with the State. Post MK-35, the State is required to provide the tools to carry out the mandate of the Constitutional Court 35. However, such devices are difficult to implement due to conflicts with indigenous peoples and communication deadlocks with related institutions. By Inquiry, indigenous peoples have become aware that their positions are parallel to the state.

Hopefully, the results of the National Inquiry can be followed up immediately, including the recognition of indigenous peoples through the ratification of the Indigenous Peoples Law which is being discussed in the

**Table 13.1** Communities to whom decisions letters were sent to

1. Adat Forest Rantau Village Pack 130 ha, Merangin district Jambi province (indigenous people Marga Serampas);
2. Adat Forest Ammatoa Kajang (313 Ha) Bulukumba District South Sulawesi Province (indigenous people Ammatoa Kajang);
3. Wana Posangke Traditional Forest (6.212 Ha) North Morowali Regency Central Sulawesi Province (indigenous people Lipu Wana Posangke);
4. Adat Forest Kasepuhan Karang (486 Ha) Lebak Regency of Banten Province (indigenous people Kasepuhan Karang);
5. Adat Forest Bukit Sembahyang (39 Ha) Kerinci District Jambi Province (indigenous people Waterfall);
6. Bukit Tinggi Adat Forest (41 Ha) Kerinci District Jambi Province (indigenous people Suangai Deras);
7. Tigo Luhah Adat Forest Sixth Permenti (252 Ha) Kerinci District Jambi Province (indigenous people Tigo Luhah Permenti);
8. Adat Forest Tigo Luhah Kemantan (452 Ha) Kerinci District Jambi Province (indigenous people Tigo Luhah Kemantan); and
9. Adat Forest Pandumaan Sipituhuta (5.172 Ha) Humbang Hasudutan District of North Sumatra Province (indigenous people Pandumaan Sipituhuta).

DPR. Until the end of 2017, the President has established 17 customary and 1 forest reserve to be designated as customary forests.[14]

## Conclusion

Komnas HAM is expected to be able to respond to the growing number of national issues today. In doing so, it must be able to stand independently and solve cases impartially. It is also required to have new breakthroughs in the settlement of such cases.

The handling of cases commonly done by Komans HAM has not been able to provide justice for the victims. The handling of cases thus far also does not give a sense of addressing the root of the problems. The dissatisfaction of the victims calls for new tools and breakthroughs in the handling of cases that can guarantee the protection and fulfillment of the rights of the victims.

Another limitation of Komnas HAM is that in the thousands of cases that have been submitted to Komnas HAM, not all have been handled properly. This is due to the lack of resources and case resolution mechanisms, leading to recommendations only, which of course cannot guarantee that a case can be completed.

The new mechanisms drafted by Komnas HAM, though not yet of widespread impact, can help to ensure that the government's attention to indigenous and tribal peoples' cases is increasingly open. The wider community became aware of the roots of the real problem. So, it encourages policy makers to take action in handling the problems of indigenous peoples and how to provide protection and fulfillment of rights for indigenous and tribal peoples in Indonesia. National Inquiry as a mechanism, mandated through NHRIs, is an effective method for dealing with structural and systemic violations involving powerful actors/institutions. It also provides an infrastructure for peace as an alternative for short and long-term resolution of conflicts related to natural resources. National Inquiry is a proven mechanism effective for case resolution. Komnas HAM can find conclusions from various cases of similar problems. In addition, this mechanism was also carried out comprehensively with NGOs and communities, making it easier for Komnas HAM to resolve a case.

[14] Data from Ministry of Environment and Forestry and HUMA 2017.

## References

The Alliance of Indigenous Peoples of the Archipelago (AMAN). 2014. *Annual Report* on a research report on typology of indigenous peoples' human rights violations, 2016, Komnas HAM.

———. 2015. Buku Panduan Pengelolaan Sumber Daya Huran dan Pemanfaatan Mekanisme Pembayaran Layanan Ekosistem di Hutan Adat. Archived on http://www.aman.or.id/wp-content/uploads/2017/01/Buku-Panduan-PSDH-PES-AMAN-2015.pdf.

Anseeuw, Ward and Liz Alden Wily. 2012. *Land Rights and the Rush for Land Findings of the Global Commercial Pressures on Land Research Project*, The International Land Coalition. Romy Patra, Penguatan Eksistensi Kelembagaan Komnas HAM dalam Sistem Ketatanegaraan Indonesia, Jurnal masalah-masalah Hukum Indonesia, Universitas Diponegoro, Jilid 41 Nomor 2, April 2012, pp. 209–217, https://doi.org/10.14710/mmh.41.2.2012.209-217.

Asia Pacific Forum of National Human Rights Institutions and Raoul Wallenberg Institute of Human Rights and Humanitarian Law. 2012. *Manual on Conducting a National Inquiry into Systemic Patterns of Human Rights Violations.*

Bolin, A. 2011. *Fenomena Global Perampasan Tanah*, Bulletin Down to Earth Tanah Papua: perjuangan yang berlanjut untuk tanah dan penghidupan, *DTE 89–90, November 2011*. Archived on http://www.downtoearth-indonesia.org/sites/downtoearth-indonesia.org/files/DTE%2089-web-Indo.pdf.

Byrne, D. 2005. Social Exclusion, 2nd Ed. Maidenhead, UK: Open University Press on Ulrika Levander, Social Exclusion an Analytical Aspect of the Social Enterprise, University of Gothenburg, Sweden, paper. Archived on http://www.euricse.eu/sites/default/files/db_uploads/documents/1254838346_n180.pdf.

Herbert, J. 2008. The legal framework of human rights in Indonesia', in Timothy Lindsey (ed), *Indonesia: Law and Society*, 2nd ed., New South Wales: The Federation Press, pgs. 456–482.

KBR. 2017. "Jokowi Sets 9 Forests for Indigenous Peoples," 25 October 2017. Archived at http://kbr.id/nasional/10-2017/jokowi_tetapkan_9_hutan_untuk_masyarakat_adat_/93100.html.

Kholis, Nur (ed). Belajar dari Pengalaman: Praktek Mediasi Hak Asasi Manusia, Sub Komisi dan Bagian Administrasi Mediasi, Komnas HAM, 2012, p. 4.

Komnas HAM. 2012. Annual Report.

———. 2016. National Inquiry Report of the Indigenous Peoples' Rights on the Territory law on State Forest. Komnas HAM.

———. 2017. Indonesia, Submission to the 3rd UPR. Archived at https://www.upr-info.org/sites/default/files/document/indonesia/session_27_-_may_2017/komnas_ham_upr27_idn_e_main_rev.pdf.

Lay, C. et al. 2002a. *Komnas HAM 1993–1997: Pergulatan dalam Otoritarianisme.* Yogyakarta, Fisipil UGM.

———. 2002b. Komnas HAM 1998–2001, Pergulatan dalam Transisi Politik. Yogyakarta, Fisipol UGM 2002.

Li, Tania M. 2011. Centering labor in the land grab debate, *The Journal of Peasant Studies*, Vol 38 Issue 2, 281–298, https://doi.org/10.1080/03066150.2011.559009. Archived on https://www.sv.uio.no/sai/english/research/projects/anthropos-and-the-material/Intranet/economic-practices/reading-group/texts/li-centering-labor-in-the-land-grad-debate.pdf.

Lindsey, T. (ed). 2008. Indonesia: Law and Society. The Federation Press.

Little and Watts in Borras, S.M. Jr, Hall, R., Scoones, I., White, B. and W. Wolford. 2011. Towards a better understanding of global land grabbing: an editorial introduction. *Journal of Peasant Studies.*

McCarthy, John F. and Krystof, O. 2015. *Responding to Food Security and Land questions: Policy Principles and Policy Choices in Kalimantan, Indonesia*, Conference Paper No 47. An International Academic Conference on Land grabbing, conflict, and agrarian-environmental transformational perspectives from East and Southeast Asia. 5–6 June, 2015. Archived on https://www.iss.nl/sites/corporate/files/CMCP_47-McCarthy___Obidzinski.pdf.

Ministry for Economic Affairs. 2011. Masterplan P3EI, Koridor ekonomi Papua – Kepulauan Maluku, Hlm 159.

Ministry of Forestry and the Environment (2009). The State of Indonesia's Forests.

Nainggolan, Y., Tito F. and Laporan P. 2015. *Indikasi Pola Pelanggaran HAM Hak Masyarakat Adat dan Harapan Korban, Studi 40 Kasus Masyarakat Adat di kawasan Hutan*, Komnas HAM 2015 (unpublished).

Patra, R. 2012. *Penguatan Eksistensi Kelembagaan Komnas HAM dalam Sistem Ketatanegaraan Indonesia*, Jurnal masalah-masalah Hukum Indonesia, Universitas Diponegoro, Jilid 41 Nomor 2, April 2012, pp. 209–217, https://doi.org/10.14710/mmh.41.2.2012.209-217.

Rahman, Noer Fauzi Rahman and Siscawati. 2014. *Indigenous and Tribal Peoples are Right Holder, Legal Subjects and Owners of Their Customary Territories: Contextually Understanding the Decision of the Constitutional Court of the Republic of Indonesia on the Case Number 35/PUU-X/2012, Supplement Journal of Wacana, Insist.*

De Schutter, Olivier. 2011. How not to think of land-grabbing: three critiques of large-scale investments in farmland, *The Journal of Peasant Studies*, Vol 38 Issue 2, 249–279. Archived on https://doi.org/10.1080/03066150.2011.559008.

Setiawan, Ken M.P. 2013. *Promoting human rights: national human rights commissions in Indonesia and Malaysia.* Doctoral Thesis. Faculteit der Rechtsgeleerdheid, Leiden University.

Setiawan, K. 2016. From Hope to Disillusion: The Paradox of Komnas HAM, the Indonesian National Human Rights Commission, *Journal of the Humanities and Social Sciences of Southeast Asia*, vol. 172, pp. 1–32.

Setiawan, Usep (ed) KNUPKA. 2005. Sebuah Keniscayaan. Study Konteks Makro atas Konflik Agraria dan Urgensi Pembaharuan Agraria, Komnas HAM 2005.

Siscawati, Mia Siscawati. 2014. In the introduction of Indigenous Peoples and the Seizing of Forestry *Jurnal Wacana Insist Journal* Number 33 of XVI.

Stokke, H. 2007. Taking the Paris Principles to Asia. A Study of Three Human Rights Commissions in Southeast Asia: Indonesia, Malaysia and the Philippines. Report, Christian Michelsen Institute. Bergen. www.cmi.no/publications/2680-taking-the-paris-principles-to-asia.

Yance Arizona Malik. 2017. Outlook Epistema, Pengakuan Hukum terhadap masyarakat Adat: Tren Produk Hukum Daerah dan Nasional, Epistema 2017. Archived on http://epistema.or.id/download/Outlook_Epistema_2017.pdf.

Zakaria, R. Yando, Emilianus Ola Kleden, Y.L. Franky and MIFEE. 2011. Tak Terjangkau Angan Malind (Mifee Not Reacheable of Malind People), Pusaka Foundation, Jakarta.

CHAPTER 14

# The Protection Capacities of NHRIs

*James Gomez and Robin Ramcharan*

From a review of the Southeast Asian NHRIs undertaken in this book, and of other NHRIs by the editors, Gomez and Ramcharan, one sees broadly that there is a gap between the mandate and capacity to provide protection and pursue remedies following the receipt of complaints and conduct of investigations. Laws drafted to establish the different national institutions do attempt to empower these entities to perform investigative services into human rights abuses. These laws also provide for varying degrees of intervention, which can range from public awareness campaigns, mediation, visiting detainees, observing court cases and submitting reports to national assemblies, the United Nations and investigations. However, they do not follow through with effective exercise of quasi-judicial functions and securing remedies for victims of violations of human rights.

Why is this so? Clearly the region's NHRIs operate in a political context that is conducive to the grudging advancement of universal human rights standards. The regression in rights is well documented in a region whose members are dominated either by one party, or a military regime, or monarchical rule or populist rulers. Indonesia is the only one to date that

J. Gomez (✉) • R. Ramcharan
Asia Centre, Bangkok, Thailand
e-mail: james@asiacentre.co.th; robin@asiacentre.co.th



J. Gomez, R. Ramcharan (eds.), *National Human Rights Institutions in Southeast Asia*,
https://doi.org/10.1007/978-981-15-1074-8_14

**Table 14.1** GANHRI ratings of Southeast Asian NHRIs

| *NHRI* | *Current rating* | *Year of rating* |
|---|---|---|
| Indonesia (Komnas HAM) | A | 2000<br>March 2007<br>March 2012<br>November 2013—special review in March 2014<br>March 2014—A<br>**March 2017-A** |
| Malaysia (SUHAKAM) | A | 2002 April 2008—recommended to be accredited B<br>November 2009—A<br>October 2010—A<br>**November 2015—A** |
| Philippines (CHRP) | A | 1999 March 2007—deferred to October 2007<br>October 2007<br>March 2012<br>**March 2017—A** |
| Timor-Leste (Provedor) | A | April 2008<br>November 2013<br>October 2018—A |
| Myanmar (MNHRC) | B | November 2015—B |
| Thailand (CHRT) | B | 2004 November 2008<br>November 2013—deferred to March 2014—deferred to October 2014—recommended to be downgraded B; given one year to establish compliance with the Paris Principles<br>**November 2015—B** |
| Timor-Leste (Provedor) | A | April 2008<br>November 2013<br>October 2018—A |

Legend:

A = Fully compliant with Paris Principles

B = Partially compliant with Paris Principles

C = Noncompliant with Paris Principles

Source: GANHRI, accreditation status as of 9 May 2019, available at https://nhri.ohchr.org/EN/Documents/Status%20Accreditation%20Chart%20%289%20May%202019%29.pdf

proudly boasts of independent institutions; however, even this remains to be seen in light of the rise of fundamentalist religious forces.

The region's NHRIs have received "A" (Indonesia, Malaysia, the Philippines and Timor-Leste) and "B" ratings (Myanmar and Thailand) from GANHRI (see Table 14.1), which monitors the application of the

Paris Principles (see generally De Beco and Murray 2015). They have all been the subject of regular reviews for their conformity with the Paris Principles, established to provide a global standard to measure and enhance the effectiveness of NHRIs.

However closer scrutiny of the effectiveness of their protection roles is warranted as the positive "ratings" of some commissions have been threatened. This was hinted at with the ICCs threat in 2008 to downgrade Malaysia's Commission due to concerns over the independence of this body. In 2015, a similar concern was raised over Thailand's National Human Rights Commission (NHRCT), which was eventually downgraded in 2016 due to failure to address long-standing functional and structural problems. The NHRCT is still functioning under the 2017 Constitution but it continues to be affected by political interference by the state. On 31 July 2019, two Commissioners resigned from their posts citing inability to perform their work in light of new regulations. Upon leaving, Commissioners Angkhana Neelapaijit and Tuenjai Deetes noted "that the NHRC's management system prevented commissioners from receiving complaints directly from the public." They also noted that new regulations prevented them from having effective relations with civil society (Prachatai 2019). With these two resignations, the Commission had less than half the number of Commissioners required.

In 2016, Myanmar's Human Rights Commission was evaluated for the first time and was awarded a "B" status by the ICC. Critics have pointed out that the Commission remains a state-sponsored mechanism to deflect attention away from past and current abuses by the military. The ANNI 2018 report noted that Myanmar's Commission has chosen a very restrictive interpretation of its mandate (ANNI 2018: 10).

While performing important work, the region's NHRIs must enhance significantly their capacity and willingness to fulfill some critical roles: (1) investigating allegations of violations, to conduct credible, impartial "hearings" on the same and to publicize these for public awareness of the pursuit of justice; and (2) secure remedies for victims of violations. NHRIs are in principle an avenue outside of the judicial mechanisms of a state that can provide quicker access to justice, through less complicated and less expensive processes that ultimately secure remedies for violations. In this regard, it is worth recalling long-standing Commonwealth Secretariat guidelines on best practices for NHRIs, including on remedies, which are now in multimedia form (Commonwealth Secretariat 2001: 24–25; Commonwealth Forum 2019). These guidelines recommended that an

NHRI "should be empowered to refer matters for prosecution" and that it "should have the power to seek effective remedies including, where appropriate, through the courts." The guidelines noted that NHRIs "must be able to provide effective remedies for violations of human rights." It continued:

> The means that are available to NHRIs to resolve complaints will affect both public perception and the ability of an NHRI to successfully foster a culture of respect for human rights. Human rights breaches may be resolved in various ways ranging from alternative dispute resolution to action in the courts. The power to conciliate and mediate between disputants is important as a means of resolving complaints expeditiously. Delays in the provision of remedies will diminish public confidence in the NHRI and deter victims from looking to the NHRI for redress. NHRI decisions should, where appropriate, be enforceable through the courts. In addition, complainants should have access to the courts should they be dissatisfied with the findings of an NHRI.

NHRIs thrive best in democratic contexts, which have appropriate checks and balances upon governmental authority. However, the NHRIs reviewed here operate in the context of troubled democratic transition processes and a regression in democracy and rights in the region. An indicator of the influence of the six NHRIs in Southeast Asia is that parliaments often seldom openly engage with and discuss their work. NHRIs remain weak and appear to be serving as forms of "appeasement" to the international community. The NHRIs in Southeast Asia are indeed the products of their individual country's political contexts and generally mirror domestic political developments and demands from the international arena.

The current regional political context does not bode well for the set-up of new NHRIs nor for an enhanced capacity to protect human rights by existing commissions. As elections have unfolded across the region over recent years (Cambodia, 2018; Malaysia, 2018; Indonesia, 2019; Thailand 2019; Myanmar expected 2020), authoritarian tendencies of the "elected" leaders have increased and NHRIs have come under attack. Cambodia's strong man Hun Sen was "reelected" in an election that was widely held to be a sham and he continues to trample on basic rights and freedoms (Ellis-Peterson 2018). Malaysia elected a new party for the first time in six decades, though the election of Prime Minister Mahathir has yet to yield systemic changes to the state apparatus, bureaucracy and cronyism (BBC 2018). Indonesia, a regional powerhouse and seemingly the one bright spot, maintained its democratic momentum with the reelection of President Jokowi in 2019. However, KOMNAS Ham now finds itself in a context of rising extremism and religious fundamentalism (McBeth 2019). An expert commentator has noted President Jokowi's likely inability to counter growing military influence over the Indonesian economy and domestic politics, and his inability to curtail crackdowns on free speech, and rising intolerance for religious and ethnic minorities, and LGBT Indonesians (Kurlantzick 2019).

In this context, significant improvements in NHRIs' performance are not to be expected. Among their challenges, as noted in the latest ANNI report, are challenges of

- Diversity in composition of NHRIs, lacking gender-balance and representatives of minorities,
- Transparency in selection of Commissioners,
- Lack of independence,
- Difficulty engaging with state actors such as the military and police forces,
- Inadequate funding and financial independence in their operations, and
- Inadequate powers to fully investigate situations and to enforce the recommendations that come from those investigations. (ANNI 2018)

The ANNI review noted the continuing dilemma for NHRIs, which are given adequate powers to investigate cases related to human rights violations but cannot achieve much beyond providing recommendations. Their ability to investigate cases involving state actors, especially the military or police forces, is restricted. The credibility of some NHRIs is also at stake because of unqualified Commissioners (MNHRC, NHRCT), unwillingness to investigate former military personnel (MNHRC) and corruption (Komnas HAM). Symptomatic of the deep challenges faced, the NHRCT was tasked with defending the government's human rights record under the 2017 Constitution of Thailand, imposed by the former military junta (Somjittranukit 2018).

These developments take place in a wider geo-political context of a rising China that challenges the international human rights movement and seeks to showcase its authoritarian political system. Authoritarian leaders in Southeast Asia have a natural affinity with China, which claims it does not interfere in other countries and offers financial incentives through its One Belt, One Road initiative. With the Western liberal bastions—USA and European Union—seemingly retreating from democracy and human rights engagement globally, China is filling this void with its own vision. At a South-South Forum on Human Rights in Beijing in December 2017, Chinese Foreign Minister Wang Yi said his government had "identified the goal of forging a new field in international relations and building a community of shared future for mankind" (Associated Press 2017) The place of current international human rights standards in this vision is uncertain, even if Foreign Minister Wang noted a place for the human rights cause. China's critical preoccupations are still developmental and internal. Its engagement with international human rights challenges and standards will remain limited for the foreseeable future (Subedi 2015). It is less shy about championing its view of human rights, prioritizing the issues such as the right to development, health, housing and nutrition. It remains to be seen to what extent it "is willing to cooperate closely with all parties in the world human rights field," as noted by Huang Kunming, a member of the Political Bureau of the CPC Central Committee and head of the Publicity Department of the CPC Central Committee at the 2018, Beijing Human Rights Forum. Huang noted that "China had combined common principles in human rights protection with the country's reality" (Xinhua 2018).

It is to be hoped that the international community will spur the development of new and improved NHRIs amidst the 2030 Agenda for the Sustainable Development Goals. A 2019 Statement by GANHRI to the 41st session of the UN Human Rights Council noted that "The fact that the existence of an independent NHRI with A-status accreditation is a global indicator for the achievement of SDG 16 further reaffirms their crucial role with regards to the 2030 Agenda," which seeks to achieve human rights for all (GANHRI 2019). In line with this a 2017 UN General Assembly Resolution called for the strengthening of NHRIs' capacity to promote and protect human rights (UN General Assembly 2017).

Meanwhile in Southeast Asia, NHRIs are struggling to live up to the high expectations inherent in their mandates and their very creation. The regression in democracy and the rule of law in the region further thwarts such expectations. In those countries without an NHRI, the prospects for setting up NHRIs are slim. While setting up Ombudsmen offices in non-NHRI countries may be appealing, their mandates tend to be limited to reviews of maladministration by public authorities and do not extend to the protection of the full panoply of human rights.

Despite this reality NHRIs in the region must persist and push the boundaries of their mandates. They must foster deeper relations with each other across the region and share best practices. They must effectively marshal international mechanisms at the UN, notably the aforementioned UN General Assembly Resolution. They must also marshall their respective governments' commitment to the SDGs, notably Goal 16, which calls for equal access to justice and inclusive institutions, to gradually enhance their capacity to protect human rights. Countries in the region that do not have NHRIs should establish one but steer away from the predicament that currently affects NHRIs in Southeast Asia.

## References

ANNI Report. 2018 *ANNI Report on the Performance and Establishment of National Human Rights Institutions in Asia*. Bangkok: Forum Asia.

Associated Press. 2017. China presents its take on human rights at global forum in Beijing. 7 December. Available at https://www.scmp.com/news/china/diplomacy-defence/article/2123305/china-presents-its-take-human-rights-global-forum.

BBC. 2018. Malaysia Election: Opposition Scores Historic Victory. 10 May. Available at https://www.bbc.com/news/world-asia-44036178.

Commonwealth Secretariat. 2001. National Human Rights Institutions: Best Practice. Commonwealth Secretariat.

Commonwealth Forum on NHRIs. 2019. Guidelines on How to Run a National Human Rights Institution.

De Beco, G., and Murray, R. 2015. *A commentary on the Paris Principles on national human rights institutions/*Cambridge: Cambridge University Press.

Ellis-Peterson, Hannah. 2018. Cambodia: Hun Sen re-elected in landslide victory after brutal crackdown. 29 July. Available at https://www.theguardian.com/world/2018/jul/29/cambodia-hun-sen-re-elected-in-landslide-victory-after-brutal-crackdown.

GANHRI. 2019. Statement of the Global Alliance of National Human Rights Institutions (GANHRI) at the 41st session of the Human Rights Council, under agenda item 8 on the presentation of the OHCHR report on the inter-sessional meeting on NHRIs and SDGs, held on 7 March 2019 (report A/HRC/41/30).

Kurlantzick, Joshua. 2019. "After Jokowi's Victory," Council on Foreign Relations. 28 May. Available at https://www.cfr.org/blog/after-jokowis-victory.

McBeth, John. 2019. "Indonesia election exposes ethnic, religious divides," Asia Times. 22 eat https://www.asiatimes.com/2019/04/article/indonesia-election-exposes-ethnic-religious-divides/.

*Prachatai*. 2019. "Two human rights commissioners resign; say new regulations made them feel restricted. 1 August.

Somjittranukit, Kornkritch. 2018. Constitution turns NHRC into government mouthpiece. Prachatai, 4 May.

Subedi, S.P. 2015. China's Approach to Human Rights and the UN Human Rights Agenda. Chinese Journal of International Law, Vol. 14, No. 3, pp. 437–464.

UN General Assembly. 2017. National Institutions for the Promotion and Protection of Human Rights. A/C.3/72/L.45. 31 October.

Xinhua. 2018. China willing to cooperate with world in human rights: official. 18 September. Available at http://www.xinhuanet.com/english/2018-09/18/c_137476749.htm.

# Index[1]



[1] Note: Page numbers followed by 'n' refer to notes.



J. Gomez, R. Ramcharan (eds.), *National Human Rights Institutions in Southeast Asia*,
https://doi.org/10.1007/978-981-15-1074-8

The manufacturer's authorised representative in the EU is Springer Nature Customer Service Centre GmbH, Europaplatz 3, 69115 Heidelberg, Germany. If you have any concerns regarding our products, please contact ProductSafety@springernature.com

Printed and bound by CPI Group (UK) Ltd, Croydon, CR0 4YY
25/09/2026
02222897-0012